A note on large numbers:
1 million	1,000,000
1 billion	1,000,000,000
1 trillion	1,000,000,000,000
1 quadrillion	1,000,000,000,000,000
1 quintillion	1,000,000,000,000,000,000
1 sextillion	1,000,000,000,000,000,000,000
1 septillion	1,000,000,000,000,000,000,000,000

This edition published in 2024 by Arcturus Publishing Limited
26/27 Bickels Yard, 151–153 Bermondsey Street,
London SE1 3HA

Copyright © Arcturus Holdings Limited

All rights reserved. No part of this publication may be reproduced, stored in a retrieval system, or transmitted, in any form or by any means, electronic, mechanical, photocopying, recording, or otherwise, without prior written permission in accordance with the provisions of the Copyright Act 1956 (as amended). Any person or persons who do any unauthorized act in relation to this publication may be liable to criminal prosecution and civil claims for damages.

Author: Claudia Martin
Illustrator: Marc Pattenden
Designer: Rocket Design (East Anglia) Ltd.
Consultants: Steve Parker, Dr. Sharon Ann Holgate, Dr. Helen Giles,
Dr. Kristina Routh, Jules Howard, Dougal Dixon
Editors: Becca Clunes and Lydia Halliday
Design Manager: Rosie Bellwood-Moyler
Editorial Manager: Joe Harris

ISBN: 978-1-3988-4660-9
CH012453US
Supplier 29, Date 0724, Print run 00007971

Printed in China

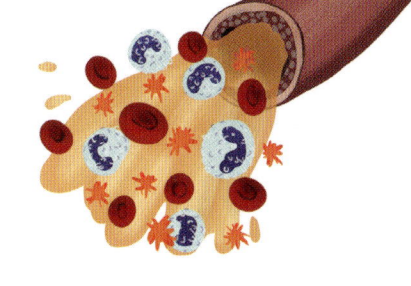

Contents

Introduction	4
Chapter 1: Matter	6
Chapter 2: Forces and Energy	30
Chapter 3: The Solar System	62
Chapter 4: Earth and the Moon	98
Chapter 5: Stars and Galaxies	120
Chapter 6: Life	140
Chapter 7: The Human Body	156
Chapter 8: Animals	172
Chapter 9: Dinosaurs	228
Glossary	248
Index	254

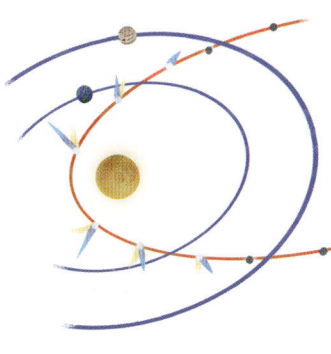

Introduction

Over the 300,000 years that modern humans have walked this planet, we have built up a store of knowledge through watching, testing, inventing, and sharing what we learn. To delve into that store, turn the pages of this book to find out about animals and plants, space and telescopes, the human body and its cells. Learn about living things from tiny bacteria to the world's largest animal, the blue whale, which grows to 29.9 m (98 ft) long. Find out about atoms, which are the building blocks of everything from hissing snakes to super-hot stars more than 2 billion km (1.2 billion miles) wide. Discover how seeds grow and black holes destroy, why balls bounce and ice melts.

Long before writing was invented, the earliest humans passed knowledge from generation to generation through talking, singing, and sometimes painting or carving pictures on rocks. Among those early facts was vital information about plants, animals, and what could be known of the human body itself. From the start, we also watched and talked about the movements of the Moon, the Sun, and other stars across the sky.

Every day, we add to our store of knowledge. We spot new planets, black holes, or galaxies. We use our knowledge of matter and forces to construct new materials and machines. We develop new medications to cure and prevent disease. We are even starting to unravel the mysteries of the extraordinary human brain. There is still much we do not know, but our thirst for knowledge will take us there in the end.

The northern clouded yellow butterfly sucks nectar from the flowers of Arctic plants. It was not until the 1670s that German scientist Maria Sibylla Merian discovered that caterpillars become butterflies through metamorphosis. It was several more decades before we learned how butterflies pollinate plants.

Although she lived at a time when most Chinese women were not allowed to study or to work outside the home, Wang Zhenyi (1768–97) educated herself in astronomy. Using a lantern (representing the Sun), table (Earth), and mirror (the Moon), she figured out a mathematical explanation for eclipses of the Moon, which is when the Moon passes into Earth's shadow.

Matter

Everything you can see or touch is made of matter, from people to plants and paperclips to planets. Matter is anything that has volume and mass. If something has volume, it takes up space. If something has mass, you can weigh it on a scale—as long as you have a scale that is sensitive enough to weigh a speck of matter or big enough to weigh a star!

All matter is made of tiny particles called atoms. The average person is made of 7 octillion atoms—that is a 7 followed by 27 zeros. There are 118 different types of atoms, such as hydrogen atoms and gold atoms. Something that is made of just one type of atom is called an element. Hydrogen and gold are two of the 118 elements. Each element has different characteristics. Hydrogen is a clear gas at room temperature, but gold is a shiny solid.

Atoms can form chemical bonds with each other, joining together to make groups of atoms called molecules. When a molecule contains different types of atoms, it is called a compound. A compound has different characteristics from the elements it contains, which is why you can see and touch many different types of materials with many characteristics, from waterproof to bendy, hard to crumbly. The human body contains more than 20 elements, forming thousands of different compounds. In the whole Universe, there are millions upon millions of different compounds, all made of those 118 different types of atoms.

Oxygen atoms (pictured) make up 65 percent of the human body's mass. Most of those oxygen atoms are joined to two hydrogen atoms, forming the compound known as water. In fact, you contain twice as many hydrogen as oxygen atoms. However, an oxygen atom weighs 16 times more than a hydrogen atom, so oxygen accounts for much more of your mass.

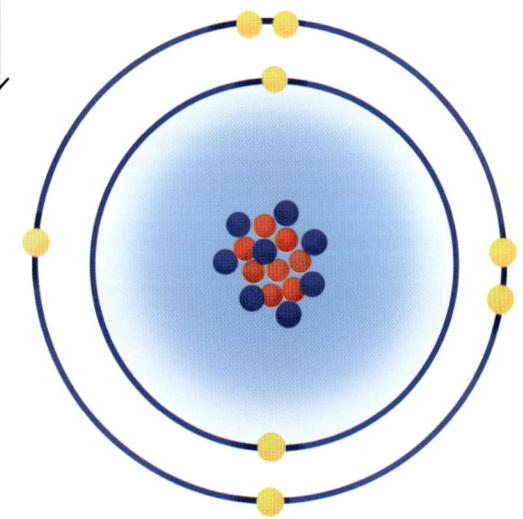

The Polish-French scientist Marie Curie (1867–1934) discovered the elements polonium and radium. These elements are found on Earth only in tiny quantities, in compounds with other elements. Polonium and radium are radioactive (see page 28), which means they give off energy.

Atoms and Molecules

Atoms are the tiny building blocks of all matter. Around 0.0000002 mm (0.000000008 in) across, they are far too small to be seen with the human eye. A group of joined atoms is called a molecule. The smallest molecules have two atoms, while the largest have millions.

ATOMS

An atom is made of even smaller particles. In the middle of an atom is its nucleus, which is made of particles called protons and neutrons. Electrons spin around the nucleus. Electrons have a negative electric charge (see page 52), while protons have a positive charge. Neutrons have no charge. Since atoms usually have an equal number of protons and electrons, these opposite forces normally balance, leaving atoms with no electric charge.

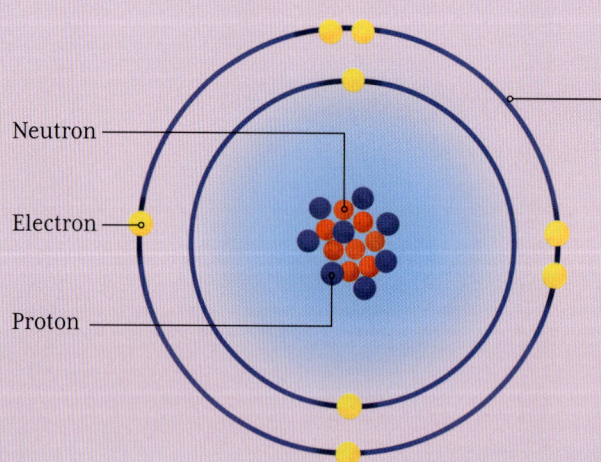

An oxygen atom usually has 8 protons, 8 neutrons, and 8 electrons.

Electrons spin around the nucleus in layers called shells. Each shell can contain only a certain number of electrons: The first shell can hold up to two electrons, the second shell up to eight, the third shell up to 18, and so on. An oxygen atom usually has 2 electrons in its first shell and 6 in its second shell.

ELEMENTS

There are 118 different types of atoms. Materials that are made of only one type of atom are known as elements, so there are also 118 elements (see page 10). Each type of atom has a different number of protons in its nucleus. An atom of hydrogen has just 1 proton in its nucleus, making it the lightest atom—and hydrogen the lightest element. The heaviest element is oganesson, which has 118 protons in each of its atoms.

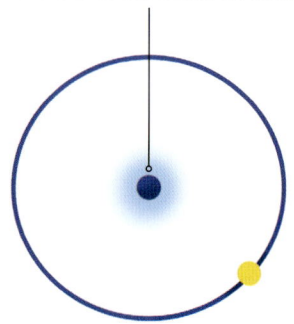

A hydrogen atom has 1 proton. It is the only atom that usually has no neutrons. With just 1 electron shell, it is one of the smallest atoms.

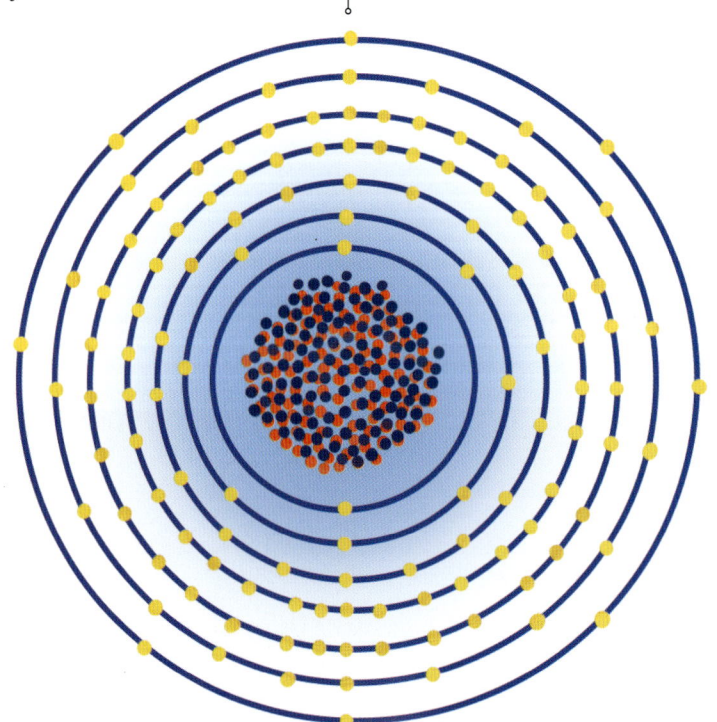

An oganesson atom has 118 protons. With 7 electron shells, it is one of the biggest atoms.

MOLECULES

Molecules form when atoms share or give away electrons, which joins them together. This is known as chemical bonding. Some molecules contain only one type of atom. For example, the oxygen you breathe is made up of molecules with two oxygen atoms (see page 166). Many other molecules contain two or more different types of atoms. These molecules are known as compounds. For example, water is a compound containing oxygen and hydrogen atoms.

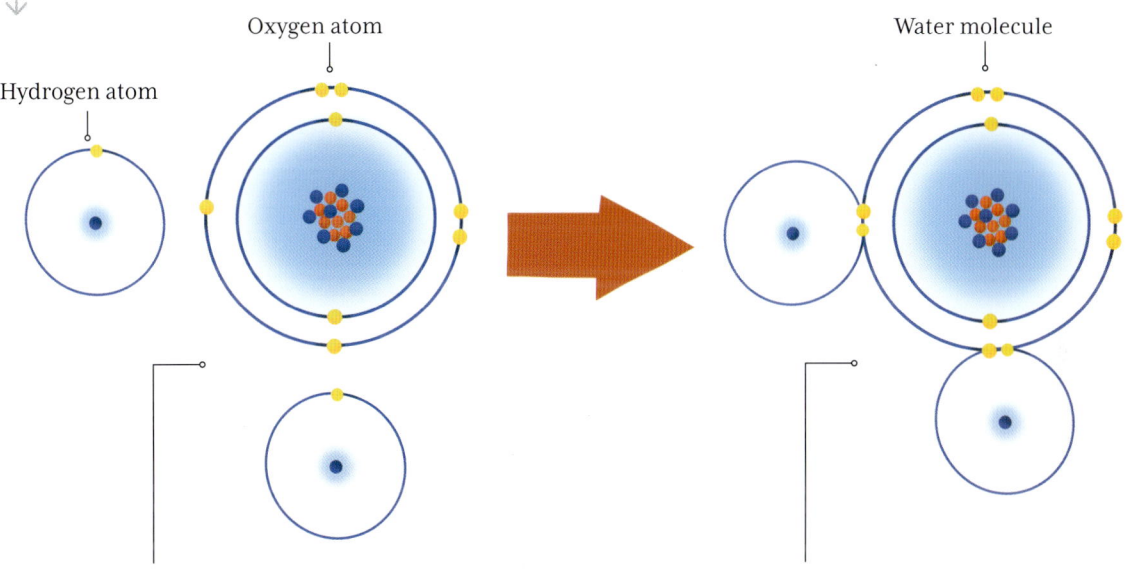

Atoms "try" to fill up their outer electron shell. Hydrogen has 1 electron in its only shell, but has room for 2. Oxygen has 6 electrons in its outer shell, but has room for 8.

Two hydrogen atoms share their electron with an oxygen atom, joining the atoms to form a water molecule. This fills the hydrogen atoms' electron shell, with 2 electrons each. It also fills the oxygen atom's outer shell, with 8 electrons.

A compound has different properties from the elements it contains. At room temperature, water is a liquid, but—on their own—oxygen and hydrogen are gases.

Scientist Profile

NAME John Dalton
DATES 1766–1844
NATIONALITY British
BREAKTHROUGH
He figured out that each molecule in a compound contains a set number of atoms of each element. For example, we now know that a water molecule always contains one oxygen and two hydrogen atoms, which scientists write as a formula: H_2O, where H is for hydrogen and O is for oxygen.

The Periodic Table

The periodic table displays the 118 elements. Elements are substances that are made of only one type of atom and cannot be broken down into simpler substances. Alone or with each other, the elements form all the materials we can see and touch.

The elements are displayed in order of their number of protons (see page 8), which is known as their atomic number. The table starts at the top left with hydrogen, which has 1 proton and atomic number 1. It ends with oganesson, at bottom right, which has atomic number 118.

The table was devised by Russian scientist Dmitri Mendeleev in 1869. He figured out that when the elements are displayed in this way, elements with similar properties fall into the same columns. He left spaces for the elements he thought must exist but had not yet been discovered.

PERIODS

The table is in seven rows, known as periods, which run across the table. (The two extra rows at the bottom are extensions of periods 6 and 7, because there is not enough room to fit them in the right places.) The elements in period 1 have one electron shell (see page 8), while those in period 2 have two shells ... up to the elements in period 7, which have seven electron shells.

ABBREVIATIONS

Each element is presented with its name and an abbreviation (shortening). Some abbreviations are obvious, such as Sc for scandium, while others are based on the element's Latin or German name, such as Au for gold (short for Latin *aurum*).

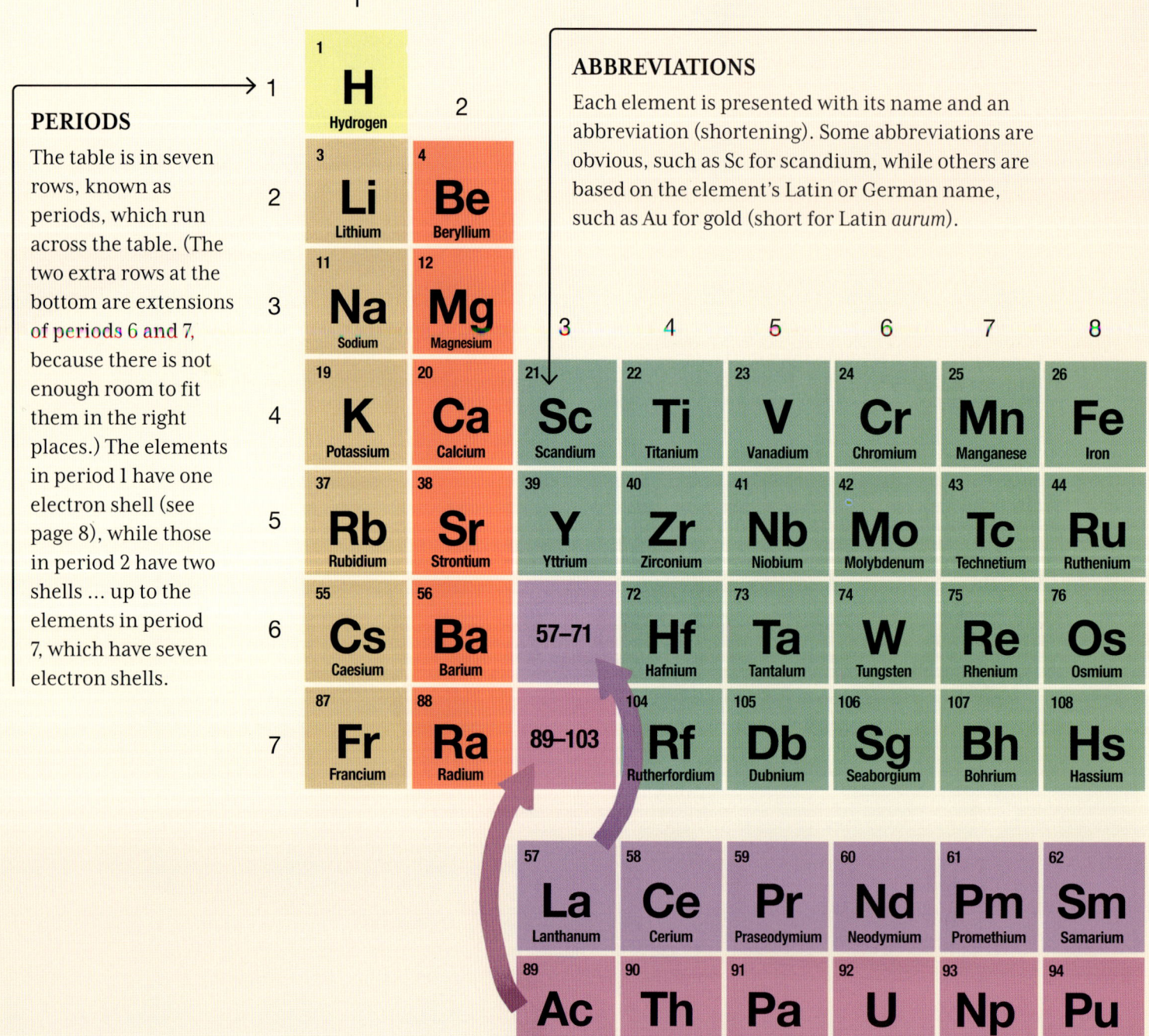

ELEMENT FAMILIES

Blocks of different shades—such as green and orange—are used to group together elements in the same family (see page 12). Elements in a family share similar properties.

KEY

- Alkali metals
- Alkaline earth metals
- Transition metals
- Lanthanides
- Actinides
- Post-transition metals
- Metalloids
- Nonmetals
- Halogens
- Noble gases

GROUPS

The table is arranged in 18 columns, known as groups, which run down the table. Elements in the same group have their electrons arranged in a similar way, which gives them similar properties. For example, elements in group 18, such as helium and neon, are mostly clear gases.

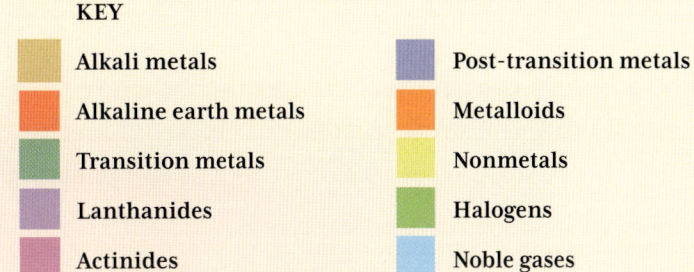

MATTER

Families of Elements

An element family is a group of elements that share properties. Their similar characteristics are due to having the same number of electrons in their outer shell. Elements in the same family are close to each other in the periodic table (see pages 10–11).

ALKALI METALS

These elements are metals. At room temperature, metals are solid materials that are typically hard, shiny, bendy, and conduct heat and electricity, which means that heat and electricity flow through them. The alkali metals are soft, shiny, lightweight, and very good conductors. They react (see page 22) easily and sometimes violently with other elements.

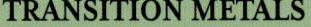

Potassium is so soft that it can be cut with a knife.

ALKALINE EARTH METALS

These metals are harder and heavier than the alkali metals. They are also shiny and very good conductors of heat and electricity. They react with other elements less easily than the alkali metals.

TRANSITION METALS

The largest family, transition metals are harder, stronger, heavier, and melt at a higher temperature than either alkali or alkaline earth metals. They are shiny and very good conductors.

LANTHANIDES

These metals are silvery-white, fairly soft, and do not melt until a high temperature. They react easily with most nonmetals, forming new compounds.

Gold is hard, shiny, and easy to shape, so it is often used for rings and necklaces.

ACTINIDES

These metals are silvery-white, fairly soft, and heavy. They react with most nonmetals. They are all radioactive (see page 28).

MATTER

POST-TRANSITION METALS
Although these elements share some characteristics with transition metals, they are softer, more breakable, and melt at lower temperatures. They usually conduct less heat and electricity.

Aluminum is often used in planes because it is very lightweight, but it must be mixed with other materials to make it stronger.

METALLOIDS
Positioned on the periodic table between the metals and nonmetals, these elements usually look like metals, but do not always behave like them. They are shiny, but brittle rather than bendy. They may conduct heat and electricity only under certain conditions.

HALOGENS
At room temperature, some halogens are gases, some liquids, and some solids. Halogens are often toxic, which means they can harm living things. They react easily with other elements, particularly alkali metals.

Chlorine is added to swimming pool water to kill germs.

NONMETALS
These elements are not metals, so they are not shiny, bendy, or conductors of heat and electricity. At room temperature, some are gases and some solids.

Along with other living things, humans are made mostly of nonmetals. By mass, your body is 65 percent oxygen, 18.5 percent carbon, 9.5 percent hydrogen, and 3.3 percent nitrogen.

NOBLE GASES
At room temperature, these elements are clear gases, with no smell or taste. They do not burn easily and do not react easily with other elements.

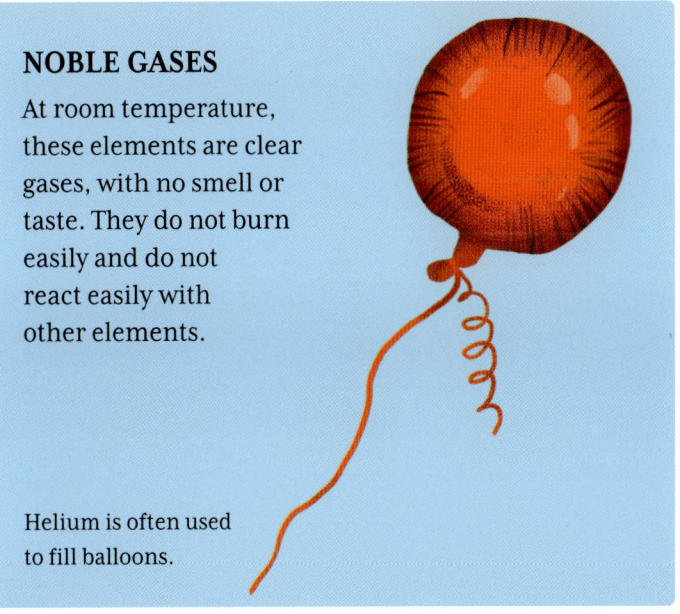

Helium is often used to fill balloons.

MATTER

Solids

Every element can exist in different states—solid, liquid, and gas—depending on its temperature. These are known as states of matter. If you look around, you will spot many solids, from books to chairs to pencils.

WHAT IS A SOLID?

All solids share some characteristics. A solid can be held. A solid object keeps the same volume at the same temperature, which means it takes up the same amount of space. Most solids have a definite shape. However, some solids—such as a wire or a rubber ball—can be stretched, bent, or flattened.

ATOMS IN A SOLID

In a solid, atoms or molecules are tightly packed and stuck to each other. The atoms cannot easily be pushed aside, which is why you cannot put your hand through a table. Unless atoms are very, very cold—at -273 °C (-459 °F)—atoms are always moving. But the atoms in a solid are tightly joined and lack the movement and energy to change position. However, they do vibrate (shake). This vibration can be seen only with the help of a super-powerful microscope.

The atoms in a solid are stuck together and cannot change their position. This means that a solid does not change its shape to fill a container.

Diamond

Diamond molecular structure

Diamond is a crystalline solid made of carbon atoms stuck together in a regular pattern known as diamond cubic. This arrangement is extremely strong, making diamond the hardest natural material. Diamonds can be shaped by cutting them using saws with diamond blades.

STICKING TOGETHER

Most atoms and molecules are attracted to each other. In a solid, this attraction makes them stick together. This "stickiness" is much weaker than the chemical bonds that join a molecule. However, the vibration of the atoms is too tiny to pull the molecules away from each other.

In most solids, the atoms and molecules are stuck to each other in a regular, repeating pattern. These are known as crystalline solids. In other solids, the atoms or molecules are stuck together more messily and irregularly. These are known as amorphous solids. Glass, wax, and rubber are amorphous solids. They tend to be less hard and strong than crystalline solids.

Scientist Profile
NAME Ida Noddack
DATES 1896–1978
NATIONALITY German
BREAKTHROUGH
Along with her husband Walter Noddack and Otto Berg, in 1925 she discovered element 75, rhenium. One of the rarest elements in Earth's crust, it is a heavy transition metal that is solid at any temperature below 3,186 °C (5,767 °F).

Glass is an amorphous solid made of molecules of the compound silicon dioxide (SiO_2), each with one silicon atom joined to two oxygen atoms. The molecules are stuck together irregularly, which makes glass less rigid. While crystalline solids melt at a particular temperature, glass softens and melts gradually over a temperature range, so it can be shaped easily when hot.

Glass

Glass molecular structure

MATTER

Liquids

When an element gets warm enough, it melts from a solid into a liquid. The most common liquid on Earth is a compound: water. Water covers more than two-thirds of Earth's surface and makes up around 60 percent of the human body.

WHAT IS A LIQUID?

Liquids can be held in a suitable container. They do not have a fixed shape. However, they do have a fixed volume, if their temperature remains the same. This means that, if you pour a carton of milk into different-shaped glasses and bowls, it will take up the same amount of space even though its shape changes.

ATOMS IN A LIQUID

In a liquid, atoms or molecules are quite tightly packed together, but not stuck to each other. This is because the atoms or molecules are warm enough—and vibrating fast enough—to break free from each other. They can move past each other, which allows liquids to flow.

If a liquid is heated, its atoms vibrate faster and move farther apart. This makes liquids expand (get bigger). We make use of this fact in liquid thermometers, in which the liquid in a tube expands, moving up a marked scale, as the temperature rises.

The atoms in a liquid can move past each other, so they flow to cover the bottom of a container.

16

SLOW FLOW

Some liquids flow faster than others. Some, such as peanut butter, flow so slowly that they can be mistaken for solids. Viscosity is the term that describes how fast a liquid flows. Low-viscosity ("runny") liquids—such as water and juice—have molecules that slide past each other easily.

High-viscosity liquids—such as oil and honey—have molecules that catch on or rub against each other, slowing them down. Usually, larger molecules—such as those in honey—have more difficulty in sliding. However, heating a high-viscosity liquid makes the molecules move farther apart and flow more easily.

Scientist Profile

NAME Carl Jacob Löwig
DATES 1803–90
NATIONALITY German
BREAKTHROUGH
He discovered bromine, which (along with mercury) is one of only two elements that are liquid at room temperature. Bromine is not found alone in nature, only in compounds with other elements.

Surface tension is a force that makes the surface of a liquid behave like a skin. Water's high surface tension is caused by water molecules being very attracted to each other. Below the surface, the molecules pull each other in all directions. However, surface molecules have only air above them, so they are pulled only downward, which draws them together to form a skin.

Surface tension allows insects called pond skaters to walk across water. Their long, hairy legs spread their weight across the "skin," so it does not break.

Gases

Even though you cannot see or smell it, you are surrounded by gas. The air is a blanket of gases including all-important oxygen, which you need to breathe. Gas is the third state of matter, but not the last ...

WHAT IS A GAS?

Gases cannot easily be held in your hands. They do not have a fixed shape. They also do not have a fixed volume. This means that, in any container, they always expand to fill all the available space.

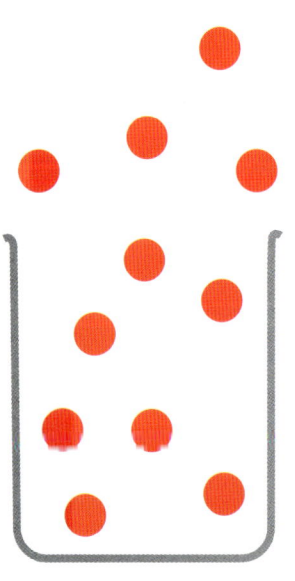

The atoms in a gas fly in all directions, quickly and freely.

FOURTH STATE OF MATTER

On Earth, we are familiar with only three states of matter, but a fourth state exists: plasma. To become a plasma, gas has to get extremely hot. On Earth, this usually happens only high in Earth's atmosphere and in lightning. Elsewhere in the Universe, plasma is very common: Stars are made mostly of plasma.

In a plasma, the atoms are so hot that they rip apart, losing electrons. Since electrons have an electric charge (see page 8), this gives plasma an electric charge. When plasma flowing from the Sun meets Earth's atmosphere, the air glows, creating lights called auroras. These can usually be seen only around the poles.

ATOMS IN A GAS

In a gas, atoms or molecules are warm enough—giving them enough energy—to dart around freely. If they are packed into a small container, they can be close to each other. If they are not in a container, they can be very far apart.

The atoms and molecules bounce off each other and against the sides of any container. The force of atoms and molecules hitting a container's walls is called "gas pressure."

As a gas gets hotter, its atoms move faster. If a warming gas is in a stretchy container—such as a balloon—the growing pressure of the gas on the inside of the balloon will make the balloon expand.

Scientist Profile
NAME William Ramsay
DATES 1852–1916
NATIONALITY Scottish
BREAKTHROUGH
In 1898, he and Morris Travers discovered the elements krypton, neon, and xenon, which are found in small quantities in air. He cooled air until it was liquid, then captured the elements as they boiled into gas at different temperatures. These three noble gases are among the 11 elements that are gases at room temperature.

MATTER

If you let go of a balloon filled with helium gas, it rises into the air. This is partly because helium is lighter than air. Helium has only 2 protons in its atoms, so it is very light. Around 78 percent of air is the heavier gas nitrogen, which has 7 protons in its atoms.

The air beneath the balloon pushes on the balloon with more force than the air above the balloon—so the light balloon moves upward. This is because the pressure of the air beneath the balloon is slightly greater than the pressure of the air above the balloon, because air gets thinner the higher you travel. This is due to the force of gravity (see page 33)—which pulls air toward Earth—getting weaker farther from Earth's surface.

Changes of State

Elements change from one state to another when they are heated or cooled. Solids melt into liquids, while liquids freeze into solids. Liquids evaporate into gases, while gases condense into liquids.

MELTING AND FREEZING

When a solid element gets warmer, its atoms gain energy. As the atoms vibrate faster, they separate from each other. The solid melts, becoming a liquid. When an element freezes, the reverse happens. As its atoms cool, they have less energy. They slow, move closer, then stick together. These changes are reversible, which means that a melted element can be frozen again—and the other way around.

Melting point is the temperature at which a particular material changes state between solid and liquid. Each element has a different melting point. The element with the lowest melting point is helium, which melts at -272 °C (-458 °F). Carbon has the highest melting point, at 3,550 °C (6,420 °F).

Water's melting point is around 0 °C (32 °F). This is the temperature at which its molecules are shaking fast enough to unstick from each other, changing from solid ice to liquid water.

MATTER

EVAPORATING AND CONDENSING

Evaporation happens when atoms in a liquid are warm enough—and moving fast enough—to break free from it. The atoms become gas. On a sunny day, evaporation makes puddles dry up within a few hours. However, evaporation happens much faster if a liquid is boiled. This is when its atoms are moving so fast that they form big bubbles of gas that rise to the liquid's surface.

Each element boils at a different temperature, known as its boiling point. Helium has the lowest boiling point, at -269 °C (-452 °F). Tungsten has the highest boiling point: 5,930 °C (10,706 °F).

Condensation happens when a gas is cooled to its boiling point or below. The gas's atoms slow and move closer together, becoming liquid. You can watch condensation happening on the outside of a cold soda glass. As the glass cools the surrounding air, the gaseous water floating in air turns to liquid water on the glass.

Scientist Profile

NAME Anders Celsius
DATES 1701–44
NATIONALITY Swedish
BREAKTHROUGH
He developed the Celsius (often written as °C) scale, which we use to measure temperature. His version of the scale measured the boiling point of water as 0 °C and the freezing point as 100 °C, but today those values are reversed.

NO CHANGE

All elements can exist in all states of matter, but not all compounds (see page 9) or mixtures (see page 24) can. That is because many larger molecules break apart when they get too hot, so they do not have a melting or boiling point. Many materials, such as the paper in this book, catch fire if you heat them. However, some common compounds—such as water and glass—do exist in all three states.

Water's boiling point is around 100 °C (212 °F). At this temperature, its molecules break free, forming bubbles of gaseous water, called water vapor, that rise into the air.

Chemical Reactions

A chemical reaction is when two or more materials react to each other, breaking or making chemical bonds between their atoms (see page 9). This makes a new material or materials. Chemical reactions formed all the millions of compounds in the Universe. Here are some examples of reactions.

RUSTING

Although most materials can touch each other without reacting, nearly all metals react to contact with oxygen. Very slowly, the metal iron reacts to the oxygen and water in damp air. The iron's surface takes oxygen atoms, becoming a reddish material called iron oxide, which we often call rust.

COMBUSTION

Also called "burning," combustion is a chemical reaction. Three things are needed for this reaction: heat, a fuel such as wood, and oxygen in the air. The reaction produces ash and the gases carbon dioxide and water vapor. A combustion reaction is useful, because it releases energy from the wood as heat, which can cook food or power machinery. It is also dangerous, since fire can kill.

BIOLUMINESCENCE

Some deep-sea creatures make their own light to attract mates or prey in the dark water. This ability is called bioluminescence. Special body parts create a chemical reaction by combining oxygen with chemicals called luciferase and luciferins. The reaction releases light.

MATTER

FINGERPRINTING

Police officers use a chemical reaction to see fingerprints at a crime scene. When we touch surfaces, we leave behind invisible fingerprints of sweat and skin oil, in the unique pattern of the ridges on our fingertips. The element iodine reacts to sweat and oil, turning fingerprints brown.

MAKING TOAST

When bread is heated, it undergoes a chemical reaction—and becomes toast. Heat causes a reaction between the bread's sugars and molecules called amino acids. They become brown molecules called melanoidins. As with many chemical reactions, we know that a reaction has taken place because of a change in the material's appearance. As with most chemical reactions, this change cannot be reversed.

Scientist Profile

NAME Stephanie Kwolek
DATES 1923–2014
NATIONALITY Polish-American
BREAKTHROUGH
In 1965, she created the material Kevlar using a reaction between two chemicals: an amine and an acid. This material is so strong that it is used to make bulletproof vests and car brakes.

Mixtures

Many materials are neither made of one pure element nor of one pure compound: They are mixtures. The paper in this book is a mixture! You can also make mixtures in the kitchen by whisking together oil and vinegar or adding raisins to cereal.

A mixture contains two or more elements or compounds. These materials have not reacted together, so their atoms are not chemically bonded. This means that the materials in a mixture keep their own characteristics. They may not be mixed in particular quantities. For example, a mixture of oil and vinegar can contain two spoons of both or two of one and three of the other.

Unlike most chemical reactions, which cannot be reversed, making a mixture is a reversible change: Its materials can be separated again. A mixture of oil and vinegar can be separated by letting the oil, which is lighter, rise to the surface. Air is a mixture that can be separated by cooling it to a liquid, then using a similar method. A mixture of a liquid and solid can be separated with a filter, which has tiny holes that let the liquid pass through.

ROCK
Different types of rocks are mixtures of different ingredients. The common rock granite is a mix of compounds containing elements such as silicon, oxygen, potassium, and aluminum. It may be studded with gemstones such as topaz, which are compounds of fluorine, aluminum, silicon, and oxygen.

SEAWATER
Pure water is a compound of hydrogen and oxygen (see page 9), but seawater is a mixture because it also contains salts and gases, including oxygen. Salts are compounds that can be made by reacting an acid with a base (see page 26). The most common salt in seawater is sodium chloride, which is better known as the "salt" we put on food.

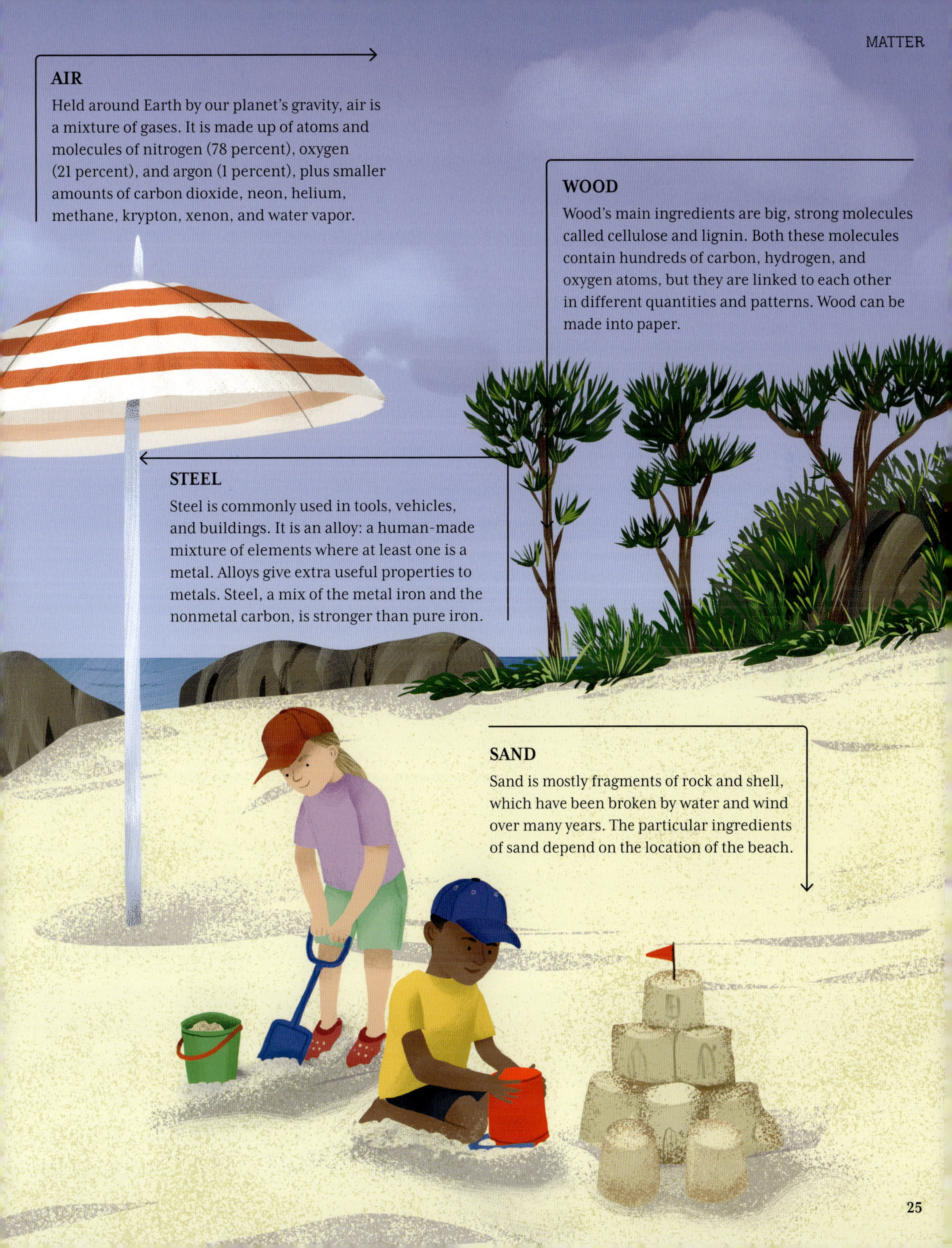

MATTER

AIR
Held around Earth by our planet's gravity, air is a mixture of gases. It is made up of atoms and molecules of nitrogen (78 percent), oxygen (21 percent), and argon (1 percent), plus smaller amounts of carbon dioxide, neon, helium, methane, krypton, xenon, and water vapor.

WOOD
Wood's main ingredients are big, strong molecules called cellulose and lignin. Both these molecules contain hundreds of carbon, hydrogen, and oxygen atoms, but they are linked to each other in different quantities and patterns. Wood can be made into paper.

STEEL
Steel is commonly used in tools, vehicles, and buildings. It is an alloy: a human-made mixture of elements where at least one is a metal. Alloys give extra useful properties to metals. Steel, a mix of the metal iron and the nonmetal carbon, is stronger than pure iron.

SAND
Sand is mostly fragments of rock and shell, which have been broken by water and wind over many years. The particular ingredients of sand depend on the location of the beach.

25

Acids and Bases

Apart from water, many of the liquids in your home are acids or bases. Acids include lemon juice and vinegar, while bases include toothpaste and soap. Strong acids and bases are extremely dangerous and must never be touched or eaten.

WHAT IS AN ACID?

Acids have a sour taste. However, strong acids eat away skin and even metal, so must never be tasted. Acids are substances that contain hydrogen atoms and—if added to water—will break apart, releasing hydrogen ions. An ion is an atom or molecule with a positive or negative electric charge because it does not have an equal number of positive protons and negative electrons (see page 8).

A hydrogen ion is a hydrogen atom that has lost its electron, leaving only its proton. This makes it out of balance: It has a positive charge. Strong acids release a lot of hydrogen ions, while weak ones release fewer. The hydrogen ions "try" to find balance by attaching to other substances they meet. This is what makes strong acids dangerous: They create chemical reactions, changing the other substance.

WHAT IS A BASE?

A base is the opposite of an acid. If it can be dissolved in water, it releases hydroxide ions, which are molecules with one hydrogen atom and one oxygen atom, which between them have 10 electrons but only 9 protons. This makes a hydroxide ion out of balance: It has a negative charge. If added to an acid, a base's negative hydroxide ions attract the acid's positive hydrogen ions. This chemical reaction neutralizes the acid, taking away its acidic nature.

Like a strong acid, a strong base is very reactive because it "tries" to find balance by bonding with other materials. A strong base easily breaks down materials such as fats and oils, which is why bases are used in soaps, detergents, and drain cleaners. Strong bases are just as dangerous as strong acids.

The strength of acids and bases is measured on the pH (short for "power, or potential, of hydrogen") scale. The strongest and most dangerous acids have a pH of 0, while the strongest bases have a pH of 14.

0 Battery acid   1 Stomach acid   2 Lemon juice   3 Vinegar   4 Tomato juice   5 Black coffee   6 Milk   7 Pure water

ACID   NEUTRAL

MATTER

When the acid hydrogen chloride (HCl) is added to water, it breaks into positive hydrogen ions and negative chloride ions.

When the base sodium hydroxide (NaOH) is added to water, it breaks into negative hydroxide ions and positive sodium ions.

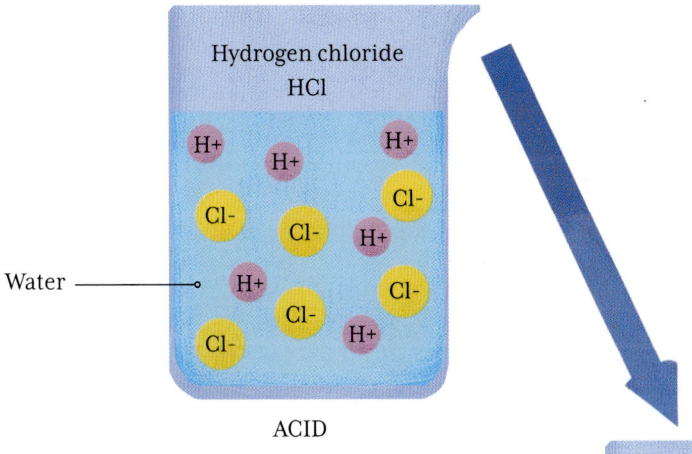

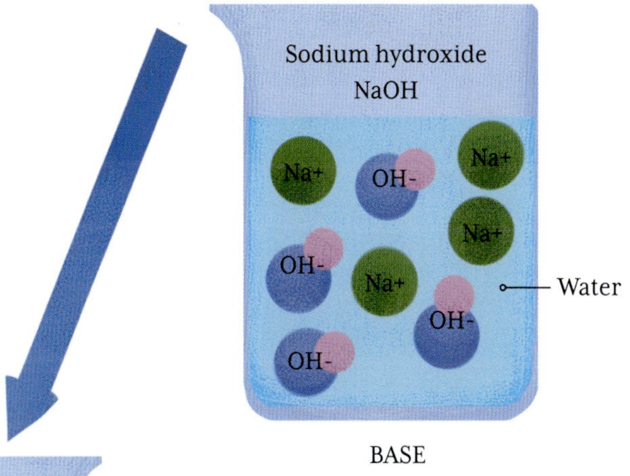

Hydrogen chloride
HCl

Water

ACID

Sodium hydroxide
NaOH

Water

BASE

If this acid and base are combined, they chemically react to create two neutral materials: water (H_2O) and sodium chloride (NaCl), better known as table salt.

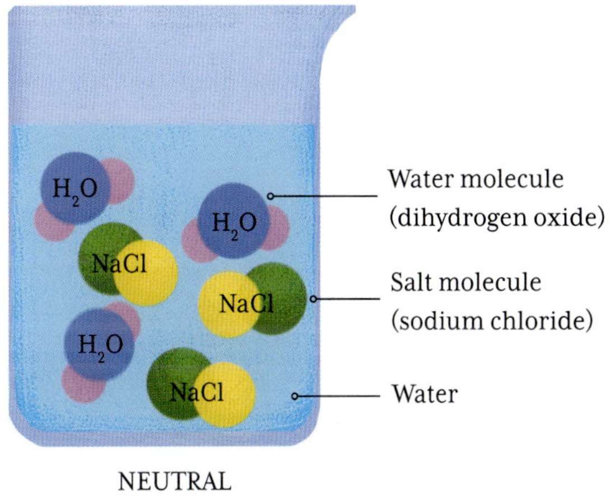

Water molecule (dihydrogen oxide)

Salt molecule (sodium chloride)

Water

NEUTRAL

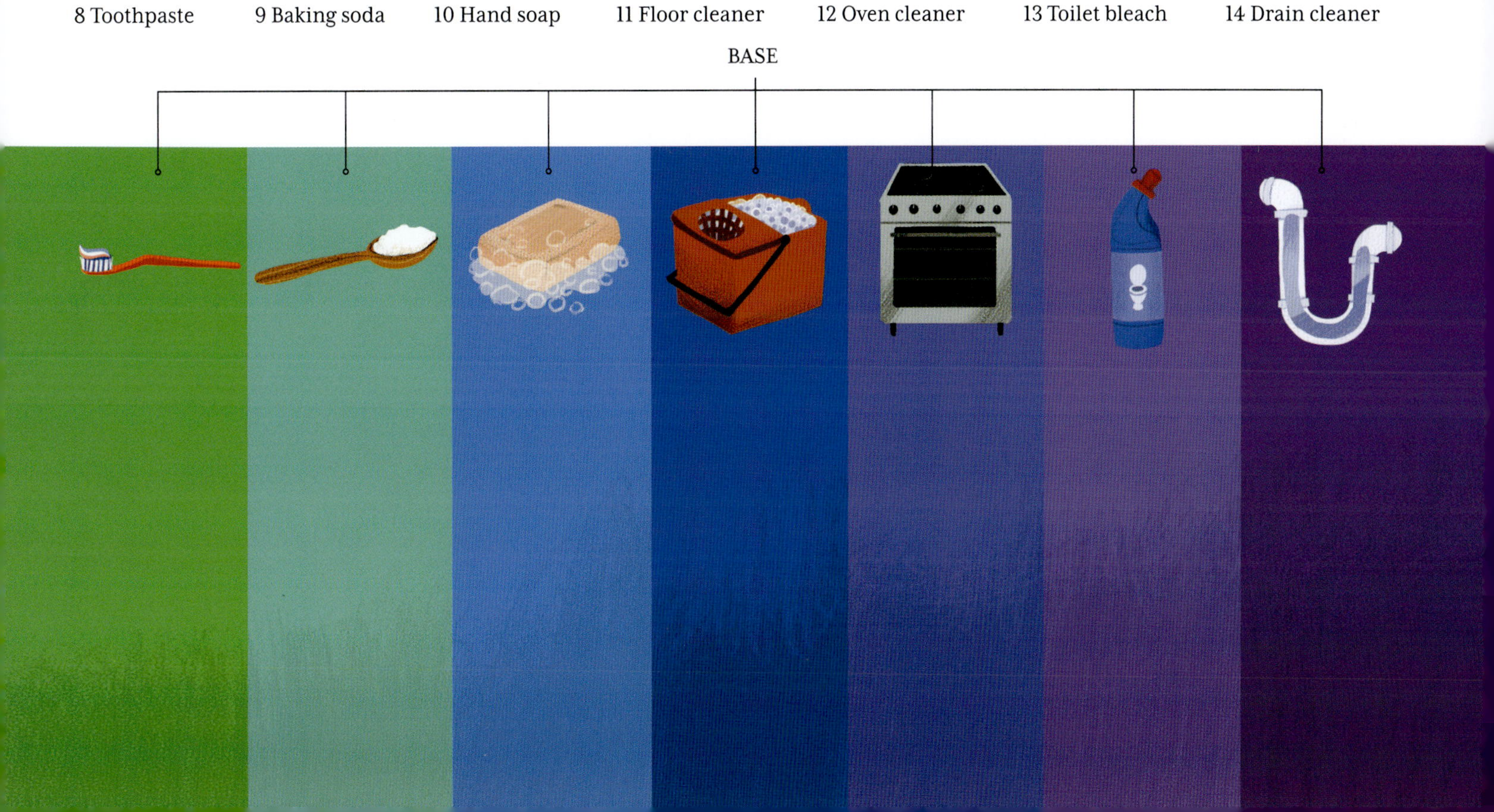

8 Toothpaste 9 Baking soda 10 Hand soap 11 Floor cleaner 12 Oven cleaner 13 Toilet bleach 14 Drain cleaner

BASE

MATTER

Isotopes

Each element has a particular number of protons, along with—usually—a matching number of electrons. However, every element can exist in different forms, called isotopes, each with a different number of neutrons in its nucleus.

NUMBER OF NEUTRONS

Hydrogen is the element with the fewest isotopes: three. Caesium and xenon have the most known isotopes: 36. Like many elements, hydrogen has one isotope that is most common, while the others are rarer. Nearly all hydrogen atoms in Earth and its atmosphere are the isotope hydrogen-1, with no neutron in their nucleus. The rarer hydrogen-2 isotope has one neutron, while the hydrogen-3 isotope has two neutrons.

Different isotopes of an element have many of the same properties, so the hydrogen isotopes are all gases at room temperature. However, since they have more neutrons, the hydrogen-2 and hydrogen-3 isotopes are heavier. They also have different melting and boiling points.

STABLE AND RADIOACTIVE

There are two types of isotopes: stable and unstable. Stable isotopes do not change over time. Unstable isotopes are also called radioactive isotopes or radioisotopes. These isotopes have too many or too few neutrons to hold the atom together. This is because neutrons and protons exert a pulling force on each other, which holds together the nucleus—but only if they are balanced.

Radioisotopes break apart, which makes them give off energy, known as radiation. A decaying radioisotope atom can—over seconds or over billions of years—lose a neutron, becoming a different isotope; or lose a proton, becoming a different element entirely.

All elements with 83 or more protons (an atomic number of 83 or more), as well as technetium (atomic number 43) and promethium (atomic number 61), have only unstable isotopes. These elements are always radioactive, either weakly or strongly.

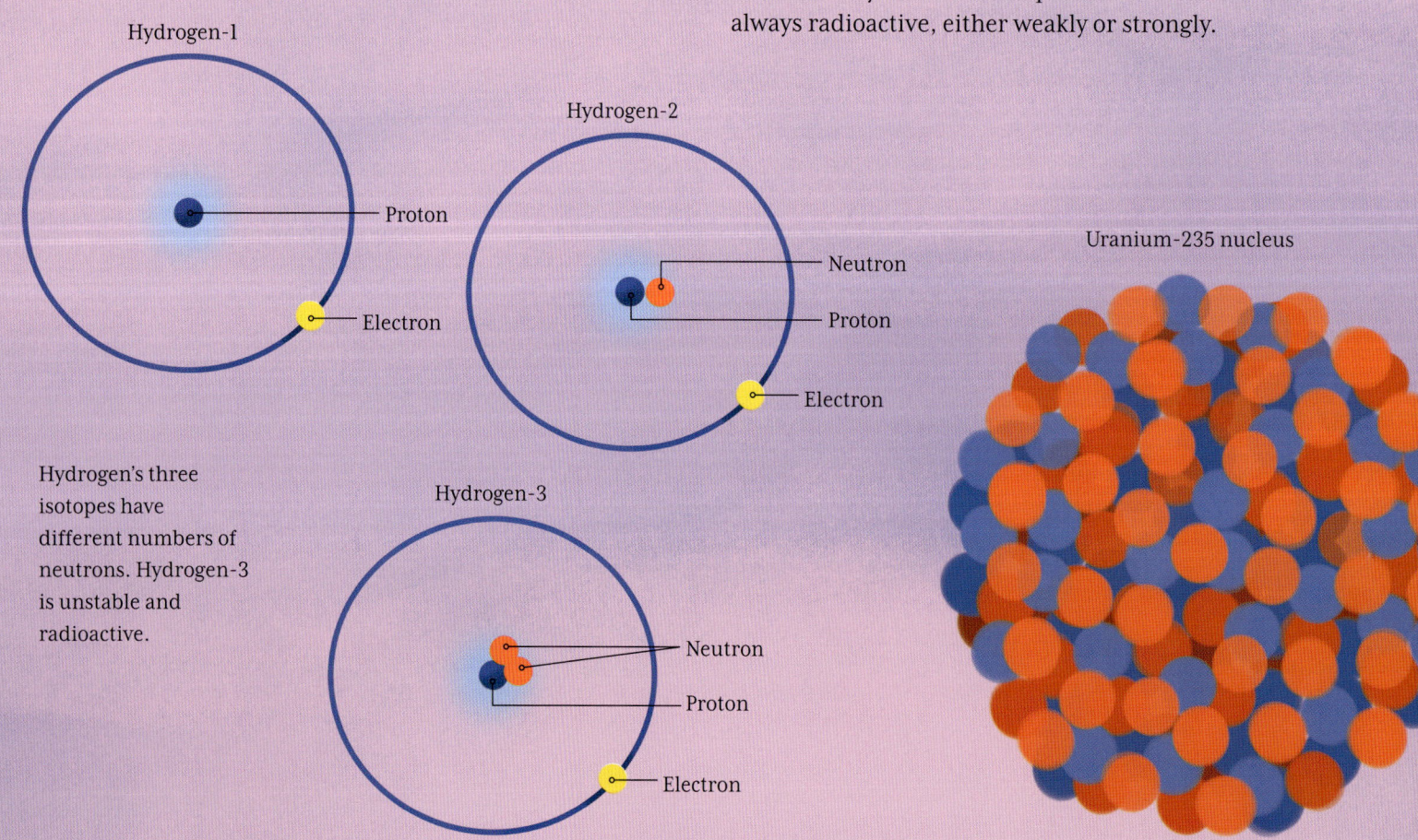

Hydrogen's three isotopes have different numbers of neutrons. Hydrogen-3 is unstable and radioactive.

MATTER

USEFUL RADIOISOTOPES

Radiation can be dangerous in large quantities, since it damages living cells. However, when radiation is carefully targeted, it can save lives. For example, the radioactive isotope lead-212 is used to kill cancer cells while limiting damage to healthy cells.

Radioisotopes are also used in power plants to release energy that is harnessed to make electricity. The current method for this is nuclear fission (which means "splitting of the nucleus"). Usually, the nuclei of uranium-235 or plutonium-239 are split. These big, unstable nuclei are easier to split—and release much more energy— than smaller, more stable nuclei.

Scientist Profile
NAME John Cockcroft and Ernest Walton
DATES 1897–1967 and 1903–95
NATIONALITY British and Irish
BREAKTHROUGH
In 1932, they were the first to split an atom's nucleus, by firing protons at lithium. This divided each lithium nucleus into two helium nuclei.

Neutron

A neutron shoots at a uranium-235 nucleus, making it split.

To start the process of nuclear fission, a nuclear power plant uses a start-up neutron source, such as californium-252. This highly radioactive isotope gives off lots of neutrons.

Uranium-235 nucleus

Neutron

Two or three neutrons are released, which shoot into more uranium nuclei and split them, repeating the process over and over again. This is known as a chain reaction.

Uranium-235 nucleus

Neutron

Strontium-93 nucleus

Two lighter elements are produced, which are themselves radioactive and must be disposed of carefully.

Xenon-140 nucleus

Energy

Energy is released in the form of radiation and heat. The heat is used to boil water to make steam, which turns a generator that converts movement energy into electrical energy.

29

Forces and Energy

Without forces, the Universe would not exist. Any push or pull on an object or particle is a force. Forces such as the electromagnetic force help to hold together atoms by pulling together their tiny electrons and protons. Without atoms, there would be no matter: no planets or people. On a larger scale, forces are responsible for matter having the form we know and take for granted. Without the force of gravity, you would float off Earth into space—and, in fact, Earth would not exist to float away from. Forces including the reaction force stop you being able to put your hand through tables, walls, and people.

In our everyday lives, we use forces—pushes, pulls, and presses—to get everything done, from squeezing toothpaste on a brush to kicking a ball. You can see forces at work as they change the speed, direction, or shape of objects. When a force moves or changes the shape of an object, that is called work. Work changes energy from one form to another or transfers energy from one object to another. When you squeeze toothpaste or kick a ball, you are doing both. You are changing energy in your muscles into movement energy in the toothpaste or ball. You are also transferring energy from you to the toothpaste or ball. Energy is the ability to do work—the ability to apply a force that moves or changes the shape of an object.

Without energy, the Universe as we know it could not exist. Without energy, there could be no movement, change—or life. Energy takes many different forms, from the light we see to the mechanical energy of a speeding train. From humans' earliest days, we have learned to harness energy so we can eat, travel, and communicate. Hundreds of thousands of years ago, we learned to harness the chemical energy in wood by burning it, which releases heat energy that cooks food. Over the last few hundred years, we have learned to harness electrical energy to power light bulbs, machines, and televisions.

When you kick a soccer ball, you are applying a force. You are transferring energy from yourself to the ball. When the ball moves into the air, you have done work!

Born in the region of modern Iraq, Ibn al-Haytham (c.965–1040) was the first to explain that it is light reflecting off objects, into our eyes, that allows us to see. He realized this when he saw light shining through a tiny hole into his darkened room, projecting an image onto the opposite wall, as happens on the eye's retina. Light is a form of electromagnetic energy.

FORCES AND ENERGY

Forces at Work

Forces are pushes and pulls. We cannot see forces, but we can see their effects on objects. Forces make objects move, speed up, slow down, change direction, or change shape. Forces are caused by interaction between objects—when an object affects another object.

There are two types of forces: contact and non-contact. Contact forces act on objects when they are touching. Every day, you probably come across contact forces including tension, friction, spring, reaction, and applied forces.

Non-contact forces act between objects when they are not touching. These include gravity, as well as electric and magnetic forces (see page 53). Forces are measured in newtons, named after Sir Isaac Newton (see page 34): 1 newton is the force needed to accelerate (speed up) a 1 kg (2.2 lb) object by 1 m (3.3 ft) per second per second.

APPLIED

An applied force is a force applied to an object by a person or another object. If you push, pull, lift, or throw an object, you are applying a force to it. Scientists define "work" as the use of force to move an object. The farther the object is moved, the greater the work done.

FRICTION

Friction is a force between objects that are moving against one another, for example when a rabbit hutch is pushed across the floor. Friction works in the opposite direction from the way an object is moving, slowing it down. The rougher the surfaces, the greater the friction. A type of friction, called air resistance, acts between a moving object and the air, slowing the moving object.

FORCES AND ENERGY

GRAVITY

Gravity pulls all objects toward each other. The greater the mass (often called "weight") of an object, the bigger the pull of its gravity, so Earth's gravity is greater than a ball's. If you throw a ball upward, its speed slows due to Earth's gravity, which pulls in the opposite direction from the ball's motion. Finally, the ball stops, then falls to Earth—speeding up again as it plummets.

TENSION

This force travels through a rope or wire that is pulled tight. An acrobat dangling from a trapeze has tension exerted on them by the trapeze's rope. A team of sled dogs also pulls a sled using tension: The force travels through their harnesses and ropes.

REACTION

When an object rests on a surface, the surface pushes back with an equal force, known as the reaction force. So when a gymnast handstands on a pedestal, the pedestal pushes back on the gymnast. The heavier the gymnast, the greater the force exerted by the pedestal.

SPRING

A spring is a coil that returns to its original shape when stretched or compressed (squeezed). An object that compresses or stretches a spring is acted on by a force that returns the spring to its original shape. If a spring is compressed by an acrobat jumping on a springboard, the spring force pushes in the opposite direction—so the acrobat bounces into the air.

33

FORCES AND ENERGY

Laws of Motion

In 1687, the English scientist Sir Isaac Newton figured out three laws of motion. His three rules describe the relationship between the forces acting on an object and the way the object moves. The laws apply to objects bigger than an atom, on Earth and in space.

FIRST LAW OF MOTION

This law states that an object that is not moving will continue to not move, unless it is acted on by a force. It also states that an object that is in motion will stay in motion with the same speed and direction, unless it is acted on by a force. This law is one of the reasons why you must wear a seatbelt in a moving car: If the car brakes suddenly, you will keep on moving forward, unless you are restrained by a seatbelt.

A soccer ball does not move, unless a force acts on it.

The applied force of a kick sends a soccer ball into the air.

The soccer ball would continue to travel at the same speed and in the same direction, but the forces of gravity and air resistance act on it, bringing it to a stop on the ground.

SECOND LAW OF MOTION

The second law explains an object's acceleration, which is the rate at which it either speeds up or slows down. Newton explained that acceleration depends on the force acting on the object and the mass (often called "weight") of the object. If you double the force on an object, you double its acceleration. However, if you double the mass of an object, you halve its acceleration. This explains why it takes more force to move a heavy object than to move a light one.

Newton's second law tells us why it is harder work to push a full shopping cart than to push an empty one.

FORCES AND ENERGY

Scientist Profile
NAME Isaac Newton
DATES 1643–1727
NATIONALITY English
BREAKTHROUGH
In 1666, before figuring out the laws of motion, Newton realized that a force attracts every object to every other object, explaining why an apple falls to Earth. He called the force gravity (from the Latin *gravitas*, meaning "weight").

THIRD LAW OF MOTION

Newton's third law tells us that, for every action, there is an equal and opposite reaction. This means that forces come in pairs: When one object exerts force on a second object, the second object exerts an equal force on the first object. The third law explains how you skateboard on level ground: As you push off against the ground with your foot, the force of your kick is matched by the force the ground exerts on your foot—which propels you forward.

The third law explains how a rocket lifts off. Its engines burn fuel, creating a downward blast of hot gas—and an opposite force, which shoots the rocket upward.

FORCES AND ENERGY

Simple Machines

A machine is a device that uses forces to perform a task. These six simple machines were invented thousands of years ago. They make work easier by changing the strength or direction of a force. Many of today's complex machines, found in factories and vehicles, contain several of these simple machines.

As well as increasing a force, a wedge also changes its direction: from downward to sideways.

WEDGE

A wedge is a triangular block. This shape means that the force applied to the wedge is less than the resulting force. If a wedge is used to split wood, the applied force is a blow across the wedge's broader side. At the sharp end of the wedge, the force is concentrated in a smaller area, making the resulting force on the wood greater. You can see wedges in tools such as axes and shovels.

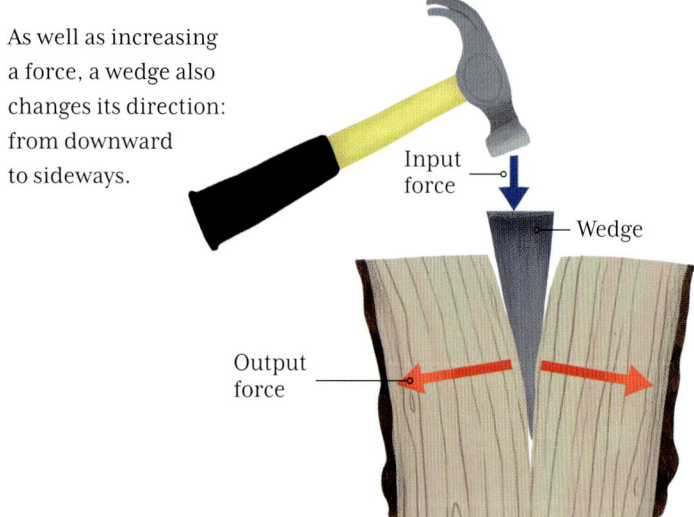

INCLINED PLANE

Also called a ramp, an inclined plane is a sloping surface. It takes less force to push a heavy box up a slope than it does to lift the box to the same height, because the slope supports some of the box's weight as it is pushed. However, you do need to move the box a greater distance, all the way up the long slope.

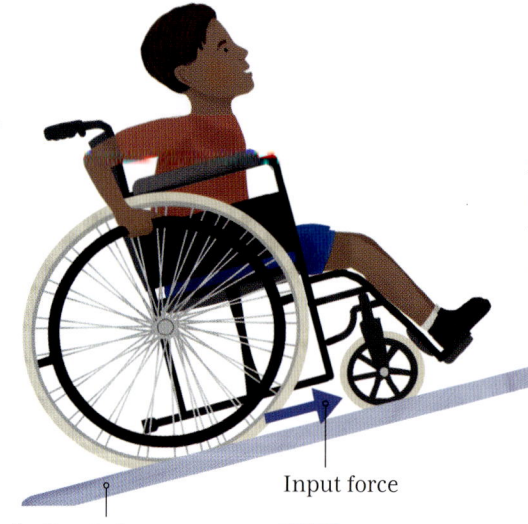

An inclined plane makes it easier for a wheelchair-user to reach a higher floor.

WHEEL

It is much easier to pull a heavy box on a wheeled cart than to pull the box along the ground, since there is less friction (see page 32) between the narrow edge of the wheel and the ground than between a box and the ground. The bigger the wheels on the cart, the farther the cart travels without you having to pull harder.

An axle is the central rod around which a wheel turns.

A wheel is bigger than its axle, so for every turn of the axle, the edge of the wheel turns farther—so a large-wheeled vehicle travels farther with less effort.

FORCES AND ENERGY

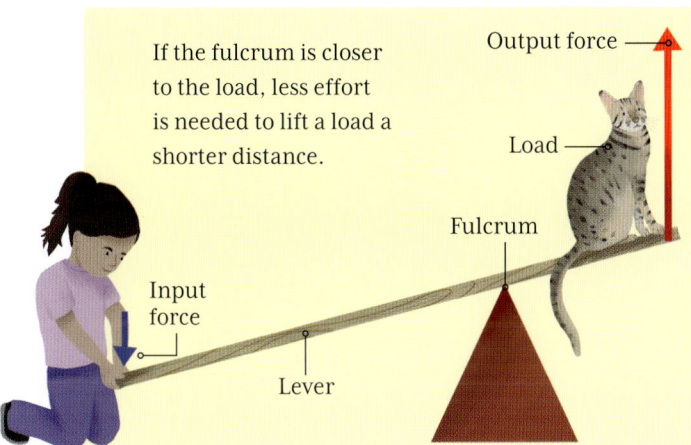

If the fulcrum is closer to the load, less effort is needed to lift a load a shorter distance.

LEVER

A lever is a straight rod or beam that can be pivoted (turned) around a turning point, called the fulcrum. If the fulcrum is closer to one end of the lever than the other, a lever makes it easier to lift a load. You must apply a downward force to the long end of the lever to lift a load resting on the opposite end. You press your end of the lever a greater distance to lift the opposite end a short distance, but this results in a greater lifting force on the load. You can see levers in wheelbarrows, scissors, and nutcrackers.

PULLEY

This simple machine is a wheel with a rope or cable looped around its rim. A pulley changes the direction of a force. If a load is attached to one end of the rope, pulling downward on the opposite end of the rope will lift the load upward.

Pulleys are often used by construction workers.

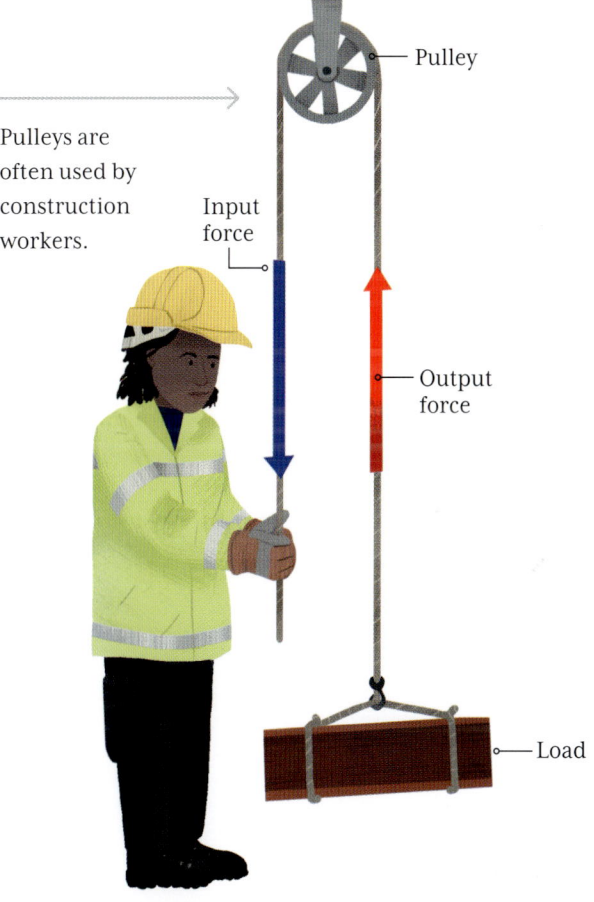

SCREW

A screw is a sharp-tipped pole with a spiraling groove, called a thread, around its edge. A screw changes a gentle turning force into a strong forward force. Less strength is needed to twist a screw into wood than to bang in a nail, because the screw spreads your effort over a longer distance—all the way along the edge of the spiral.

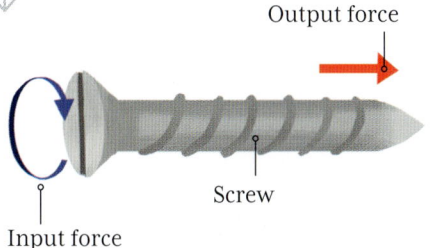

Each turn of the screw produces only a tiny movement of the screw tip into wood, so the work takes longer but requires less strength than banging in a nail.

Scientist Profile
NAME   Elisha Otis
DATES   1811–61
NATIONALITY   American
BREAKTHROUGH
In 1852, he invented the safety elevator, which uses a system of pulleys and weights to carry passengers from floor to floor. He devised a safety brake to stop the elevator from falling if its cable breaks.

FORCES AND ENERGY

Energy

Without energy, living things could not grow, and objects could not move.
Energy is the ability to do work, from climbing steps to blasting a rocket into space.
Energy cannot be created or destroyed, but it can be changed from one form to another.
There are two main types of energy: potential and kinetic.

POTENTIAL ENERGY

Potential energy is stored energy. It could be released later
as kinetic energy. Everything holds potential energy.

NUCLEAR

This form of potential energy is stored inside the nucleus of atoms (see page 28). Nuclear energy holds the protons and neutrons in the nucleus together. It can be released when nuclei split or join together.

CHEMICAL

Chemical energy is stored in the bonds between groups of atoms, called molecules. It can be released when molecules undergo a chemical reaction (see page 22), breaking their bonds. Your body uses chemical reactions to release the energy in food molecules. The energy in fuels such as wood is released by a combustion reaction, also known as burning.

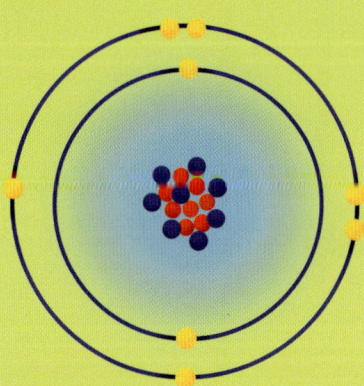

GRAVITATIONAL

This energy is stored in an object that could fall from a height, due to the force of gravity. It can be released—as mechanical energy—if the object falls. Usually, work must be done to give gravitational potential energy to an object: If you lift a bowling ball to a high shelf, chemical energy stored in your muscles is changed into gravitational potential energy.

ELASTIC

Elastic potential energy is stored inside an elastic object—such as a spring, bowstring, or rubber band—that has been stretched or squeezed. It can be released as mechanical energy by letting go of the object, so it springs back into shape. Work must be done to give elastic energy to an object, by pulling or pressing it.

KINETIC ENERGY

Kinetic energy is the energy of motion. It is the energy an object or particle has due to its movement.

MECHANICAL

This is the energy of objects in motion. A plummeting rollercoaster, flowing river, and turning windmill all have mechanical energy. An object with mechanical energy can do work: It can apply a force to move an object. For example, a moving hammer can bang in a nail.

THERMAL

Thermal energy is the movement of atoms. All atoms are moving: slowly if they are cool, but fast if they are hot (see page 20). If something has a lot of thermal energy, it feels hot. The Sun is the most powerful source of thermal energy in our Solar System.

RADIANT

Also known as electromagnetic radiation (see page 40), this energy travels through space in the form of waves. Radiant energy is given off by the Sun and other stars, as well as by light bulbs. It includes light, the only form of energy that can be seen by the human eye.

SOUND

Sound energy is made when mechanical energy—such as a drumstick hitting a drum—makes an object vibrate (shake). Sound travels through the air as a wave of vibrating molecules, a little like the way a wave travels across the ocean. This form of energy can be heard by living things (see page 165).

ELECTRICAL

Electrical energy is the movement of electrically charged particles (see page 52). By powering machines, heaters, light bulbs, and speakers, electrical energy can be changed into mechanical, thermal, radiant, or sound energy.

FORCES AND ENERGY

Electromagnetic Radiation

Electromagnetic radiation is the energy given off by the Sun and other stars. This energy travels through space as fast as anything can travel: 1,080,000,000 km/h (670,600,000 miles per hour), known as the speed of light. When the Sun's electromagnetic radiation reaches Earth, we feel some as heat and see some as light, but there are other forms that we can neither feel nor see.

RADIO WAVES

Radio waves have wavelengths between 30 cm and 100,000 km (12 in and 62,000 miles). As well as being released by the Sun, radio waves can be made by radio transmitters. These devices give waves particular patterns to carry information—sounds and images—for radios, televisions, computers, and phones.

MICROWAVES

Earth's atmosphere absorbs (soaks up) some of the Sun's energy with microwave wavelengths, between 1 mm and 30 cm (0.039 and 12 in), so much of it does not reach Earth's surface. Microwave ovens also make microwaves, which can travel into food, spinning molecules in the food— which heats them up and cooks the food.

INFRARED

Infrared wavelengths make up around half of the Sun's radiation that reaches Earth's surface. These wavelengths can be felt by humans as heat, because these photons are soaked up by the molecules they meet, making the molecules move faster (see page 20). Infrared wavelengths are used to send signals by remote controls for televisions and toys.

VISIBLE LIGHT

Photons with wavelengths between 0.0004 and 0.0007 mm (0.000016 and 0.00003 in) are the only things that human eyes can see (see page 164). You see objects because these photons bounce off

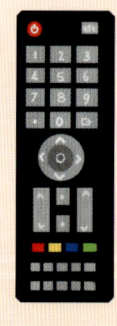
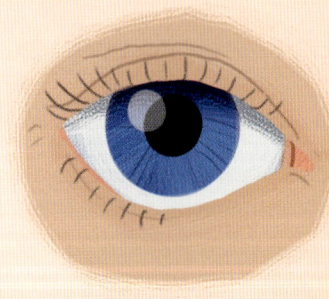

FORCES AND ENERGY

Electromagnetic radiation is made up of tiny particles called photons. Photons are packets of energy. This energy is "electromagnetic" because it is released by electrically charged particles: electrons and protons, which are found in atoms (see page 8). When atoms smash together in the core of the Sun (see page 66), their electrons release photons. These photons travel to the Sun's surface, then are released into space.

Electromagnetic radiation can behave both like a stream of photons and like a wave. Photons holding different amounts of energy have different wavelengths. Wavelength is the distance between the peaks of waves. The lowest-energy photons have the longest wavelengths. Different forms of electromagnetic radiation are made up of photons with different wavelengths, from low-energy radio waves to high-energy gamma rays.

ULTRAVIOLET
X-RAYS
GAMMA RAYS

them, then enter your eye through a hole called the pupil. The photons are absorbed by cells that cover the retina at the back of the eye, making the cells send electrical signals to your brain. Your brain makes sense of the signals, so you "see" the objects.

This radiation can harm human skin, causing sunburn and permanent damage, so it is essential to wear sunscreen to protect yourself from the ultraviolet photons that are not absorbed by the atmosphere. Ultraviolet wavelengths are used in water treatment plants to kill bacteria and viruses in wastewater from toilets and baths.

All X-rays are blocked by Earth's atmosphere. Medical X-ray machines produce photons that travel through the body and are absorbed in different amounts by different tissues. Those that pass out the other side create an image that shows the "shadows" made by different tissues. Doctors avoid X-raying too often, since repeated exposure can be harmful.

Most of these photons, with wavelengths less than 0.00000000000001 mm (0.0000000000000004 in), are blocked by Earth's atmosphere. They make atoms in living things give off electrons, which damages cells. Targeted gamma rays, given off by radioisotopes (see page 28), are used to kill cancerous cells, as well as microorganisms on medical equipment.

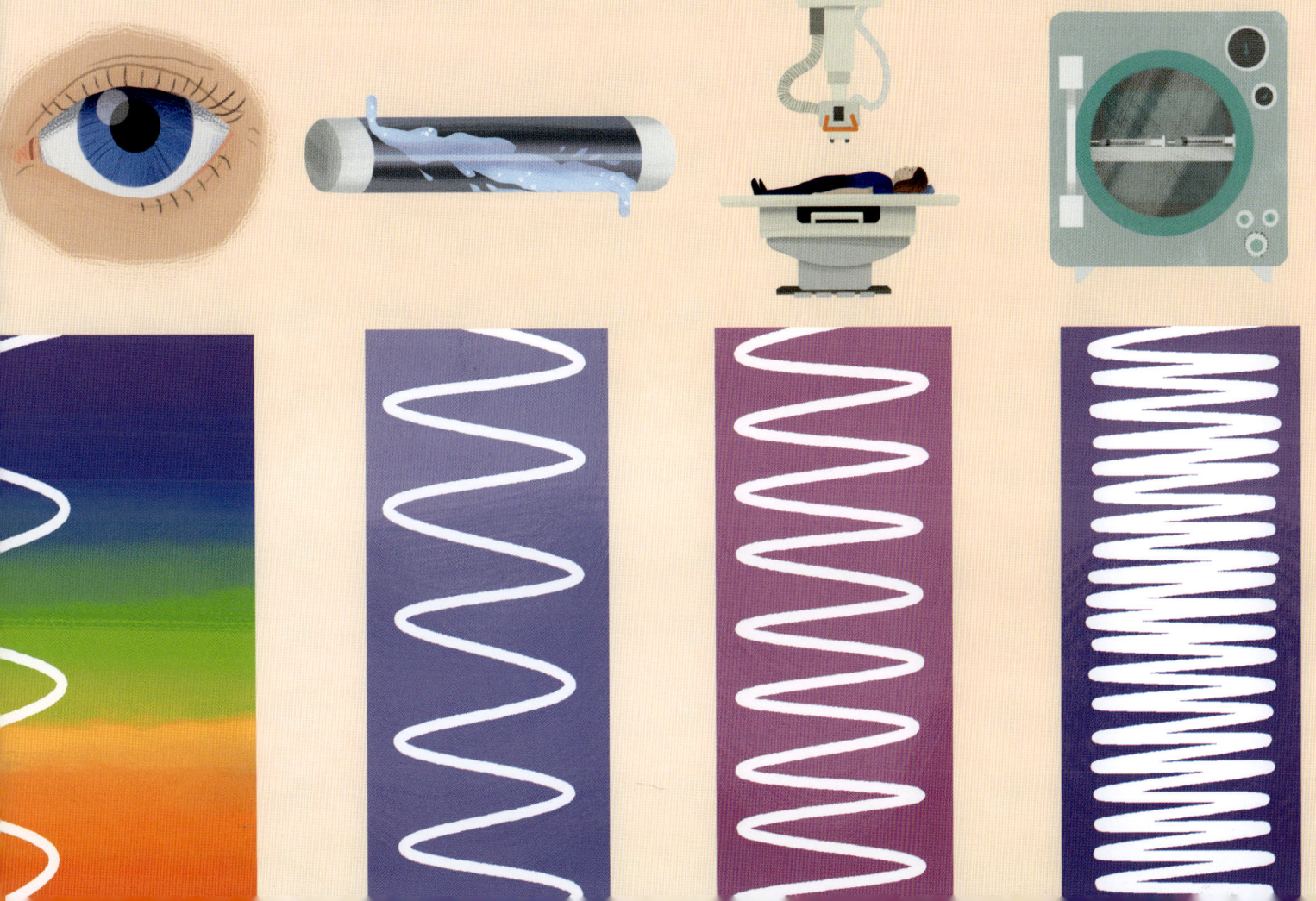

41

FORCES AND ENERGY

Light

Visible light is the form of electromagnetic radiation that humans can see. Without it, we would not be able to watch the world around us. On Earth, the main source of light is the Sun, but visible light is also given off by light bulbs, flames, and very hot objects.

THE SPECTRUM

The wavelength of visible light—the light that most humans can see—ranges from around 0.0004 to 0.0007 mm (0.000016 to 0.00003 in). Some animals can see a different range of electromagnetic radiation. For example, bees can see ultraviolet wavelengths as short as 0.0003 mm (0.000012 in). Flower petals have markings that can be seen only in ultraviolet light, which guide bees toward nectar.

Visible light is made up of all the colors of the rainbow: red, orange, yellow, green, blue, indigo, and violet. However, your eyes see the mixture of all these colors as white, which is why sunlight usually looks colorless. This range of colors is known as the spectrum. Each color is made of photons with a slightly different range of wavelengths, with red photons having the longest wavelengths and violet photons the shortest.

Refraction lets us see the different colors of light. This can happen when sunlight passes through raindrops in the air, making a rainbow, or when it passes through a pyramid-shaped glass block called a prism. Longer wavelengths refract less, so the prism bends each color by a different amount—allowing us to see each one.

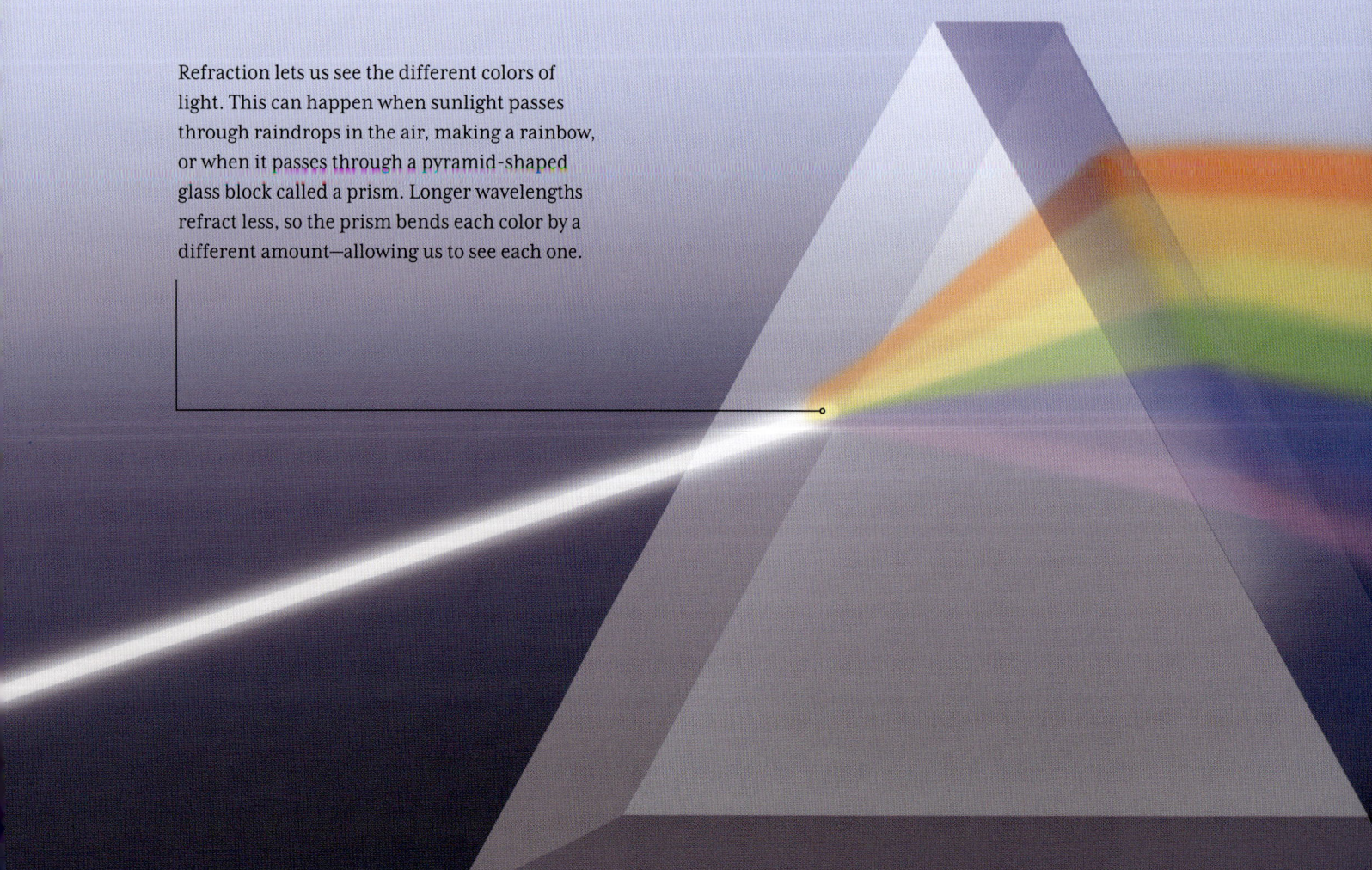

FORCES AND ENERGY

WHAT WE SEE

Light travels in a straight line. It can pass through some materials, such as glass and water. These materials are known as transparent. Objects that light cannot pass through are known as opaque. They cast a shadow. Light reflects (bounces back) from them and into our eyes, so we can see them. Shiny materials, such as metal, reflect more light than rougher materials, such as rock, which absorb (soak up) more light.

Objects look different colors because of the way they absorb or reflect different wavelengths of light. When an object looks a particular color, that wavelength of light is being reflected into our eyes, while the other wavelengths are being absorbed.

BENDING LIGHT

When light enters a transparent material such as glass or water at an angle, it changes direction. This is known as refraction. It is caused by light slowing down as it enters a material that is denser (more tightly packed with molecules). Both glass and water are denser than air. This is why a drinking straw in a glass of water appears to bend where it enters the water.

It is easier to understand refraction if you imagine sunlight as a line of friends walking side by side into the ocean. If the line of friends meets the ocean at an angle rather than straight on, and each person slows down when they step into the water, one end of the line slows down before the other, so the line becomes crooked.

A red object absorbs all wavelengths except red, which it reflects into your eyes.

A white object reflects all wavelengths into your eyes, which see it as white.

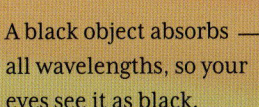

A black object absorbs all wavelengths, so your eyes see it as black.

Scientist Profile
NAME Ibn Sahl
DATES c.940–1000
NATIONALITY Persian
BREAKTHROUGH
In 984, he figured out the law of refraction. This is an equation that tells us how much light bends when it enters transparent materials.

Optical Telescopes

Optical telescopes can gather and focus more visible light than the human eye. This means they create brighter and magnified (or larger) images of distant objects. Due to the time light takes to travel from a space object to a telescope, an optical telescope allows us to look back in time.

FOCUSING LIGHT

Some optical telescopes used by astronomers are located on Earth, in observatories on mountaintops where their view is not spoiled by clouds, pollution, or city lights. Other optical telescopes, such as the Hubble Space Telescope, orbit above Earth's atmosphere to get an even clearer view.

Powerful optical telescopes are usually reflecting telescopes. They have a curved primary mirror, which gathers light. The wider the primary mirror, the more light it can collect to make dim objects look brighter. The primary mirror reflects light onto a flat secondary mirror, which reflects and focusses the light into an eyepiece. Here, it passes through a lens that magnifies the image.

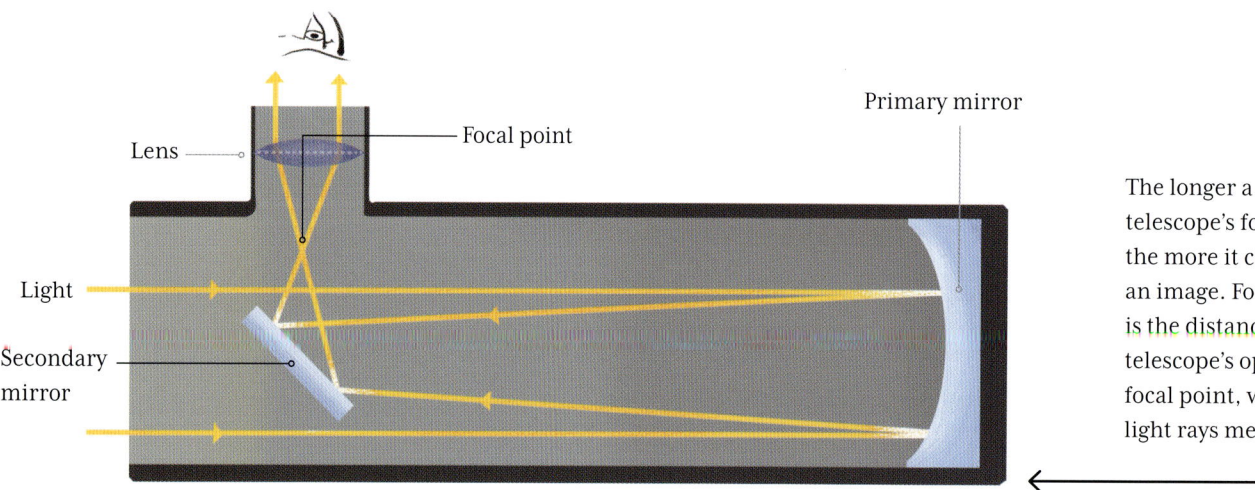

The longer a reflecting telescope's focal length, the more it can magnify an image. Focal length is the distance from the telescope's opening to the focal point, where the light rays meet at a point.

Extremely Large Telescope Facts

OBJECT	Ground-based telescope
DETECTS	Visible light and infrared
MIRRORS	5 mirrors with a 39.3-m (129-ft) wide primary and 4-m (13-ft) wide secondary
MASS	200,000 kg (440,000 lb) primary mirror
SIZE	74 x 86 m (243 x 282 ft) dome
LAUNCH	2028
LOCATION	3,046 m (9,993 ft) above sea level in Antofagasta, Chile

SEEING THE PAST

The most powerful optical telescopes can detect the light from stars billions of light-years away. For example, in 2022, the Hubble Space Telescope spotted the star Earendel, which is currently 28 billion light-years away. Yet the light from that star had taken only 13 billion years to reach the telescope.

When that light was emitted by the star, not long after the Big Bang (see page 138), Earendel was just 4 billion light-years from the young Milky Way. The expansion of the Universe has since carried the star much farther away. In fact, Earendel is probably now dead, but Hubble is seeing the star as it was when it first formed. The further away a telescope can look, the further back in time we can see.

When completed, the Extremely Large Telescope (ELT) will be the world's largest optical telescope. It has five mirrors, creating a focal length of 743 m (2,438 ft) by bouncing light between them. The telescope is on a mountain in Chile's Atacama Desert, where the dry air creates few clouds.

FORCES AND ENERGY

Radio Telescopes

A radio telescope usually has a curved "dish" that collects radio waves from space objects such as the Sun, quasars, and pulsars. Since radio waves from such distances are weak, a very large dish is needed to gather them. Many radio telescopes are in groups, so they can work together.

COLLECTING WAVES

Radio telescopes, also called antennas, are located far from towns and cities, so that they are not disturbed by the radio waves emitted from radio stations, phones, and other electronic equipment. The most powerful radio telescopes have a dish that is curved in a shape, called a parabola. The dish can usually be tilted to face different areas of the sky.

The parabola shape reflects incoming radio waves onto a single point above it, called the focus. Positioned at the focus is a "subreflector," which reflects the waves into a funnel called a feed horn at the dish's middle. The waves bounce back and forth against the sides of the funnel, creating a pulse. A device called a receiver turns the pulse into an electrical signal, which travels along wires to a computer so it can be stored and studied.

FORCES AND ENERGY

TELESCOPE TALK

Some radio telescopes collect information—such as photos—sent back to Earth from space telescopes, or from probes visiting other planets. First, the space telescope or probe turns its photos into an electrical signal by converting it into a pattern of numbers—just 1s and 0s. Any information can be turned into long streams of 1s and 0s, which are the "language" used by all computers and electronic devices. A 1 turns the electrical current on, while a 0 turns it off.

The electrical signal is turned into radio waves by a device called a transmitter. Electricity flowing into the transmitter makes electrons vibrate up and down, producing radio waves. The particular pattern of the waves represents all the 1s and 0s. When the waves reach Earth, they are turned back into 1s and 0s—then into images.

Very Large Array Facts

OBJECT	Ground-based telescope
DETECTS	Radio waves
DISHES	28 telescopes with 25-m (82-ft) wide dishes
MASS	209,000 kg (460,000 lb) per telescope
SIZE	Telescopes moved along a Y shaped track, with each track arm 21 km (13 miles) long
LAUNCH	1980
LOCATION	2,124 m (6,969 ft) above sea level in New Mexico, United States

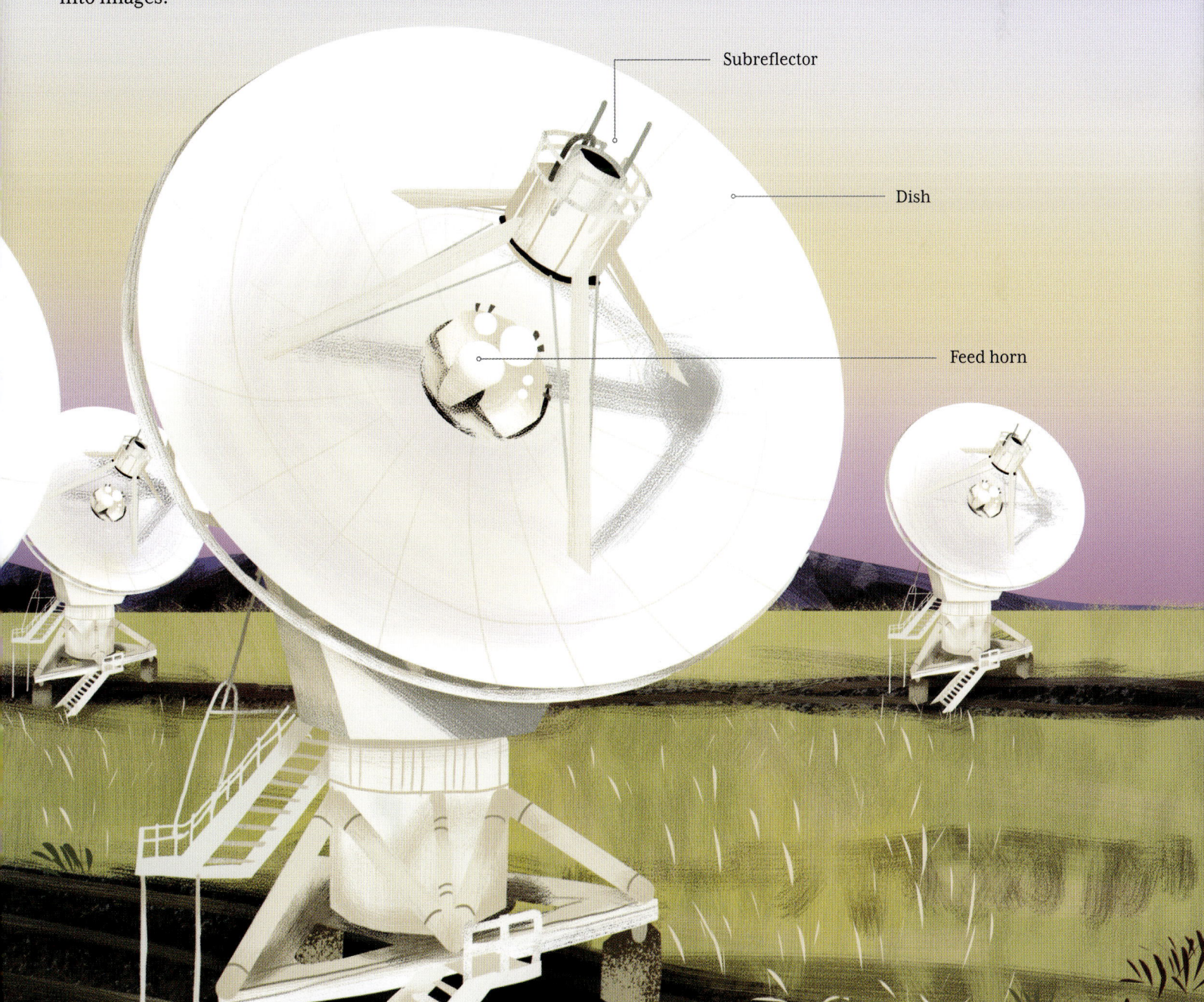

Subreflector

Dish

Feed horn

Space Telescopes

Space telescopes can detect electromagnetic radiation without it being blocked or distorted by Earth's atmosphere. The first space telescope was blasted into Earth orbit in 1961. Today, space telescopes are in orbit around both the Sun and Earth.

PLANCK
From 2009 to 2013, Planck studied the microwave radiation that fills space, called the cosmic microwave background. Planck's findings suggested that the Big Bang, which created this radiation, was slightly longer ago than previously thought—around 13.798 billion years.

CHANDRA X-RAY OBSERVATORY
Launched into Earth orbit in 1999, Chandra was named after astronomer Subrahmanyan Chandrasekhar. Its mirrors are made of material that reflects X-rays instead of letting them pass through, so the rays can be focused like visible light.

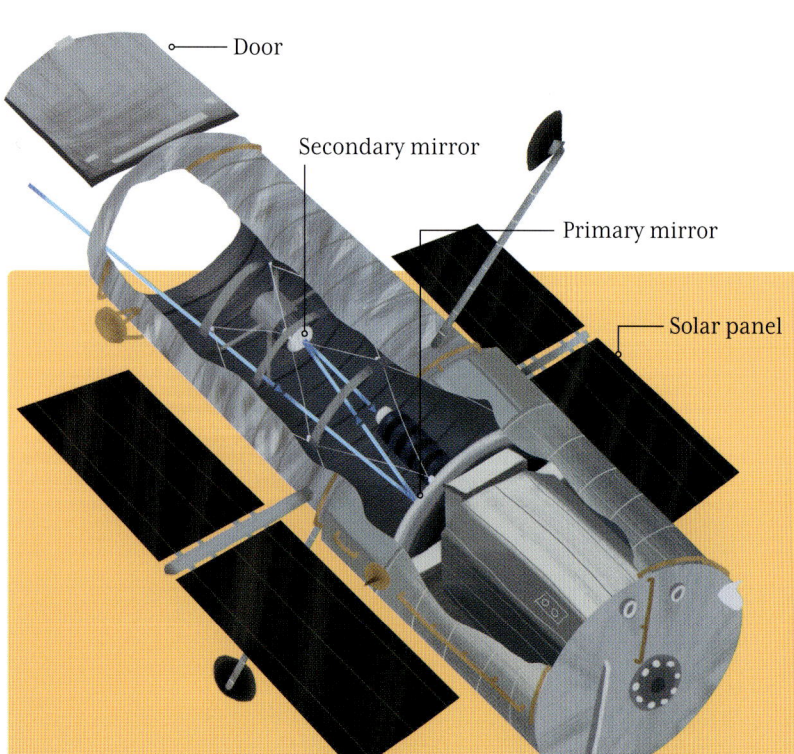

Door
Secondary mirror
Primary mirror
Solar panel

HUBBLE SPACE TELESCOPE
Hubble uses a 2.4-m (7.9-ft) primary mirror to detect mostly visible light, as well as some ultraviolet and infrared. Since being launched into Earth orbit in 1990, it has sent home more than 1 million images in the form of radio waves.

FORCES AND ENERGY

JAMES WEBB SPACE TELESCOPE

This Sun-orbiting telescope sees very faint, distant objects in infrared, allowing it to look far back in time to the very earliest galaxies and stars. A sunshade prevents the telescope warming up, so it is undisturbed by its own infrared radiation.

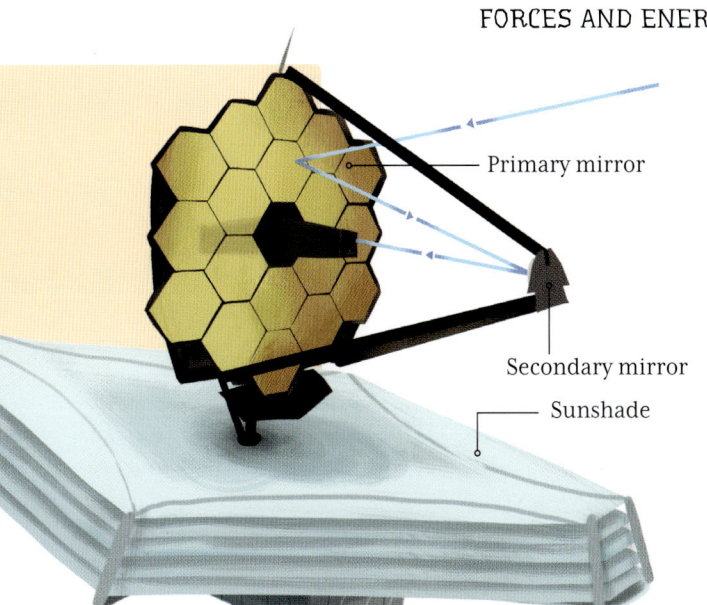

— Primary mirror
— Secondary mirror
— Sunshade
— Radio antenna

CHEOPS

CHEOPS stands for CHaracterising ExOPlanets Satellite. Launched in 2019, it focuses on nearby bright stars orbited by exoplanets. As the exoplanets pass in front of their star, it uses visible light observations to determine their size, mass, and materials.

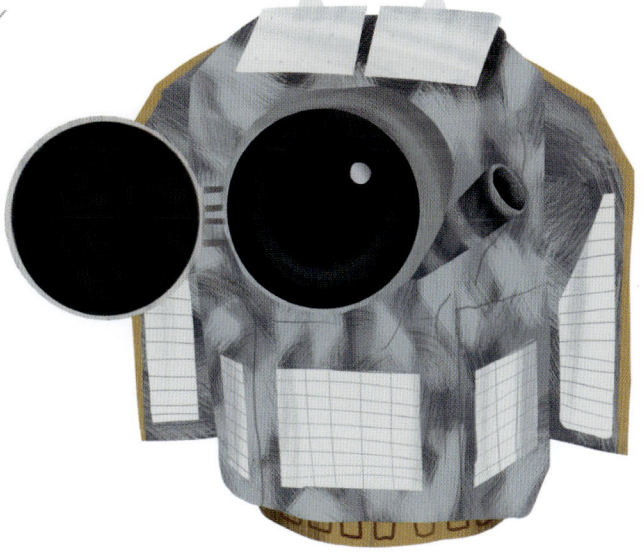

James Webb Telescope Facts	
OBJECT	Space telescope
DETECTS	Infrared and visible light
MIRRORS	3 mirrors, with a 6.5-m (21.3-ft) wide primary and 74-cm (29-in) wide secondary
MASS	6,500 kg (14,300 lb)
SIZE	21 x 14 m (69 x 46 ft)
LAUNCH	2021
LOCATION	Around 1.5 million km (1 million miles) from Earth

FERMI SPACE TELESCOPE

Named after the 20th-century physicist Enrico Fermi, this telescope has been observing gamma rays since 2008. It is searching for the sources of some mysterious rays, which may come from colliding galaxies or dark matter.

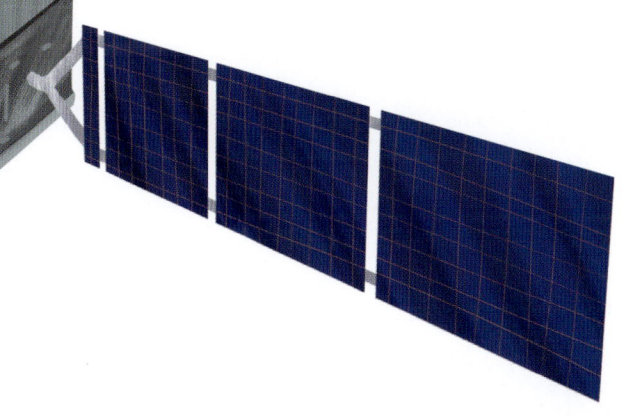

49

FORCES AND ENERGY

Heat

You feel heat when you stand in the sunshine. But what is heat? Heat is thermal energy (see page 39) that is flowing from one object to another. Heat always flows from hotter objects to colder ones—making them warm up. As you warm up in sunshine, you feel heat!

HEAT OR TEMPERATURE?

We often use the words "heat" and "temperature" as if they mean the same thing. However, heat is a transfer of energy. Temperature is a measure of how much of that energy is in an object. The temperature of an object is determined by how fast its molecules are moving (see page 20). The faster they are moving, the higher the object's temperature.

Energy called heat flows from a hotter object to a colder one. As this happens, the molecules in the hotter object slow down and the molecules in the colder object speed up, until they reach the same temperature.

We measure temperature using the Kelvin (°K), Celsius (°C), or Fahrenheit (°F) scales. Heat can be measured in calories. A calorie is the energy needed to raise the temperature of 1 g (0.04 oz) of water by 1 °K (1 °C; 1.8 °F).

CONDUCTION

There are three ways that heat can transfer from one object or material to another. The first is conduction, which is how heat travels through solids; from a solid to a solid, liquid, or gas; or through liquids and gases that are not flowing.

In conduction, hot molecules or atoms vibrate or hit into colder molecules or atoms. Like balls that bounce into other balls, they pass on some of their movement: The colder molecules or atoms start to move faster, while the hotter molecules or atoms start to move slower.

Conduction happens more easily with solids, particularly metals, because their atoms are close together. Other materials—such as air—are poor conductors, since their molecules or atoms are widely spaced, so they bang into each other less. In fact, air is often used as an insulator: a material that stops heat conducting. Double-glazed windows often have a layer of air sandwiched between two pieces of glass to keep homes warm.

Scientist Profile

NAME Josef Stefan
DATES 1835–93
NATIONALITY Austrian
BREAKTHROUGH:
All objects radiate heat if their temperature is above absolute zero, the lowest possible temperature, which is 0 °K (-273 °C; -460 °F). Stefan figured out an equation that explains how the heat radiated by a hot object is greater than the heat radiated by a cool object.

FORCES AND ENERGY

CONVECTION

The second way that heat transfers is convection, which happens in liquids or gases that are moving. Convection is the rising motion of warmer areas of a liquid or gas, and the sinking motion of cooler areas. When a pan of water is heated on a stove, the water at the bottom of the pan is heated first. As this portion of the water's molecules speed up, they spread out, making it less dense. This less dense water rises, while the denser, cooler water at the top of the pan sinks, then is heated. This process repeats and repeats.

RADIATION

The third way that heat transfers is radiation, which can happen even when there is no solid, liquid, or gas to travel through. In radiation, heat travels as electromagnetic waves (see page 40) known as infrared.

When an infrared wave hits an object, heat energy is released, making its molecules move faster and so warming the object up. Radiate means "to spread out in all directions," just like heat travels from the Sun.

Conduction transfers heat through a spoon.

Radiation transfers heat from the Sun.

Convection transfers heat through soup.

FORCES AND ENERGY

Electricity

Electricity powers light bulbs, computers, and cars. Electricity is a form of kinetic energy: It is the movement of particles called electrons. The form of electricity that powers machines is called current electricity: It is a constant flow of electrons through an electric circuit.

MOVING ELECTRONS

As we discovered on page 8, the nuclei of atoms are orbited by particles called electrons, which have a negative electric charge. In nuclei are particles called protons, which have a positive charge. Like charges repel (push away), while opposite charges attract (pull): Positively and negatively charged particles attract each other, while two positively charged or two negatively charged particles repel.

A special type of force called the electromotive force (see "Electricity and Magnetism") can free an electron from its atom. Some types of materials—including metals such as copper—release electrons from their atoms more easily. These materials are called good conductors of electricity (see page 12). In a copper wire, it is quite easy to create a flow of electrons from atom to atom—an electric current.

MAKING A CIRCUIT

Electric current can flow through a circuit made of a loop of conducting material, such as a copper wire. Switching "on" a machine or light closes a circuit, allowing electrons to flow.

If we add a traditional light bulb to a circuit, electrons flow through the light bulb's filament, a thin wire made of a metal called tungsten. This makes the filament so hot that it glows, which changes electrical energy to thermal and light energy.

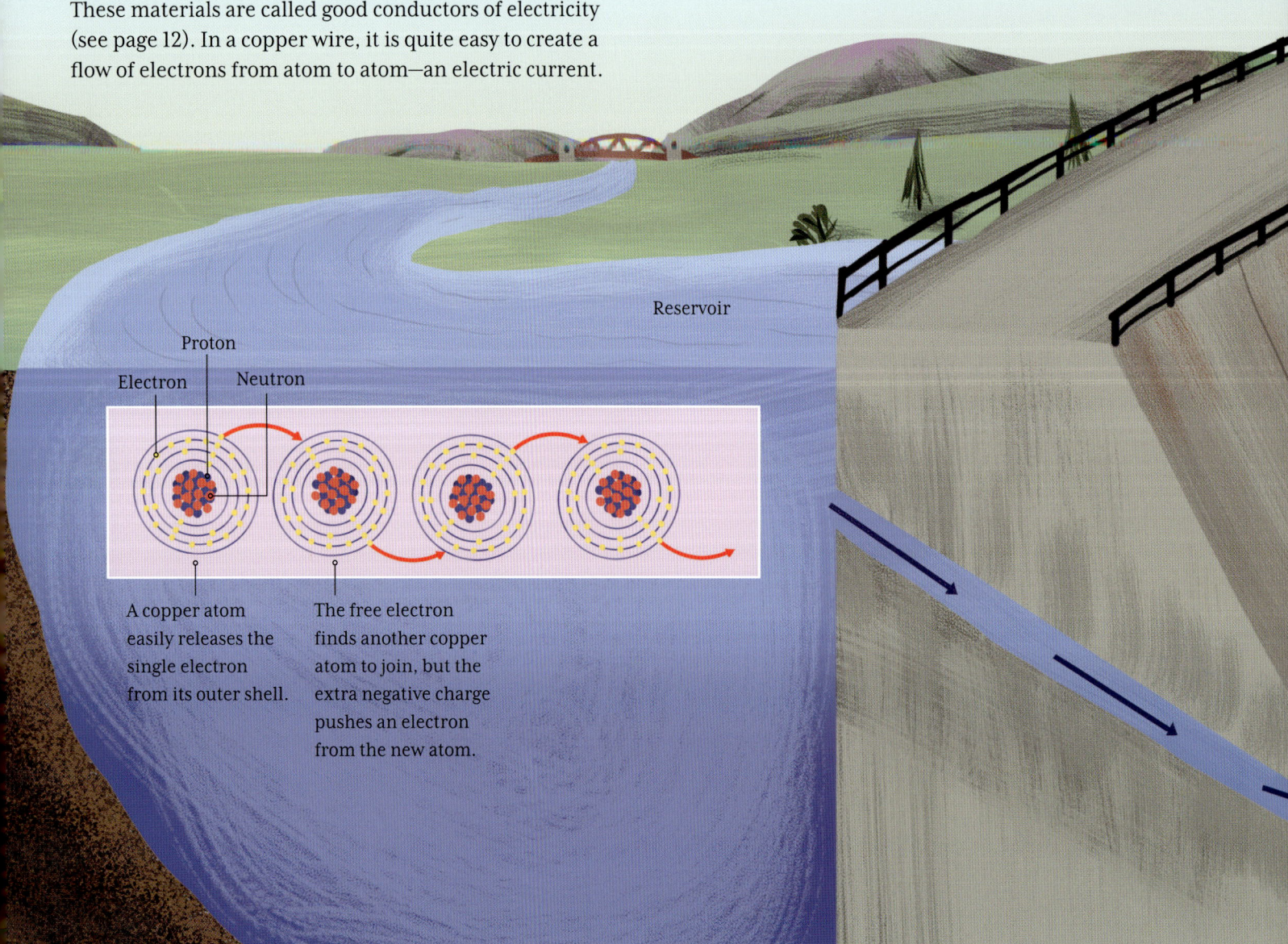

Reservoir

Electron — Proton — Neutron

A copper atom easily releases the single electron from its outer shell.

The free electron finds another copper atom to join, but the extra negative charge pushes an electron from the new atom.

FORCES AND ENERGY

ELECTRICITY AND MAGNETISM

Electricity and magnetism (see page 54) are two different but closely related things, both of them aspects of the electromagnetic force. Both electric and magnetic forces generate force fields (areas where their force can be felt), which repel objects with the same charge, or attract objects with the opposite charge.

The electric force acts between all electrons, whether or not they are moving. The magnetic force acts between moving electrons. A flow of electrons (electricity) can produce magnetism, while magnetism can produce electricity. We use this fact in electrical generators. Inside a generator, a coil of wire is spun inside a magnetic field. The magnetic field creates an electromotive force that makes electricity flow.

Scientist Profile
NAME Michael Faraday
DATES 1791–1867
NATIONALITY English
BREAKTHROUGH
He used a magnet and a coil of wire to create the first electrical generator, in 1831.

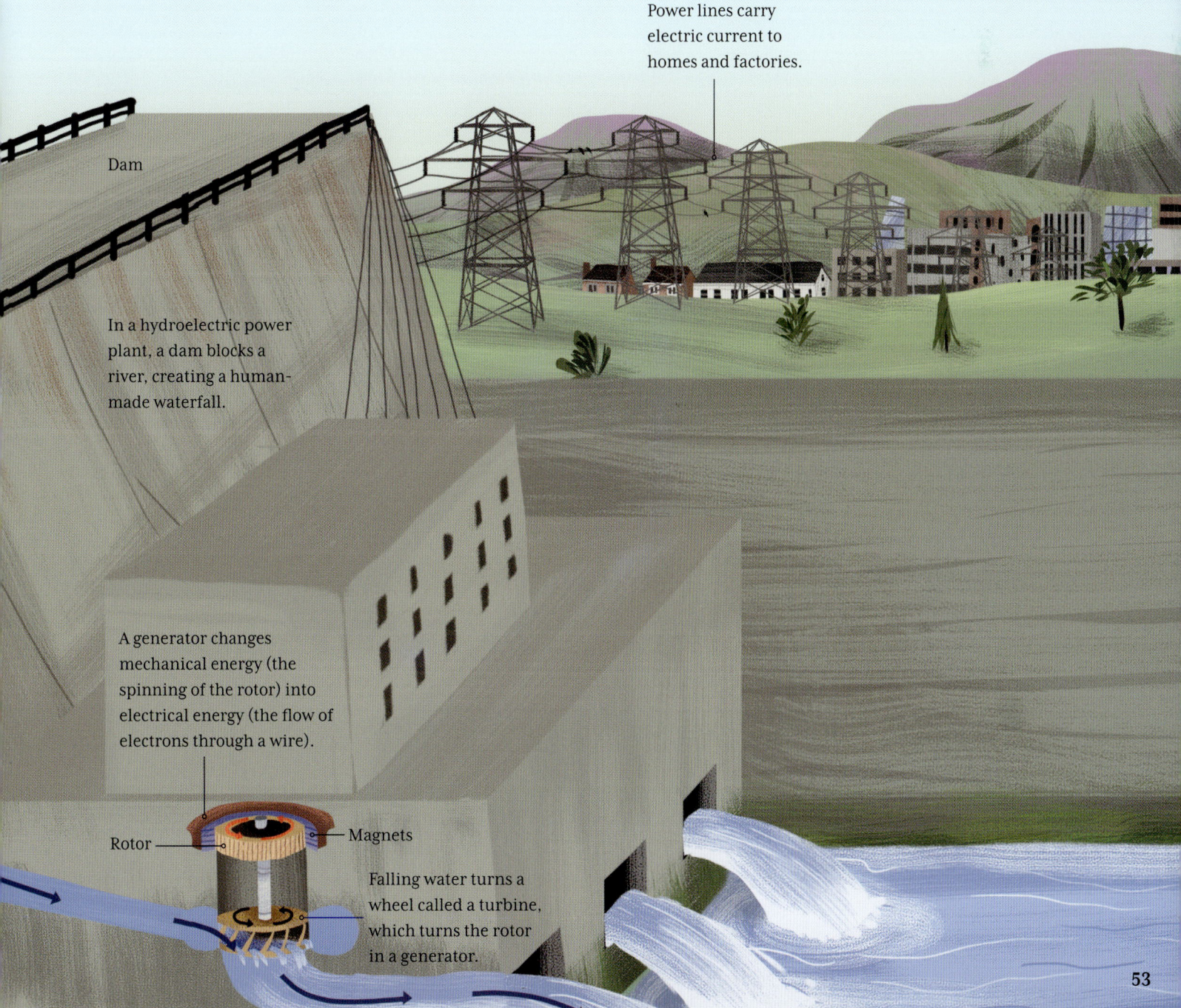

Power lines carry electric current to homes and factories.

Dam

In a hydroelectric power plant, a dam blocks a river, creating a human-made waterfall.

A generator changes mechanical energy (the spinning of the rotor) into electrical energy (the flow of electrons through a wire).

Rotor — Magnets

Falling water turns a wheel called a turbine, which turns the rotor in a generator.

FORCES AND ENERGY

Magnetism

A magnet attracts and repels other magnets. It also attracts particular metals, such as iron, nickel, and cobalt. A magnet is surrounded by a magnetic field, an area where this force of attraction and repulsion can be felt.

WHAT IS A MAGNET?

A magnet is an object that has a magnetic field. Each magnet has a north pole and a south pole, which are two points on its surface where its surrounding magnetic field is strongest. Opposite poles attract, and like poles repel: The north and south poles of two magnets attract each other, while matching poles repel each other.

A maglev (short for "magnetic levitation") system uses magnets to propel a train. In China, Shanghai's maglev train runs at up to 430 km/h (267 miles per hour).

MAKING A MAGNET

A magnetic field is created by the spinning of particles called electrons (see page 52). Electrons act like tiny magnets. In most atoms, these tiny magnets come in pairs that spin in opposite directions so their magnetism cancels each other out. However, atoms such as those of the metals iron, nickel, and cobalt have a half-filled outer shell of electrons (see page 8), so all the electrons are unpaired—giving each atom a magnetic field. These metals are called ferromagnetic.

Yet all the electrons in all the atoms in a whole chunk of iron may not line up with each other, so a piece of iron is not necessarily a magnet. However, you can turn a ferromagnetic metal into a magnet by stroking it, in

FORCES AND ENERGY

one direction, with an existing magnet, making all its electrons line up. Together, all these tiny magnets produce a powerful magnetic force.

Magnets always attract ferromagnetic metals that have not already been turned into magnets. This is because the magnet pulls on the nearest unpaired electrons in the material, turning their unlike poles toward it—creating an attraction.

MAGNETIC EARTH

Earth is like a giant magnet due to the movement of electrons in the churning, molten iron that makes up much of its core (see page 106). Like all magnets, Earth has a north pole and a south pole. Compass needles are magnets that spin so they point toward Earth's magnetic north pole.

Scientist Profile

NAME	Francisca Nneka Okeke
BIRTH	1956
NATIONALITY	Nigerian

BREAKTHROUGH
She discovered how the Sun affects the electrojet, a river of electric current that circles Earth in the outer atmosphere. The electrojet is caused by electrons in the atmosphere moving in Earth's magnetic field.

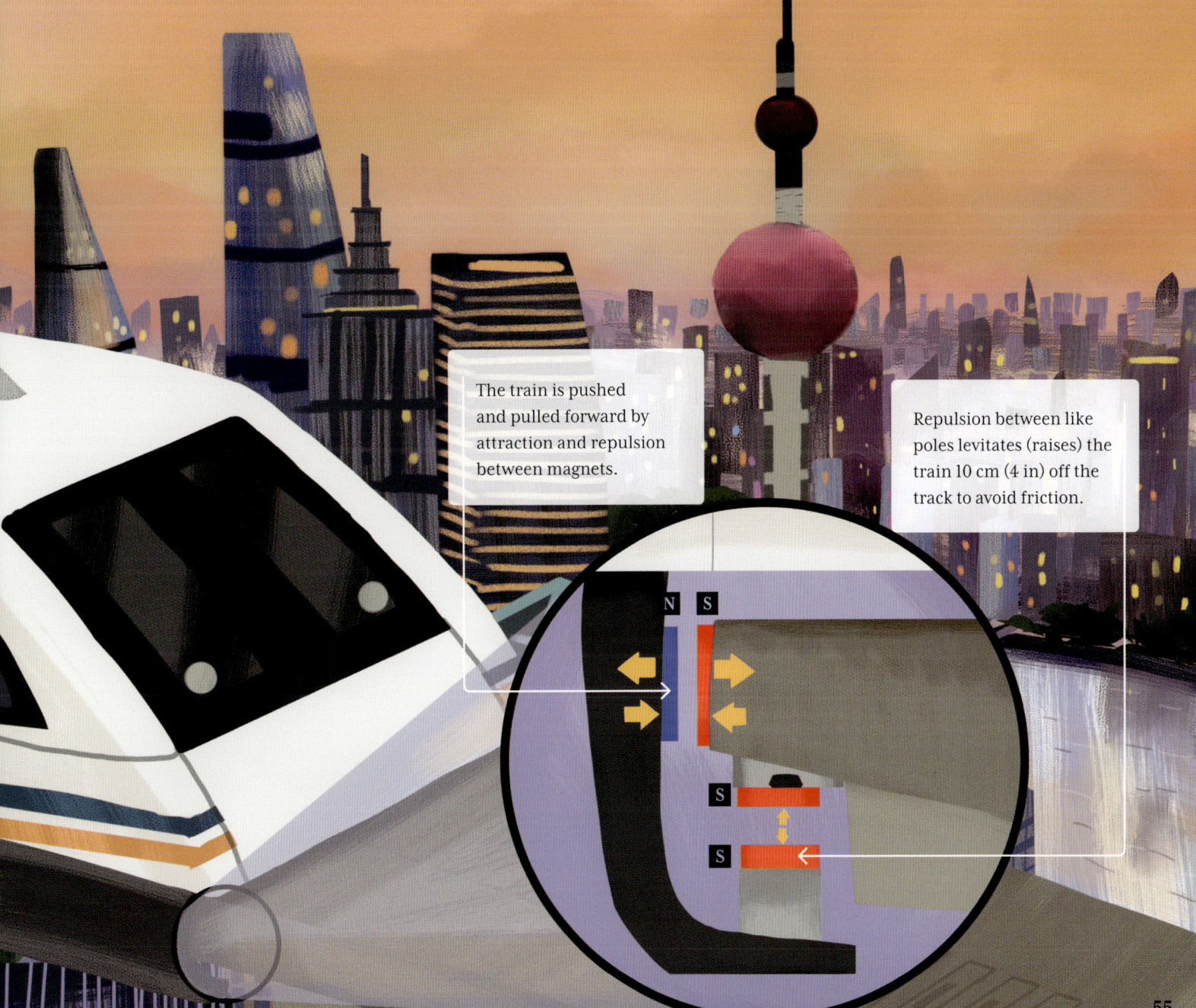

The train is pushed and pulled forward by attraction and repulsion between magnets.

Repulsion between like poles levitates (raises) the train 10 cm (4 in) off the track to avoid friction.

FORCES AND ENERGY

Cars

The first successful car was invented in 1885. It could travel at 16 km/h (10 miles per hour). Today, there are nearly 1.5 billion cars on Earth. The very fastest of them can reach 1,228 km/h (763 miles per hour).

Petroleum-powered cars turn the chemical energy (see page 38) in oil into mechanical energy. They do this in an internal combustion engine, in which this liquid fuel is burned, producing hot gases that push down pistons, which turn a rod called a crankshaft, which turns the car's wheels. The problem with burning oil is that it releases the gas carbon dioxide, which worsens climate change (see page 110).

To fight against climate change, more and more cars are powered by electricity rather than oil. They contain a lithium-ion battery, which stores chemical energy in the bonds between its molecules. A chemical reaction (see page 22) changes the chemical energy into electrical energy by releasing electrons. This type of battery needs recharging—by supplying electrical energy that is stored as chemical energy—after driving up to 560 km (350 miles).

1959: VOLVO AMAZON
The three-point safety seatbelt was invented by Nils Bohlin, a Volvo car company employee. The Volvo Amazon was one of the first cars fitted with three-point seatbelts—attached to the car at the passenger's shoulder and on either side of the lap—as standard.

1885: BENZ PATENT-MOTORWAGEN
This was the first practical car and the first put into production: Around 25 were built. Invented by German engineer Carl Benz, it had an internal combustion engine and three wire and wooden wheels.

1908: FORD MODEL T
This was the first car built on a factory assembly line, where a car is constructed by a series of workers or machines as it moves along. Assembly lines made building cars cheaper and quicker, so more people could afford them. Powered by an internal combustion engine, the Model T reached 72 km/h (45 miles per hour).

FORCES AND ENERGY

1997: THRUST SSC
The fastest car in the world, Thrust SSC was designed for breaking speed records and is not driven on ordinary roads. It has a jet engine, which pushes the car forward by releasing a backward blast of hot gas, making use of Newton's third law of motion.

2008: TESLA ROADSTER
Although many early cars were electric, in the 20th century most people lost interest in electric cars because they were slower and needed recharging. From the early 21st century, interest in electric cars grew. The Tesla Roadster was the first assembly-line, all-electric car to use a lithium-ion battery.

2021: HONDA LEGEND
Self-driving cars are controlled by a computer, which gets information on roads and traffic from cameras and sensors. Fully self-driving cars are not yet on sale, but the Honda Legend was the first assembly-line car in complete control of driving—yet only at low speeds.

FORCES AND ENERGY

Computers

Most people use a computer every day, when doing homework on a laptop or searching the web on a smartphone. A computer is a machine that works with information. For computers to use information easily, all words, numbers, pictures, and sounds are turned into a simpler form: just 0s and 1s.

DIGITAL DEVICES

Computers are digital, which means they work with digits (numbers): 0s and 1s. All information, which computer scientists call data, is turned into 0s and 1s by a computer. For example, the letter A becomes 01000001. Computers are powered by electricity. Inside a computer is a microprocessor, which contains billions of tiny electric circuits, which can be turned on and off by switches called transistors. A 0 turns a transistor off, but a 1 turns it on. Patterns of 0s and 1s turn these billions of circuits on and off in countless patterns, completing all a computer's work.

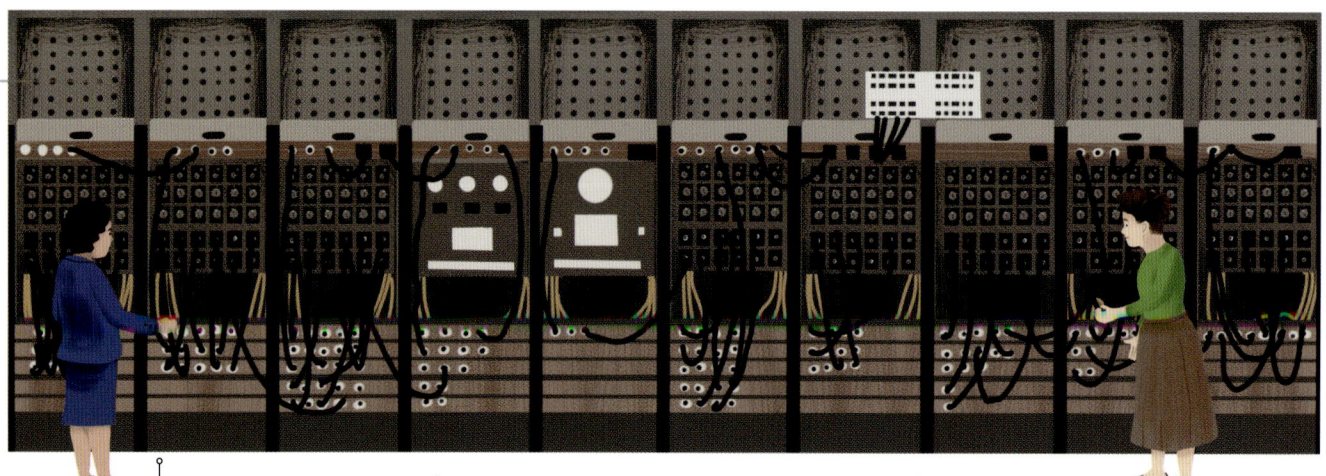

Built in 1945, ENIAC (Electronic Numerical Integrator and Calculator) was the first successful electronic digital computer. It had around 18,000 circuits, which were so large the computer was 30 m (100 ft) long.

PROGRAMMING

A program is a set of instructions that tells a computer what to do in which order. We write programs in programming languages, such as C and Perl, in which commands are given by simple combinations of words and symbols—which can more easily be turned into 0s and 1s by a computer. A combination of programming and data makes software. Different pieces of software let you search the web, send emails, or paint pictures.

The first programmer was English mathematician Ada Lovelace (1815–52). However, she wrote programs for a machine that was never fully built: Charles Babbage's steam-powered, clockwork Analytical Engine.

FORCES AND ENERGY

THE WEB

The web is all the world's websites that you can access using the internet. The internet is a worldwide network—formed by wires, cables, and wireless links (which use radio waves; see page 40)—through which computers send data. The web was invented by English computer scientist Tim Berners-Lee in 1989, when he created hypertext transfer protocol (HTTP). This sets out how websites are sent through the internet, from the computer where their data is stored to your computer, so you can see them.

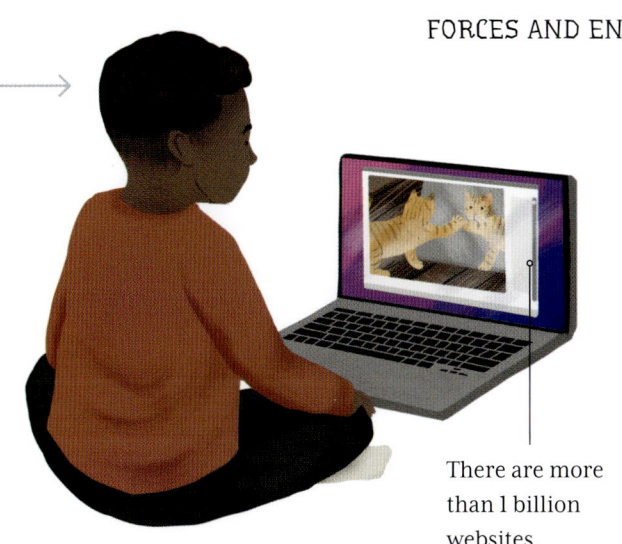

There are more than 1 billion websites.

ROBOTS

Robots are machines that contain a computer, which instructs them to carry out actions. The first successful industrial robot, Unimate, was built in 1959. It was a moving arm on a factory assembly line. Today, we have robotic toys and traffic signals, as well as robots that help surgeons operate.

Service robots assist humans in workplaces, restaurants, and stores.

ARTIFICIAL INTELLIGENCE

Artificial intelligence (AI) is software that allows computers to perform complex tasks, such as solving problems or writing stories. Although AI software makes it seem as if computers are thinking for themselves, they are only following programs that instruct them how to choose between options. In addition, AI software includes lots of data to check against. For example, weed-spotting AI software, used by farming robots, includes lots of photos of weeds.

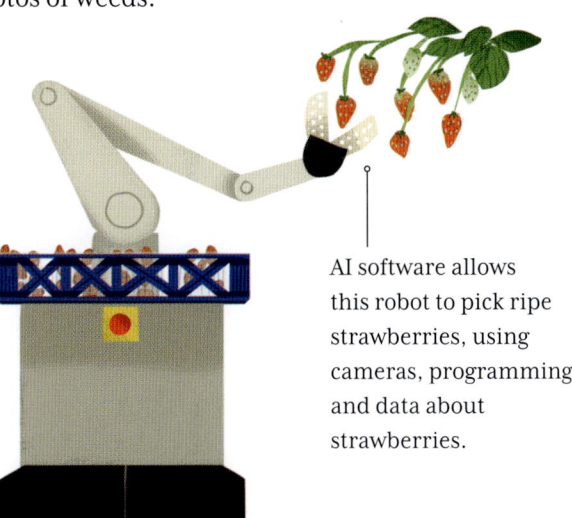

AI software allows this robot to pick ripe strawberries, using cameras, programming, and data about strawberries.

Scientist Profile

NAME   Alan Turing
DATES   1912–54
NATIONALITY English
BREAKTHROUGH
In 1950, long before computers could run complex programs, he designed a test to judge how well a computer can mimic human thinking: A human asks questions—via a computer screen—to both a human and a computer, then guesses which is which.

FORCES AND ENERGY

Our Energy Sources

We harness energy to make electricity, power vehicles, heat and cool homes, and cook food. Sources of this energy fall into two types: renewable, which means they will never run out; and non-renewable—which means they will. Currently, around one-fifth of the world's energy comes from renewable sources.

Renewable energy sources include those created by natural processes, such as sunlight, wind, moving water, and geothermal heat. These sources have the extra benefit of not usually causing pollution. In addition, biomass sources—such as plants—are usually renewable, because they can be replanted. However, some biomass—such as wood—is not sustainable, which means it is being used at too great a rate to meet future needs.

Non-renewable sources include fossil fuels: coal, oil, and natural gas. Although fossil fuels were made by natural processes, they form too slowly to be considered renewable. It takes millions of years for them to form underground from dead animals and plants. Another problem with fossil fuels is that, when burned, they release carbon dioxide, which worsens climate change (see page 110). Nuclear energy (see page 29) is also non-renewable, as it uses rare elements that must be mined. However, if carried out carefully, harnessing nuclear energy does not create pollution.

WIND
In wind farms, the wind's mechanical energy turns turbine blades, which spins rotors in generators, which then make electrical energy. Wind farms are sited in windy places, such as hilltops and the coastal ocean.

WATER
The mechanical energy of falling or flowing water is harnessed in hydroelectric (see page 52) and tidal (pictured) power plants. Tidal energy uses tides—the rising and falling of sea levels due to the Moon's gravity—to turn turbines and spin rotors in electrical generators.

FORCES AND ENERGY

FOSSIL FUELS
Fossil fuels are dug or pumped from the ground, then burned in power plants to boil water into steam, which turns turbines that power electrical generators. Oil is also burned in vehicle engines. In homes, natural gas is burned to cook food and heat water for washing and heating systems.

BIOMASS
Biomass means "material from living things." In some countries, plants or animal waste are burned to cook food and heat homes. Biomass can also be burned in power plants to heat water. Plants such as sugarcane (pictured) are made into liquid fuel that is burned in some vehicle engines.

SUNLIGHT
Solar panels convert the Sun's radiant energy into electrical energy. On house roofs, solar thermal panels convert sunlight into heat, which warms water for washing and heating systems.

GEOTHERMAL HEAT
Geothermal means "Earth heat." In certain places, Earth's crust (see page 100) is so hot that it can heat water, which is used to make electricity or pumped into heating systems. In these systems, hot water flows in pipes to radiators, which heat rooms through convection and radiation.

The Solar System

At the heart of the Solar System is the Sun. It is a star, a sphere of hot gas. At 1,390,000 km (864,000 miles) wide, the Sun is the largest object in our region of space, until the next star, which lies more than 40 trillion km (25 trillion miles) away. Massive objects have powerful gravity, which is the force that pulls all objects toward each other. The pull of the Sun's gravity holds trillions of other objects around it, and most of them are moving around the star in roughly circular paths called orbits. Together, the Sun and these objects are known as the Solar System.

The seven largest objects orbiting the Sun are the seven largest planets. Planets are large, rounded objects that orbit a star. The biggest of all of these is the giant planet Jupiter. The eighth and smallest planet, Mercury, is smaller than the Solar System's two largest moons, Ganymede and Titan. Moons are objects that orbit a planet, held by the strength of their planet's gravity. Orbiting the Sun itself are also at least nine—and perhaps many more—dwarf planets, which are smaller than true planets, but still have enough gravity to pull them into a rounded shape.

Around 4.6 billion years ago, the Solar System formed from a cloud of dust and gas. Perhaps shaken by the explosion of a nearby star, the cloud collapsed into a flat, spinning disk. Gravity pulled more and more material into the core of the disk. Here, the pressure grew so intense that hydrogen atoms started to smash together, forming a different type of atom—helium—and releasing energy that we can see as light and feel as heat. This was the birth of the Sun, which has shone ever since. Clumps formed in the remaining disk, eight of them growing large enough to become planets. Smaller clumps became moons, dwarf planets, rocky asteroids, and fiery comets.

Sun   Mercury   Ganymede   Pluto

The Sun is 285 times wider than Mercury, the smallest planet. At 4,880 km (3,032 miles) across, Mercury is 2,504 km (1,556 miles) wider than the largest dwarf planet, Pluto, but 388 km (241 miles) less wide than the largest moon, Jupiter's Ganymede.

The Solar System took shape from a spinning disk of gas and dust, with the bright Sun at its core. The disk spun counterclockwise (anticlockwise), which is why all the planets still orbit the Sun in that direction.

THE SOLAR SYSTEM

The Sun's Family

From nearest to farthest from the Sun, the planets are Mercury, Venus, Earth, Mars, Jupiter, Saturn, Uranus, and Neptune. On Mercury, the Sun appears three times larger than when it is viewed from Earth. From Neptune, the Sun would look one-thirtieth the size it appears from Earth.

The four inner planets—Mercury, Venus, Earth, and Mars—are made of metal and rock. As the Solar System formed, only these materials—which do not melt until they get extremely hot—could stay solid so close to the Sun. The inner planets are smaller than the outer planets, because there was less of these materials to go around. Due to their small size, the inner planets have weaker gravity than the outer planets, so they are not orbited by ring systems or many, if any, moons.

The outer planets are made of materials such as hydrogen and methane, which turn easily to gas. As the Solar System formed, the Sun blew these gassy materials into the Outer Solar System, where they formed the four giant planets. None of the outer planets has a solid surface—they are mostly gas and liquid.

MERCURY
Not much bigger than Earth's Moon, Mercury is the smallest planet. It also has the fastest orbit, moving at an average speed of 170,486 km/h (105,935 miles per hour).

VENUS
Venus is the second largest of the inner planets, with almost as great a size and mass (or weight) as Earth. Along with Mercury, it is one of the two planets with no moons.

EARTH
The largest inner planet, Earth, is nearly three times wider than Mercury. Earth is the only Solar System planet that is known to be home to living things.

SATURN
The second largest planet has a larger ring system than any other planet. The system may have formed when one of Saturn's moons was shattered by an asteroid.

MARS
Mars is the inner planet with the most moons—two. At Mars's closest approach to Earth, it is 57.6 million km (35.8 million miles) away, around 20 million km (12 million miles) farther away than Venus when it passes us.

NEPTUNE
Neptune has the slowest orbit of the eight planets, moving at an average speed of 19,548 km/h (12,147 miles per hour). The only Solar System planet that can never be seen without a telescope, it was the last to be discovered, in 1846.

JUPITER
The largest planet, Jupiter, is thirty times wider than the smallest planet, Mercury. Jupiter's mass is 2.5 times the mass of all the other planets combined.

URANUS
The third largest planet is slightly wider than Neptune, but has a lower mass. Although Uranus is faintly visible to the human eye, it was the first planet to be discovered using a telescope, in 1781.

THE SOLAR SYSTEM

The Sun

The Sun is a medium-sized star, one of more than 100 billion stars in the Milky Way Galaxy. Our star has been shining for around 4.6 billion years—and will shine for another 5 billion years. It supplies Earth with the perfect amount of light and heat to make our planet suitable for life.

BALL OF PLASMA

More than two-thirds of the Sun's mass is hydrogen gas, while the rest is mostly helium gas. Yet this is not ordinary gas, like the air we breathe on Earth. It has turned to plasma. Like everything from people to planets, plasma is made of atoms. In plasma, the atoms are so hot they have broken apart, releasing particles called electrons. Since electrons carry a tiny electric charge, plasma also has an electric charge.

- Core
- Radiation zone
- Convection zone
- Photosphere
- Chromosphere
- Corona

Although the photosphere is no more solid than the rest of the Sun, beneath this layer the star is opaque (not see-through). This makes the photosphere the star's visible surface.

ENERGY JOURNEY

Every second, the Sun gives off enough energy to power all the machines on Earth for 500,000 years. This energy begins its journey in the Sun's core. Here, hydrogen atoms fuse into helium atoms. This process is called nuclear fusion. It will continue for another 5 billion years, when the Sun will run out of hydrogen and start to die (see page 126), destroying all the planets.

Nuclear fusion releases energy in the form of tiny particles called photons. The photons travel outward through the Sun's layers, passing first through the radiation zone. Here the photons move by a process called radiation—they bounce from atom to atom. Next, the photons travel through the convection zone, moving through a process called convection—they are carried by currents of hot plasma, which rise, cool, then sink.

After thousands of years, the photons reach the Sun's surface, the photosphere. Now they travel through the layers of gas that form the Sun's atmosphere—the chromosphere and corona—and out into space.

WONDERFUL WAVES

When the Sun's photons reach Earth, about 8 minutes after leaving the star, we see some as light and feel some as heat. Yet light and heat are only a part of the energy given off by the Sun. Photons carrying less energy form radio waves and microwaves, while high-energy photons form ultraviolet, X-rays, and gamma rays. All the forms of the Sun's energy are together known as the electromagnetic spectrum.

The Sun Facts
- **OBJECT**: Star
- **MASS**: 333,000 Earths
- **SIZE**: 1.39 million km (0.86 million miles) across
- **ROTATION**: Around 27 days
- **TEMPERATURE**: 15 million °C (27 million °F) at the core; 5,500 °C (9,930 °F) at the photosphere
- **LOCATION**: 28,000 light-years from the middle of the Milky Way Galaxy

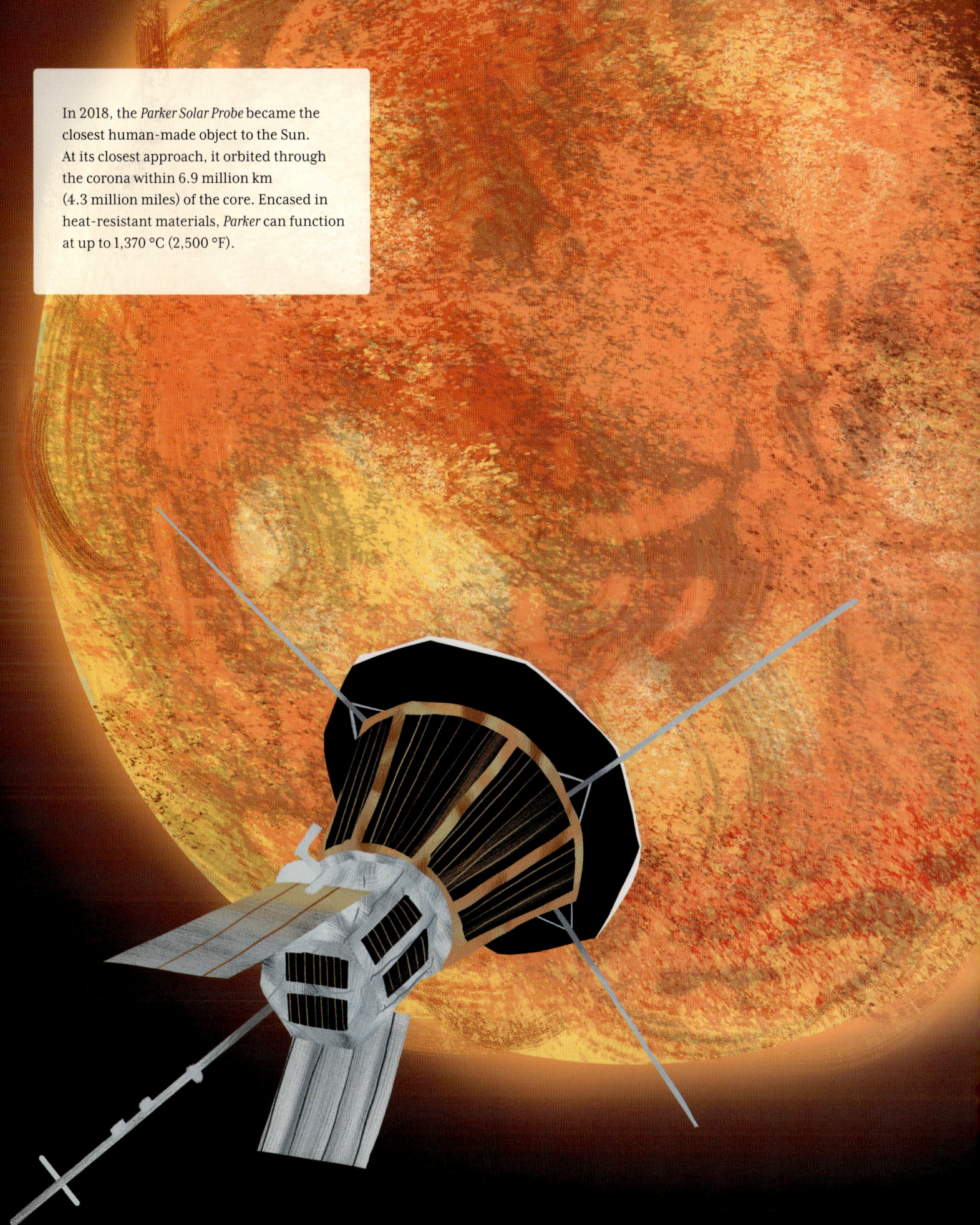

In 2018, the *Parker Solar Probe* became the closest human-made object to the Sun. At its closest approach, it orbited through the corona within 6.9 million km (4.3 million miles) of the core. Encased in heat-resistant materials, *Parker* can function at up to 1,370 °C (2,500 °F).

THE SOLAR SYSTEM

The Sun's Activity

The Sun's appearance changes constantly. Coming and going are dark spots, known as sunspots, as well as flares and loops. This activity can be viewed only using special equipment—never look directly at the Sun, as its brightness can cause blindness.

MAGNETIC FIELDS

The Sun's activity is caused by its magnetic fields, which are areas with powerful magnetic force. On Earth, we know magnetism as a force that makes magnets attract (pull) or repel (push away) each other. Magnetism can be caused by the movement of electric charges. Since the Sun's plasma is electrically charged (see page 66), its movements create moving magnetic fields.

As the Sun's magnetic fields tangle, cross, and stretch, plasma and energy erupt from the Sun's surface. Over an 11-year period, known as the solar cycle, this activity peaks, then calms. At the peak, there may be around 150 sunspots on the photosphere. At the Sun's calmest, there may be just one or two. When solar activity peaks, more intense auroras (see page 106) can also be seen in Earth's skies.

SUNSPOTS

Sunspots appear darker than the surrounding photosphere because they are cooler. They last for a few days or weeks, appearing where magnetic fields are particularly strong, which prevents some of the Sun's heat reaching the surface.

A sunspot has a dark central area, known as the umbra, which is surrounded by a less dark, warmer area known as the penumbra. The temperature of an umbra can be around 3,500 °C (6,330 °F)—about 2,000 °C (3,600 °F) less hot than the rest of the photosphere.

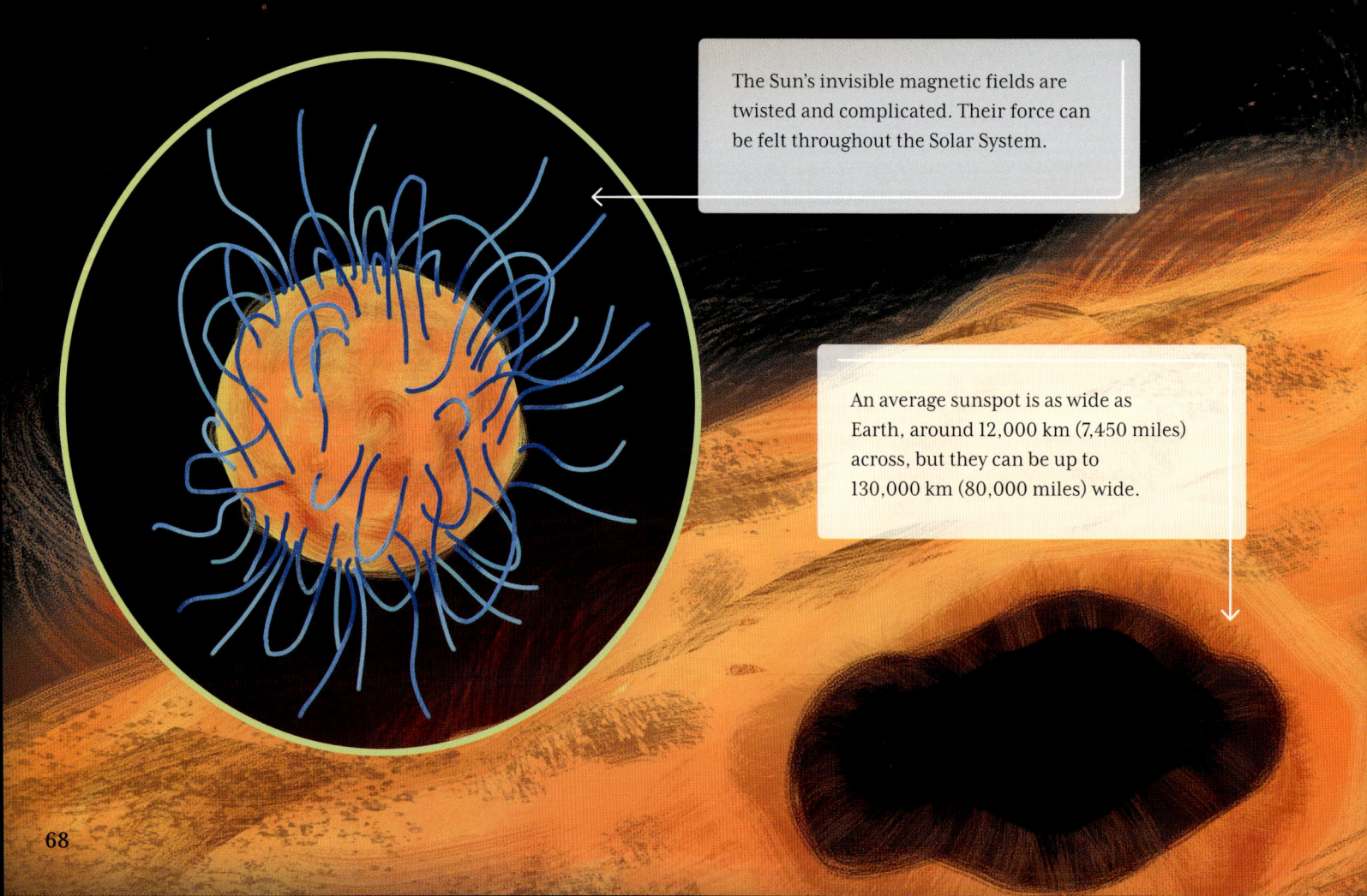

The Sun's invisible magnetic fields are twisted and complicated. Their force can be felt throughout the Solar System.

An average sunspot is as wide as Earth, around 12,000 km (7,450 miles) across, but they can be up to 130,000 km (80,000 miles) wide.

LOOPS AND FLARES

Loops happen when a loop of magnetic field drags a curl of plasma into the corona. Loops often erupt from areas of the photosphere with lots of sunspots. Flares happen when magnetic fields suddenly either cross or untangle, creating an explosion of plasma and energy.

Major flares often happen at the same time as coronal mass ejections (CMEs), which are bubbles of intense energy that explode into space at up to 11 million km/h (7 million miles per hour). When solar activity is at its peak, there may be three CMEs per day. On Earth, unusually intense CMEs can cause problems with radio communication. In 1859, a massive CME damaged electrical systems, making some spark into flame.

Most solar flares last between 6 and 11 minutes.

A coronal loop may be up to 1 million km (620,000 miles) long.

Mercury

Mercury is named after the Roman messenger god, known for his swift journeys. The planet's journey around the Sun is so fast that it makes one orbit in about 88 Earth days. This planet has been watched by humans since ancient times, even though its closeness to the Sun makes it difficult to see.

LOOKING FOR MERCURY

Like the other planets, Mercury does not give off light, but can be seen from Earth because sunlight reflects off its surface. It looks like a yellowish "star." During parts of the year, the planet can be seen in the west, just after sunset. At other times, it can be seen just before sunrise, near where the Sun will rise in the east.

FAST AND SLOW

The closer an object is to the Sun, the more it feels the pull of the Sun's gravity. As the closest planet to the Sun, Mercury orbits faster than the other planets so that it is not pulled into the star. This is like a cyclist peddling round the steeply sloping, curving track of a cycling arena. If the cyclist keeps peddling fast, they will not fall down the slope—but as soon as they slow down, gravity pulls them downhill.

Like all the planets, Mercury also rotates, turning around its own axis (an invisible line running through its poles). The Sun's intense gravity slows Mercury's rotation, so it spins just once every 59 Earth days. In fact, three Mercury days (rotations) are exactly equal to two Mercury years (orbits).

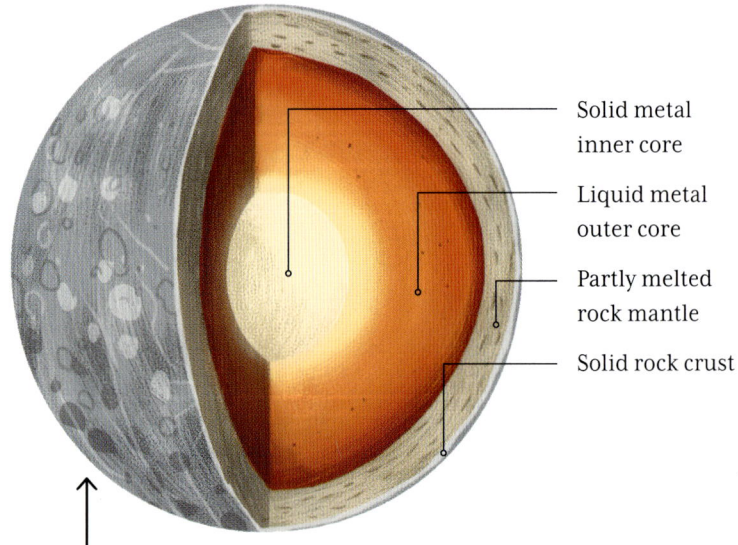

Mercury's metal core is around 2,000 °C (3,600 °F). It is surrounded by partly melted rock, known as the mantle, which is topped by a solid rock crust.

LITTLE ATMOSPHERE

Earth has a thick atmosphere, a blanket of gases held by the planet's gravity. Mercury has almost no atmosphere as its gravity is too weak to hold on to much gas so near the Sun. The Sun heats Mercury's surface to 427 °C (800 °F) during the day. Yet without an atmosphere to hold in heat, at night Mercury's surface falls to -179 °C (-290 °F). These extreme temperatures make Mercury unsuitable for life.

Mercury's lack of an atmosphere also meant that there was nothing to slow down space rocks as they battered the planet during the early years of the Solar System. As a result, the planet has more impact craters—bowl-shaped dips caused by crashes with asteroids and comets—than any other planet. Mercury has thousands of craters, the largest of them, called the Caloris Basin, is 1,550 km (960 miles) across.

Mercury Facts

OBJECT	Planet
MASS	0.055 Earths
SIZE	4,880 km (3,032 miles) across
MOONS	0
ROTATION	59 days
ORBIT	88 days
TEMPERATURE	An average of 167 °C (333 °F) on the surface
LOCATION	An average of 57.9 million km (36 million miles) from the Sun

Mercury has been visited by fewer space probes than the other inner planets, because it orbits the Sun so quickly that a probe needs to travel very fast to meet it, then brake sharply to resist the Sun's pull. The *MESSENGER* probe was the first to orbit Mercury, in 2011–2015.

THE SOLAR SYSTEM

Venus

Although it is the second closest planet to the Sun, Venus is the hottest planet in the Solar System due to its thick atmosphere. Venus is also the only planet that rotates more slowly than it orbits the Sun, meaning that a Venus day is longer than a Venus year.

BEAUTIFUL AND DEADLY

Venus is named after the Roman goddess of beauty. Since the planet is the brightest object in Earth's night sky after the Moon—and can even sometimes be seen in daylight—the planet has been watched or worshipped by many peoples since ancient times. Venus's brightness is due to sunlight reflecting off its thick clouds.

For much of the year, Venus can be seen in either the evening or early morning sky, never appearing to move far from the Sun since it orbits closer to the star than we do.

While clouds on Earth are made of water drops, Venus's clouds are made of drops of sulfuric acid. On Earth, this dangerous acid is used to clean drains. These clouds float in Venus's thick atmosphere, which is mostly carbon dioxide. This gas traps the Sun's heat, making it hot enough on Venus's surface to melt metals such as lead.

Venus's terrific heat (which would boil away any water) and its carbon dioxide atmosphere (which would be deadly to animals in such quantities) make it completely

Venus Facts
OBJECT	Planet
MASS	0.815 Earths
SIZE	12,104 km (7,521 miles) across
MOONS	0
ROTATION	243 days
ORBIT	225 days
TEMPERATURE	An average of 464 °C (867 °F) on the surface
LOCATION	An average of 108.2 million km (67.2 million miles) from the Sun

unsuitable for life. The longest any space probe has functioned on Venus's hostile surface is 127 minutes, a time achieved by the *Venera 13* probe in 1982.

WRONG DIRECTION

All the Solar System planets orbit counterclockwise (anticlockwise) and all except Venus and Uranus also rotate counterclockwise when viewed from above their north pole. Venus rotates clockwise, but it must originally have rotated the other way, since it formed in a counterclockwise-spinning disk. If the disk had spun the other way, the planets would orbit and rotate the other way, too. In addition to rotating the wrong way, Venus also rotates more slowly than any other Solar System planet, each spin taking 243 days.

Astronomers believe that, early in its life, Venus must have been hit by a planet-sized object, which reversed its rotation or even flipped it upside down. Since Venus rotates the opposite way from Earth, on Venus the Sun appears to rise in the west and set in the east. However, the planet's clouds would always block any view of the Sun from the surface.

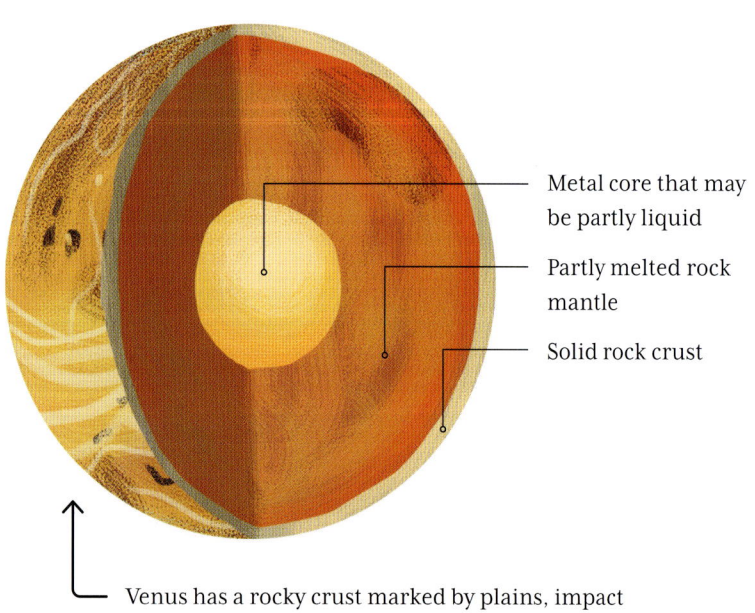

- Metal core that may be partly liquid
- Partly melted rock mantle
- Solid rock crust

Venus has a rocky crust marked by plains, impact craters, and more than 1,600 volcanoes. Beneath the crust is a mantle of denser rock, 2,840 km (1,760 miles) thick, surrounding a metal core of iron and nickel.

From Earth, our view of Venus's surface is blocked by clouds, but space probes have sent home detailed images of its surface. The pale region that stretches nearly two-thirds of the way around the planet is called Aphrodite Terra, after the Greek goddess of love. It is a highland area with deep valleys. The planet's dark "pimples" are volcanoes.

Mars

The fourth planet is named after the Roman god of war. It gained this name due to its blood-like shade. Mars can be seen as a small red light without the help of a telescope. The planet rotates in around the same time as Earth does, but its orbit takes 322 days longer.

RED PLANET

Mars's redness is caused by the shade of its surface rocks, as well as the large quantities of red dust in its atmosphere. Mars's extreme dustiness is due to the blasting of its rocks by storms and probably—long ago—by water (see page 76). The battering broke some of Mars's rock into fine pieces. The planet's current dryness allows this light dust to be whipped 30 km (19 miles) high by winds of up to 100 km/h (62 miles per hour).

The surface of the Martian rocks is reddish due to containing lots of iron oxide, which is often known as "rust" when it occurs on Earth. Here, rust forms when iron is in contact with oxygen in the air. Mars and Earth formed from similar materials, but while most of Earth's iron sank to its core, much of the Martian iron remained nearer the surface. Although Mars's atmosphere does not currently have enough oxygen to rust the iron in its rocks, it may once have contained more.

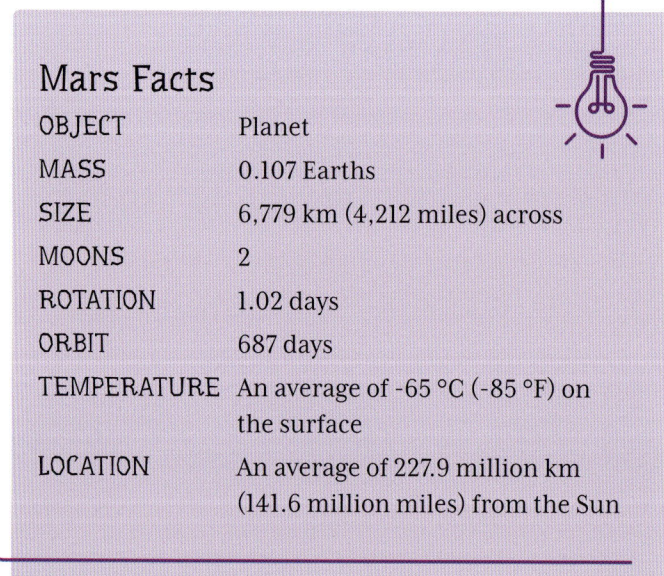

Mars Facts

OBJECT	Planet
MASS	0.107 Earths
SIZE	6,779 km (4,212 miles) across
MOONS	2
ROTATION	1.02 days
ORBIT	687 days
TEMPERATURE	An average of -65 °C (-85 °F) on the surface
LOCATION	An average of 227.9 million km (141.6 million miles) from the Sun

TALLEST VOLCANO

Mars is home to the tallest volcano, which is also the tallest mountain, in the Solar System—Olympus Mons. It is 21.9 km (13.6 miles) tall, more than twice the height of Earth's highest mountain, Mount Everest. The volcano may have started to form over 3 billion years ago on top of an extremely hot area in the mantle, which forced melted rock to the surface. The most recent lava flows are around 115 million years old.

TWO MOONS

The two Martian moons are called Phobos ("fear") and Deimos ("panic"), named after the sons of the Greek god of war, Ares, who followed their father onto the battlefield. Phobos is 22.2 km (13.8 miles) wide, while Deimos is 12.6 km (7.8 miles) across. Both moons are too small to be pulled into a sphere-shape by their own gravity.

Phobos orbits closer to its planet than any other moon—just 9,377 km (5,827 miles) away. Thanks to the pull of Mars's gravity, it is getting closer by around 2 cm (0.8 in) every year—and in around 50 million years will smash into the planet.

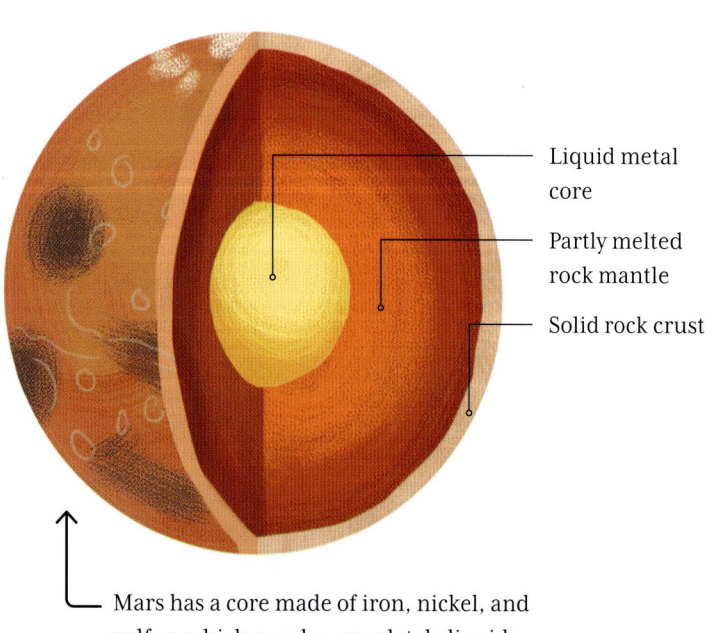

- Liquid metal core
- Partly melted rock mantle
- Solid rock crust

Mars has a core made of iron, nickel, and sulfur, which may be completely liquid. Surrounding this is a rocky mantle up to 1,880 km (1,168 miles) thick, wrapped in an iron-rich rocky crust.

Mars's most visible feature is a series of canyons, the Valles Marineris, that stretch 4,000 km (2,485 miles) across the planet. The canyons cracked as magma pushed up the crust. Mars's moons, Phobos (bottom right) and Deimos (top right), may once have been asteroids orbiting in the Asteroid Belt, but were pulled toward Mars by its gravity.

THE SOLAR SYSTEM

History of Mars

Today, Mars is dry, cold, and unsuitable for life. Yet the planet was once very different—even Earth-like. No evidence of ancient life has been found on Mars, but long ago, the planet was warm and watery enough to be suitable for living things.

4.5 BILLION YEARS AGO

Mars formed at the same time as Earth. Over the next few million years, the young Mars's volcanoes spewed out gases, creating a thick atmosphere held by the planet's gravity. Due to the churning iron in its core, Mars had a magnetic field that protected

4 BILLION YEARS AGO

Clouds of water droplets floated though Mars's atmosphere. Rain filled the lakes and oceans, which covered one-third of the planet's surface. Today, evidence of oceans and rivers can be seen in the rocks that they wore away, and the sand they carried.

On Earth, life is possible because we have liquid water and an oxygen-rich atmosphere. Mars's dryness and thin atmosphere make life extremely unlikely there today. Yet astronomers believe that, billions of years ago, Mars had oceans and rivers. It also had a thick atmosphere, although we are not sure if it was as oxygen-filled as Earth's.

Mars's past suitability for life does not necessarily mean that life did exist there. However, astronomers wonder if the planet might have been home to tiny living things, such as bacteria. Such simple living things were the earliest life forms on Earth. If tiny living things did once exist—or even still exist—evidence might be found deep in the Martian soil. Armed with drills, rovers search Mars constantly for that evidence.

3.7 BILLION YEARS AGO

The churning of Mars's core slowed, possibly due to cooling or a series of asteroid strikes. The planet lost its magnetic field. All but 1 percent of the atmosphere was stripped away by the solar wind. With so little atmosphere to press down on it, the planet's liquid water drifted off into space or froze into ice.

TODAY

With no warming blanket of atmosphere, the temperature on Mars drops to -153 °C (-243 °F) at the poles. There is still enough water to cover the planet in an ocean 35 m (115 ft) deep. Yet all this water is frozen in the soil and at the poles, which are capped by sheets of ice around 1,000 km (620 miles) across.

The Asteroid Belt

Between the orbits of Mars and Jupiter, millions of asteroids are circling the Sun. Like the inner planets, asteroids are made mostly of rock and metal. The largest of the asteroids, called Ceres, is big enough to be considered a dwarf planet.

MAKING THE BELT

The Asteroid Belt contains material that was left over during the formation of the Solar System. The immense gravity of Jupiter stopped this material from clumping together into a planet. Instead, the differently sized and shaped chunks orbit in a ring-shaped region between 329 million and 479 million km (204 million and 298 million miles) from the Sun.

The mass of all the material in the Asteroid Belt is only 0.5 percent of Earth's mass. The four largest asteroids—Ceres, Vesta, Pallas, and Hygeia—make up more than half the Belt's mass. To be called an asteroid, an object has to be at least 1 m (3.3 ft) across, although plenty of smaller objects and dust also orbit in the Asteroid Belt. Up to 1.7 million asteroids are wider than 1 km (0.6 miles).

Despite their small size, more than 300 asteroids are known to have moons. These moons were probably made by collisions, which broke off fragments that stayed close to their parent asteroid. Just 200 km (124 miles) wide, Elektra has the most known moons of any asteroid—three.

WATERY CERES

At around 939 km (583 miles) wide, Ceres has powerful enough gravity to have pulled itself into a rough sphere, earning itself the title of "dwarf planet." It is the only agreed dwarf planet that orbits entirely inside the orbit of Neptune.

Ceres is rocky, but it is also approximately half water. This makes it one of the most watery objects in the Solar System, a little less watery than Earth. Much of Ceres's water is mixed with rock, forming mud or clay. However, astronomers think the dwarf planet may have pockets of salty water beneath its surface. This water could possibly be home to tiny life forms, but no space probe has yet landed on Ceres to find out.

Ceres has a large ice volcano, known as a cryovolcano, as well as the remains of several others. None of Ceres's cryovolcanoes is currently active, but they once erupted icy, muddy water. These eruptions were possibly caused by collisions with other asteroids, which melted icy material and broke the crust.

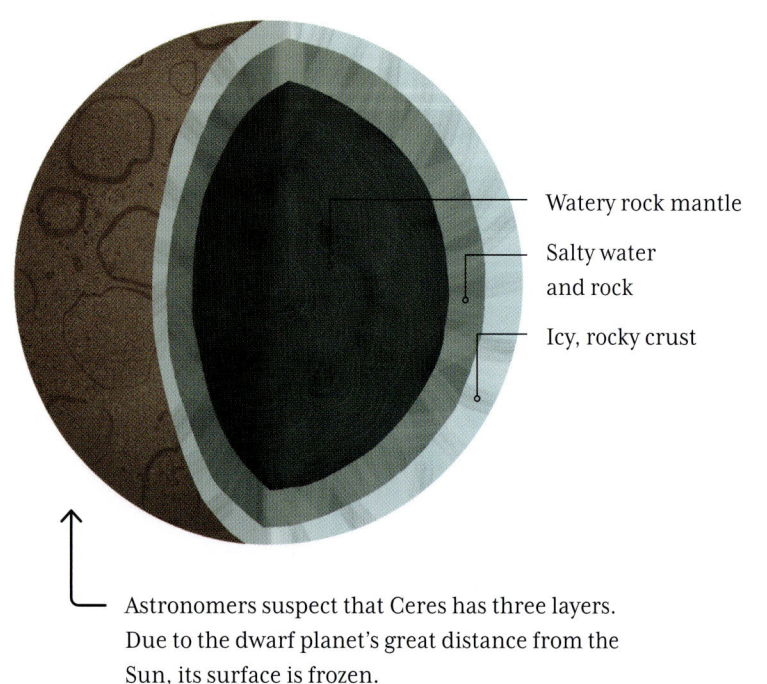

- Watery rock mantle
- Salty water and rock
- Icy, rocky crust

Astronomers suspect that Ceres has three layers. Due to the dwarf planet's great distance from the Sun, its surface is frozen.

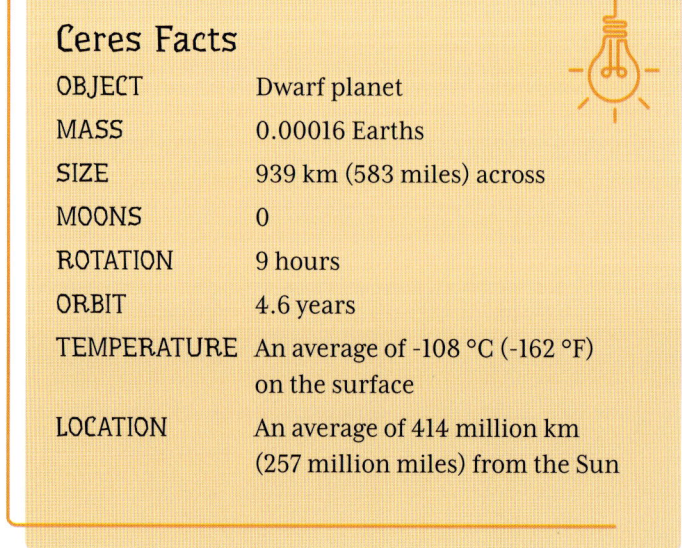

Ceres Facts

OBJECT	Dwarf planet
MASS	0.00016 Earths
SIZE	939 km (583 miles) across
MOONS	0
ROTATION	9 hours
ORBIT	4.6 years
TEMPERATURE	An average of -108 °C (-162 °F) on the surface
LOCATION	An average of 414 million km (257 million miles) from the Sun

On average, there are around 100,000 km (62,000 miles) between any two asteroids in the Asteroid Belt. However, collisions between asteroids occur every few million years. Fast collisions shatter asteroids, while slower crashes may join them.

Jupiter

The largest planet is named after the king of the Roman gods. Like its sister planet Saturn, Jupiter is a gas giant, made mostly of hydrogen and helium. It has the largest ocean in the Solar System, but it is an ocean of hydrogen and helium rather than water.

GAS GIANT

Jupiter and Saturn are called gas giants because hydrogen and helium are gasses at room temperature on Earth. Yet on these planets, hydrogen and helium take different forms—gas, liquid, and metallic. Jupiter's atmosphere is mostly hydrogen and helium gas. The atmosphere mingles with the planet's interior, where the gas is so tightly squeezed that it becomes liquid. Deeper inside the planet, electrons are squeezed out of the hydrogen and helium atoms. This means that electricity starts to flow, as if the swirling fluid were a metal.

Jupiter has no solid surface on which a spacecraft could land. The only solid portion of Jupiter is its core, which is probably iron and rock with a temperature of 24,000 °C (43,000 °F). However a spacecraft flying into Jupiter would be destroyed by pressure and heat long before it reached the core.

Jupiter's faint rings were not discovered until 1979, when they were spotted by the *Voyager 1* space probe. They are made of orbiting dust that was thrown from the planet's moons.

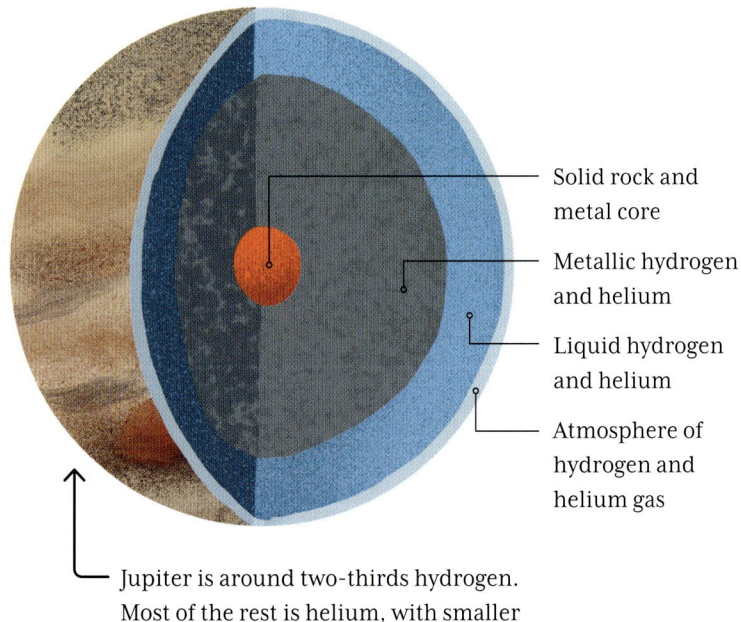

- Solid rock and metal core
- Metallic hydrogen and helium
- Liquid hydrogen and helium
- Atmosphere of hydrogen and helium gas

Jupiter is around two-thirds hydrogen. Most of the rest is helium, with smaller amounts of materials such as ammonia.

SPEEDY SPINNER

Jupiter spins around its axis faster than any other Solar System planet, at around 45,000 km/h (28,000 miles per hour). This speedy spin makes the planet bulge at the equator, a little like how a ball of dough starts to flatten into a pizza when spun. Jupiter is 9,276 km (5,764 miles) wider across its equator than across its poles.

Jupiter's fast spin creates powerful winds, which blow east to west and west to east in alternating bands. These winds separate Jupiter's clouds—which are made of materials such as ammonia—into horizontal stripes.

The orange stripes, called belts, are regions of cool, sinking gas that has been stained by sunlight. The light stripes, called zones, are warmer, rising gas.

Where belts and zones meet, circling storms can form. The largest storm, called the Great Red Spot, is around 16,000 km (9,940 miles) across—wider than Earth. Its winds spiral at up to 432 km/h (268 miles per hour). The storm has been observed by astronomers since at least 1831, when it was even larger than it is today.

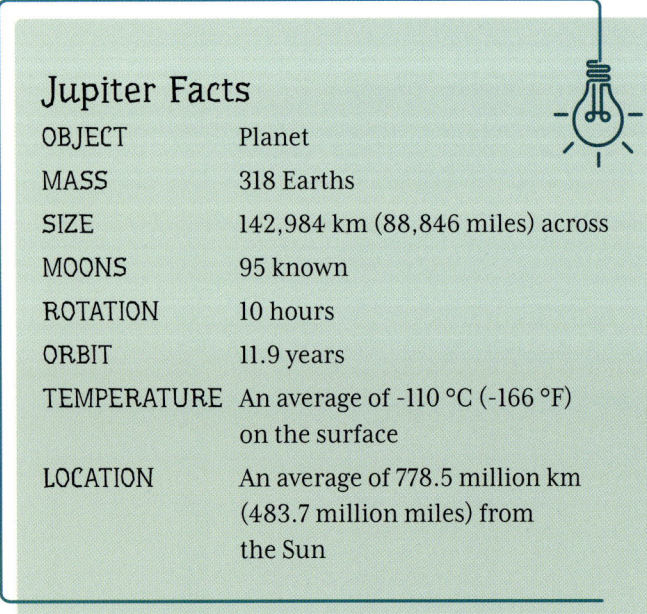

Jupiter Facts

OBJECT	Planet
MASS	318 Earths
SIZE	142,984 km (88,846 miles) across
MOONS	95 known
ROTATION	10 hours
ORBIT	11.9 years
TEMPERATURE	An average of -110 °C (-166 °F) on the surface
LOCATION	An average of 778.5 million km (483.7 million miles) from the Sun

> The Great Red Spot can be seen around 25,000 km (15,500 miles) south of Jupiter's equator. Although the storm is usually red, it has been known to change to orange, salmon, and beige.

THE SOLAR SYSTEM

Jupiter's Moons

Jupiter has 95 known moons, not including its moonlets, around 1 m (3.3 ft) across, and possibly hundreds of small moons that orbit many millions of kilometers away. The four largest moons—Ganymede, Callisto, Io, and Europa—were discovered by Galileo Galilei in 1610.

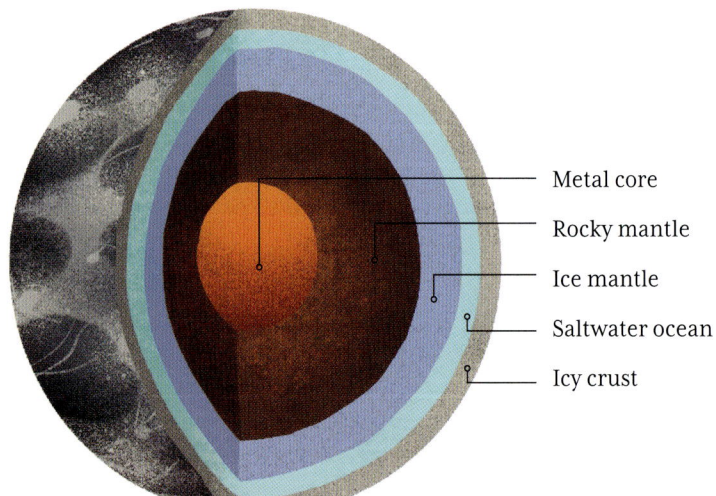

- Metal core
- Rocky mantle
- Ice mantle
- Saltwater ocean
- Icy crust

GANYMEDE

The Solar System's largest moon, Ganymede, formed soon after Jupiter, from the gas and dust spinning around its parent planet. Beneath its icy crust, the moon has a saltwater ocean, which could possibly be home to tiny life forms.

CALLISTO

At 4,820 km (2,995 miles) wide, Jupiter's second largest moon is the Solar System's third largest, after Saturn's moon Titan. Callisto is one of the most cratered objects in the Solar System, with hundreds of impact craters up to 1,800 km (1,120 miles) wide.

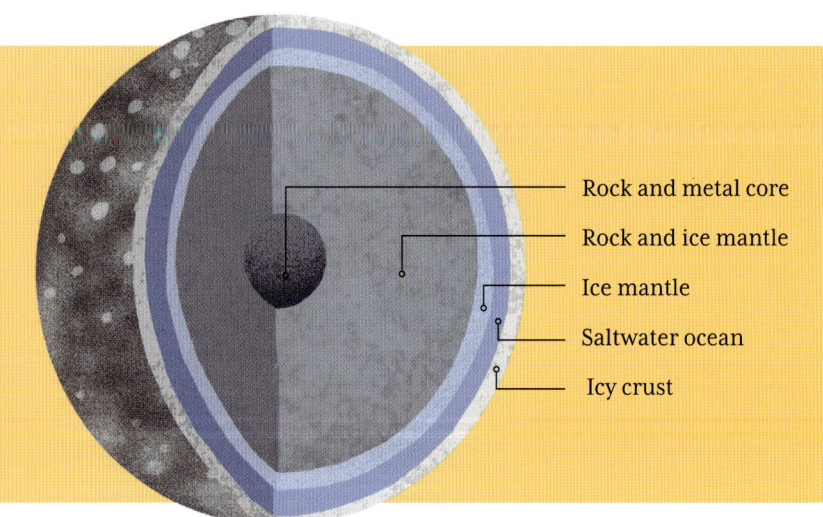

- Rock and metal core
- Rock and ice mantle
- Ice mantle
- Saltwater ocean
- Icy crust

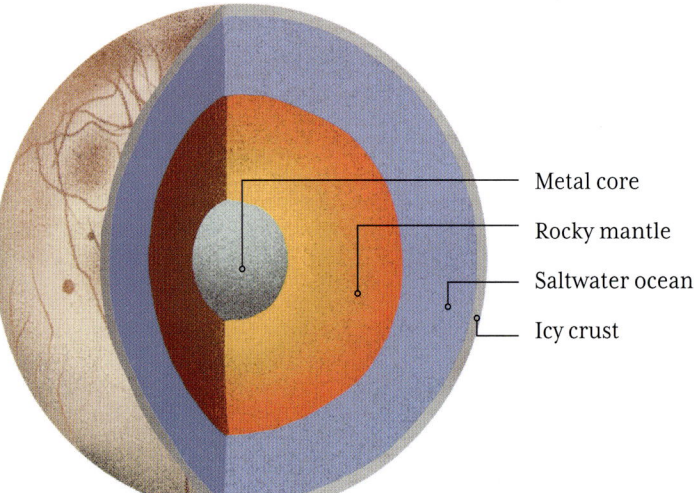

- Metal core
- Rocky mantle
- Saltwater ocean
- Icy crust

EUROPA

The smallest of the four moons discovered by Galileo, Europa is 3,122 km (1,940 miles) wide. It has a strangely uncratered surface, which suggests that a deep, warm ocean beneath the icy crust allows it to spring back into shape when struck. Long cracks in the crust may be caused by water welling up.

Ganymede Facts

OBJECT	Moon
MASS	0.025 Earths
SIZE	5,268 km (3,273 miles) across
ROTATION	7 days
ORBIT	7 days around Jupiter
TEMPERATURE	An average of -163 °C (-261 °F) on the surface
LOCATION	An average of 1,070,400 km (665,116 miles) from Jupiter

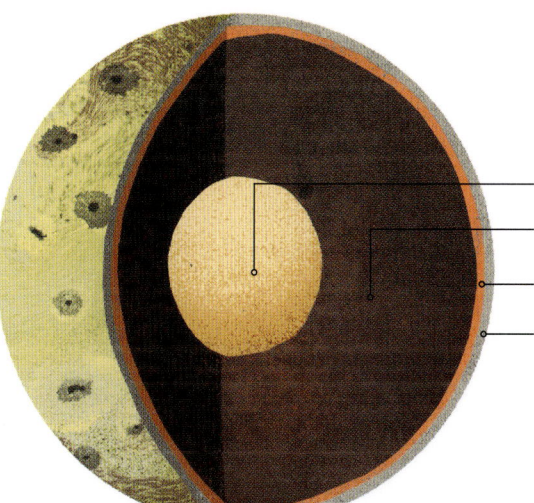

- Metal core
- Rocky mantle
- Ocean of melted rock
- Rock and sulfur crust

IO

Io is much closer to Jupiter than the other Galilean moons, around 421,700 km (262,032 miles) from the planet. This has made it hotter and less icy. It is made mostly of iron and rock. Like its sister moons, it is named after a lover of Zeus, the Greek counterpart of Jupiter.

IO'S VOLCANOES

Io has more active volcanoes—around 400—than any other object in the Solar System. The moon is stretched and squeezed by a tug of war between Jupiter's gravity and the gravity of the other Galilean moons. This causes friction in Io's interior, making its rock melt and burst from the surface.

GALILEO GALILEI

When the Italian astronomer Galileo Galilei heard about the invention of the telescope by spectacle-maker Hans Lippershey, he set about making his own. He immediately turned his telescope to the sky, becoming the first person to see a moon orbiting an object other than Earth. The four moons he spotted are called the Galilean moons.

Saturn

The sixth planet from the Sun can be seen as a yellowish point of light in the night sky during most of the year. More than nine times wider than Earth, Saturn is the second biggest planet. It is named after the Roman god of time, wealth, and farming.

DIFFERENT SISTER

Despite its similar materials to Jupiter, Saturn's atmosphere does not display the bright stripes of its sister gas giant. Saturn's stripes are fainter and paler. This is because Saturn's distance from the Sun—and its smaller size, which gives it less inner heat—makes its atmosphere cooler. The upper atmosphere is filled with crystals of frozen ammonia, which give Saturn a more even—and yellowish—appearance.

Saturn is also a lot less dense than Jupiter, which means its atoms and molecules are less tightly packed together. Although Saturn's core is dense, its average overall density is much less dense than water. This means that—if there were a swimming pool big enough to hold Saturn—it would float, for the same reason that a rubber ring floats in water.

HOT INSIDE

Saturn's core is as hot as 11,700 °C (21,000 °F). Due to its huge size, the planet grew massively hot during its formation, because of the crashing of material. Although Saturn has since cooled, plenty of heat remains. Like the other giant planets, it gives off more heat than it receives from the Sun. In fact,

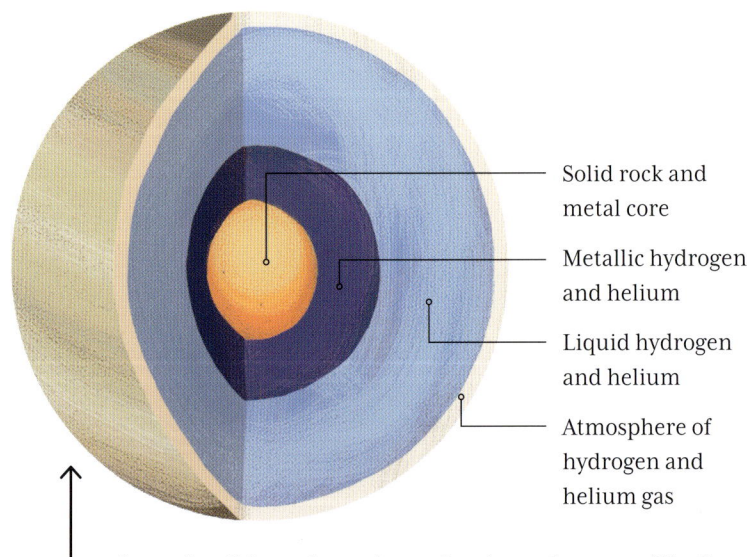

- Solid rock and metal core
- Metallic hydrogen and helium
- Liquid hydrogen and helium
- Atmosphere of hydrogen and helium gas

Saturn's solid core has at least nine times the mass of Earth. The rest of Saturn is around three-quarters hydrogen and one-quarter helium, with traces of other materials.

Saturn gives off twice the heat it receives. Due to its vast distance, Saturn gets 1 percent as much sunlight as Earth.

DIAMOND THUNDERSTORMS

Once every orbit, which takes 29.5 years, white streaks can be seen wrapping around Saturn's northern hemisphere for a few weeks. Known as the Great White Spot, these streaks are thunderstorms caused by rapidly rising, hot gas. On Earth, quickly rising, hot, wet air also causes thunderstorms. When lightning in Saturn's storms strikes methane in the atmosphere, it turns to carbon. The carbon hardens into diamonds as it falls—creating diamond rain.

Saturn's thunderstorms happen when its northern hemisphere is most tilted toward the Sun. Like all the planets except Mercury, which is almost upright, Saturn's axis is tilted. While Earth's axis tilts by around 23 degrees (see page 104), Saturn's tilts a little more, by nearly 27 degrees. Astronomers think that all the planets were upright when they formed, but were tipped by crashes with asteroids.

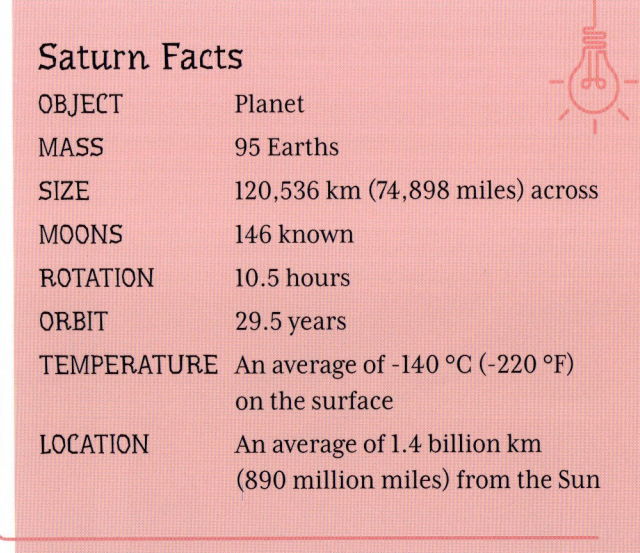

Saturn Facts

OBJECT	Planet
MASS	95 Earths
SIZE	120,536 km (74,898 miles) across
MOONS	146 known
ROTATION	10.5 hours
ORBIT	29.5 years
TEMPERATURE	An average of -140 °C (-220 °F) on the surface
LOCATION	An average of 1.4 billion km (890 million miles) from the Sun

Cassini was the first space probe to orbit Saturn, from 2004 to 2017. When the Great White Spot appeared in 2010–11, *Cassini* took photos. At the end of its mission, the probe was deliberately destroyed by being flown into Saturn, so it would not accidentally damage Saturn's moons.

THE SOLAR SYSTEM

Saturn's Rings

Saturn has the Solar System's brightest and largest ring system, stretching 400,000 km (248,000 miles) from the planet's surface. The rings are made mostly of chunks of ice, which orbit the planet around its equator. The rings' brightness is due to their iciness, which makes them reflect sunlight.

The rings may have formed less than 100 million years ago, when one of Saturn's moons was shattered by an asteroid, or perhaps when a comet was torn apart by the planet's gravity. The chunks of moon or comet were held in orbit by Saturn's gravity. Slowly, the jumbled rubble shifted into rings, divided by gaps where Saturn's moons and tinier moonlets pulled away much of the material.

Saturn's main, most densely packed rings are named A, B, and C. Visible from Earth only through a telescope, the rings were named in the order they were seen. A and B were first seen blurrily by Italian astronomer Galileo Galilei in 1610, through his newly built telescope. The C ring was spotted in 1850. Inside and far beyond these main rings are fainter rings that were discovered with powerful modern telescopes, or by space probes.

A RING

This ring stretches between 63,940 and 78,540 km (39,730 and 48,800 miles) from Saturn's surface. It is 10 to 30 m (33 to 98 ft) thick. Most of its chunks are smaller than 10 m (33 ft) across, but together they weigh many trillions of kilograms—around 0.000003 Earth masses.

ENCKE GAP
Saturn's innermost named moon, Pan, orbits inside A ring. Just 35 km (22 miles) wide, Pan keeps this narrow division, known as the Encke Gap, largely free from material.

CASSINI DIVISION
Around 4,700 km (2,920 miles) wide, this dark region between A and B rings was spotted by Italian astronomer Giovanni Cassini in 1675. The gap was created by the gravity of Saturn's innermost major moon, Mimas, even though the moon orbits 67,000 km (41,630 miles) farther from Saturn.

B RING
The biggest and brightest ring, B ring, is 25,580 km (15,895 miles) wide. It does not have any gaps, although many moonlets orbit within it. These create differences in its thickness, which ranges from 5 to 2,500 m (16 to 8,200 ft) high.

C RING
C ring begins 16,420 km (10,200 miles) from Saturn's surface. It is fainter than A and B rings, because its icy chunks are covered by dark dust. Its material orbits faster than chunks in the A and B rings, at around 76,000 km/h (47,220 miles per hour).

Uranus

The seventh planet from the Sun was named after the Greek god of the sky, while most of its 27 known moons were named after characters in the works of the English playwright William Shakespeare. The planet also has a faint ring system, made of ice and dark dust.

ICE GIANT

Uranus and its sister planet Neptune are known as ice giants. Yet they are not made of ice, but mostly of flowing water, ammonia, and methane. Scientists call these materials "ices" because—unlike hydrogen and helium, which have to be super-cold to freeze— they have freezing points above -182 °C (-279 °F). For example, water's freezing point is 0 °C (32 °F). Below this temperature it is ice. The interior of Uranus is so hot, up to 4,700 °C (8,490 °F) at the rocky core, that most of its "ices" form a super-hot ocean.

Due to its immense distance from the Sun, Uranus takes 84 years to make one orbit. The planet orbits the Sun on its side, with its ring system pointing nearly directly "upward," probably because it was knocked over by a collision with another planet when it was very young.

Due to this strange orientation, each of the planet's poles has nearly 42 years of sunlight when it faces the Sun, followed by almost 42 years of darkness.

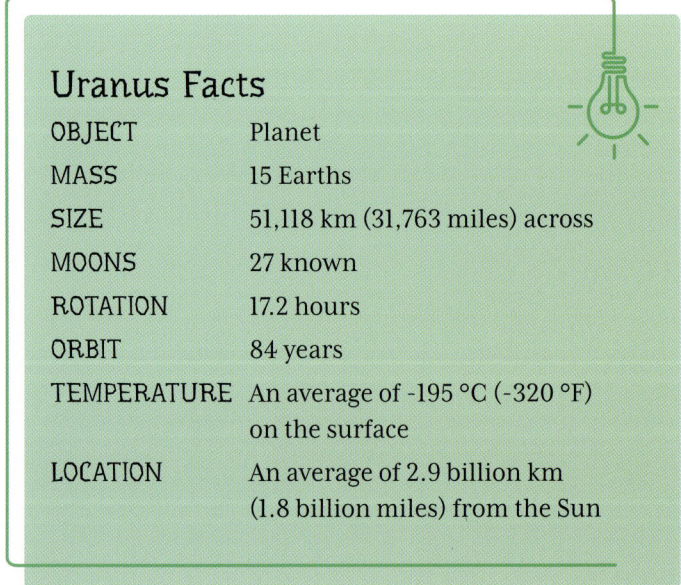

Uranus Facts
OBJECT	Planet
MASS	15 Earths
SIZE	51,118 km (31,763 miles) across
MOONS	27 known
ROTATION	17.2 hours
ORBIT	84 years
TEMPERATURE	An average of -195 °C (-320 °F) on the surface
LOCATION	An average of 2.9 billion km (1.8 billion miles) from the Sun

MANY MOONS

Uranus's largest moon, called Titania, is the eighth largest moon in the Solar System, after Neptune's moon Triton at number seven. Yet the combined mass of all 27 of Uranus's moons is less than the mass of Triton. Around 1,577 km (980 miles) across, Titania is named after the queen of the fairies in Shakespeare's comedy *A Midsummer Night's Dream*. Titania has a rocky core surrounded by frozen water.

Titania is one of Uranus's five large, rounded moons. These orbit between 129,390 and 583,520 km (80,400 and 362,580 miles) from Uranus. The five moons formed at the same time as Uranus from its leftover material.

Orbiting closer to Uranus, within 100,000 km (62,000 miles) of the planet, are 13 small, irregularly shaped moons. They probably formed at the same time as the planet's rings, perhaps when a larger moon was shattered by an asteroid.

Much farther from the planet, up to 20 million km (12.4 million miles) away, are at least nine more small moons. These were probably passing objects captured by Uranus's gravity.

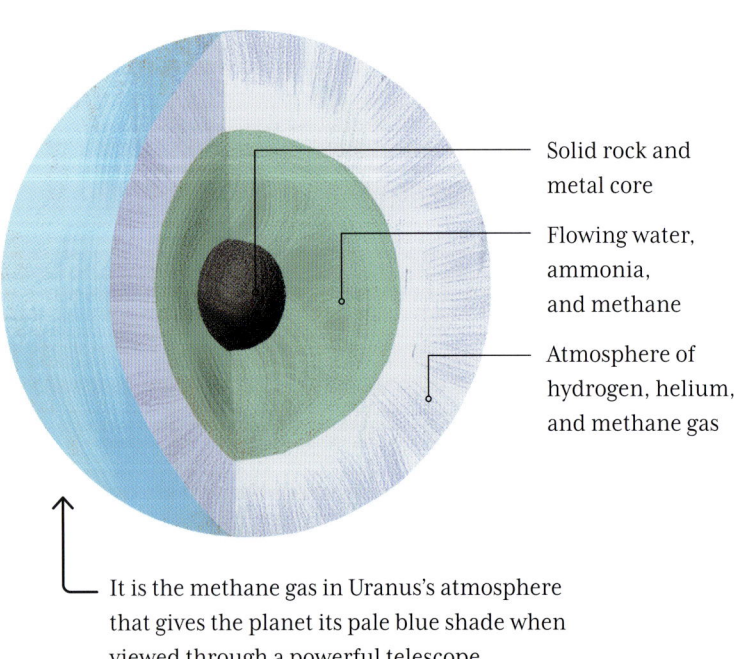

- Solid rock and metal core
- Flowing water, ammonia, and methane
- Atmosphere of hydrogen, helium, and methane gas

It is the methane gas in Uranus's atmosphere that gives the planet its pale blue shade when viewed through a powerful telescope.

Uranus and its largest moon, Titania, can be seen from the icy surface of Oberon. Oberon is the second largest and most distant of the planet's five major moons. It is named after the king of the fairies in Shakespeare's *A Midsummer Night's Dream*.

Neptune

The eighth planet is bluer than its sister ice giant, Uranus. The two planets have similar materials, but Neptune's less-hazy atmosphere makes its shade deeper. Neptune was named after the Roman god of the sea, while its 14 known moons take the names of Greek gods and spirits of water.

DIFFICULT TO FIND

Too distant to be seen with the naked eye, Neptune was found through the teamwork of astronomers and mathematicians. In the early 19th century, French astronomer Alexis Bouvard decided that the gravity of an undiscovered outer planet must be pulling on Uranus, affecting its orbit. French mathematician Urbain Le Verrier calculated where the new planet must be. Finally, German astronomer Johann Galle used this calculation to spot the eighth planet through a telescope, in 1846.

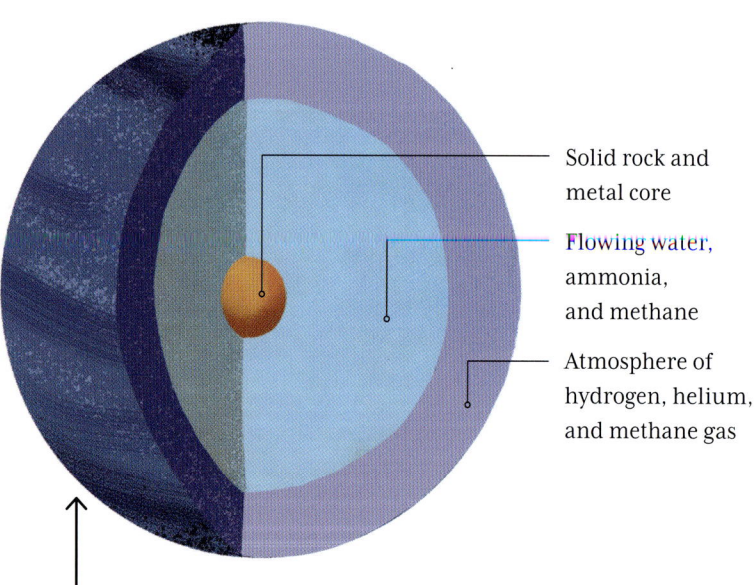

Solid rock and metal core

Flowing water, ammonia, and methane

Atmosphere of hydrogen, helium, and methane gas

Neptune has a similar structure to Uranus. However, its greater mass makes it slightly smaller, as its greater gravity compresses (squeezes) its materials.

WINDIEST PLANET

Neptune has the fastest winds in the Solar System—up to 2,200 km/h (1,367 miles per hour). These are caused by the planet's intense inner heat, 5,100 °C (9,210 °F) at the core, combined with its distance from the Sun, which makes its upper atmosphere around -214 °C (-353 °F). As on Earth, Neptune's winds are movements of gas in the atmosphere. Hot gas rises (like hot water rising in a saucepan), forcing cold gas to sink. Neptune's huge differences in temperature result in high-speed winds and vast storms. The largest storm seen on Neptune, the Great Dark Spot, was 13,000 km (8,000 miles) across.

STRANGE MOONS

Around 2,710 km (1,680 miles) wide, Neptune's largest moon, Triton, is the seventh largest Solar System moon, after four of Jupiter's moons, one of Saturn's, and Earth's Moon. Triton is the only one of Neptune's moons large enough for its gravity to pull it into a rounded shape. The next largest moon, Proteus, is only 420 km (260 miles) across. The most distant known moon, Neso, orbits up to 77 million km (47.8 million km) from Neptune, farther from its parent planet than any other known moon.

Unlike other large moons, Triton orbits its planet in the opposite direction from the way Neptune is rotating—clockwise rather than counterclockwise. This means that Triton cannot have formed at the same time, nor from the same spinning clump of gas and dust as Neptune. The moon may once have been a dwarf planet in the Kuiper Belt, but was pulled by Neptune's gravity. Triton has an almost identical structure to the largest Kuiper Belt dwarf planet—Pluto (see page 92).

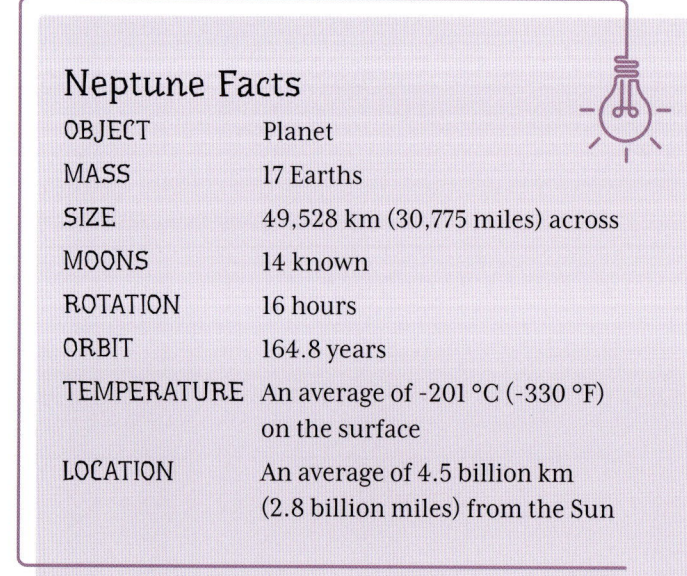

Neptune Facts

OBJECT	Planet
MASS	17 Earths
SIZE	49,528 km (30,775 miles) across
MOONS	14 known
ROTATION	16 hours
ORBIT	164.8 years
TEMPERATURE	An average of -201 °C (-330 °F) on the surface
LOCATION	An average of 4.5 billion km (2.8 billion miles) from the Sun

Neptune's biggest moon, Triton, makes up more than 99 percent of the mass of all the objects orbiting the planet, including its rings. There are five main rings, made of dusty ice.

THE SOLAR SYSTEM

The Kuiper Belt

Named after Dutch astronomer Gerard Kuiper, the Kuiper Belt is a ring of objects between 4.5 billion and 7.5 billion km (2.8 billion and 4.7 billion miles) from the Sun. As the Solar System formed, Neptune's gravity stopped these rocky, icy objects from grouping into a true planet. Yet at least five of the largest objects are big enough to be called dwarf planets.

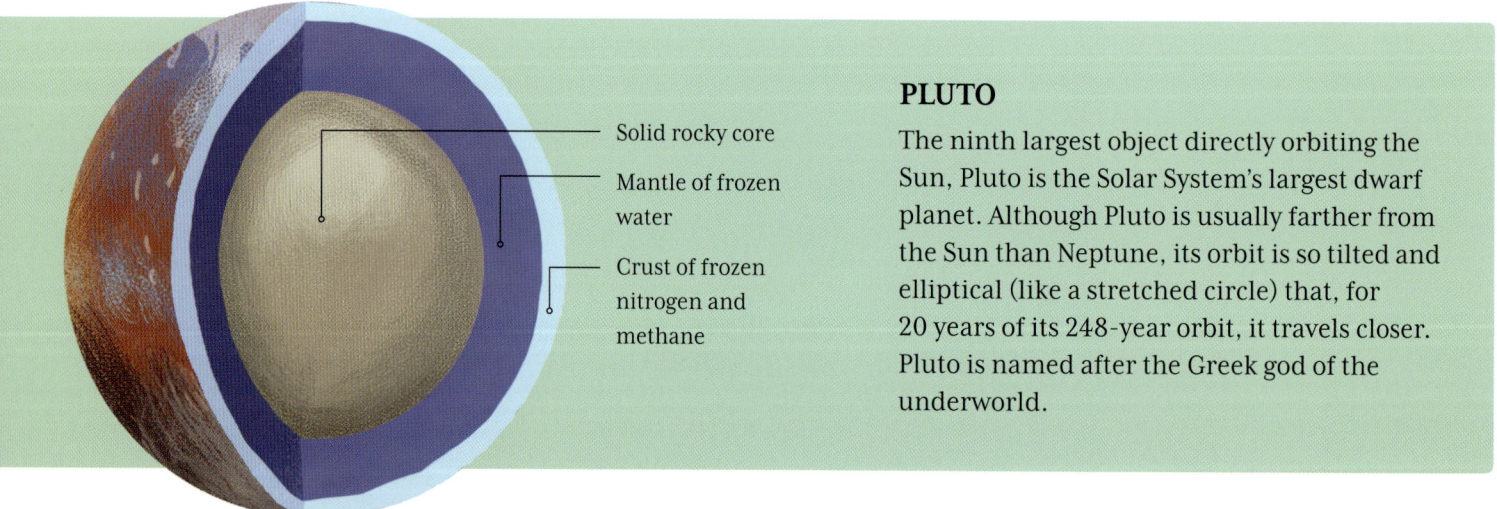

- Solid rocky core
- Mantle of frozen water
- Crust of frozen nitrogen and methane

PLUTO

The ninth largest object directly orbiting the Sun, Pluto is the Solar System's largest dwarf planet. Although Pluto is usually farther from the Sun than Neptune, its orbit is so tilted and elliptical (like a stretched circle) that, for 20 years of its 248-year orbit, it travels closer. Pluto is named after the Greek god of the underworld.

Pluto Facts

OBJECT	Dwarf planet
MASS	0.002 Earths
SIZE	2,376 km (1,476 miles) across
MOONS	5 known
ROTATION	6.4 days
ORBIT	248 years
TEMPERATURE	An average of -229 °C (-380 °F) on the surface
LOCATION	An average of 5.9 billion km (3.7 billion miles) from the Sun

PLUTO'S MOONS

Pluto's five known moons are named after characters and things linked with the underworld of Greek myths. At 1,212 km (753 miles) wide, Charon is the largest moon. It is so big compared with Pluto that both objects orbit a point in space a little outside of Pluto, where the pulls of their gravities are balanced.

Pluto

Charon

Nix

Styx

Kerberos

Hydra

THE SOLAR SYSTEM

HAUMEA

Up to 2,100 km (1,300 miles) long, Haumea is the second largest Kuiper Belt object. Unlike other dwarf planets, it is not even close to being a sphere. Its gravity pulled it into a rounded shape, but it was flattened by its speedy rotation of 1,600 km/h (995 miles per hour). Haumea has two known moons and a ring system.

MAKEMAKE

This dwarf planet was named after a creator god of the Pacific Ocean's Rapa Nui people. It has a red surface, like parts of Pluto, caused by sunlight heating methane in its crust. Makemake is about 1,430 km (890 miles) wide and has one known moon.

QUAOAR

Around 1,110 km (690 miles) wide, Quaoar was spotted in 2002 using a big telescope at the Palomar Observatory in California, USA. The dwarf planet was named after the creator god of California's Tongva people, while its moon, Weywot, was named after Quaoar's son.

ORCUS

Orcus was named after the Roman god who punished the dead if they had broken promises. It has one known moon, Vanth, named after a winged spirit who guided souls to the underworld. About 910 km (570 miles) wide, this dwarf planet was discovered in 2004.

THE SOLAR SYSTEM

Comets

Comets are icy objects with orbits that take them both far from and close to the Sun. When near the Sun, comets get so hot they grow glowing tails of gas and dust, which are sometimes so bright they can be seen without a telescope.

CREATING COMETS

One of the most famous comets is Halley's Comet, named after the English astronomer Edmond Halley, who was the first to conclude that the bright objects seen in the sky in 1531, 1607, and 1682 were the same comet. The word "comet" comes from the ancient Greek word for "long-haired," referring to these objects' long, glowing tails.

Comets probably started their lives with a regular orbit somewhere in the Kuiper Belt (see page 92), Scattered Disk, or Oort Cloud (see page 96). However, they were disturbed by the gravity of the outer planets or a star, flinging them into extremely elliptical (like stretched circles) orbits around the Sun—and making them comets.

At their closest approach to the Sun, comets may be a few million kilometers away. Some even crash into the Sun and are destroyed. At their most distant, some comets journey trillions of kilometers from the Sun. Comets with shorter orbits, known as short-period comets, have orbits lasting between 3 and 199 years. Long-period comets have orbits of 200 to thousands of years. There are about 4,000 known comets, but there are probably many more currently too far away to be spotted.

In 1066, Halley's Comet passed within 14.5 million km (9 million miles) of Earth. In England, the comet was seen as an omen, a sign of important events. A few weeks later, England's King Harold was beaten in battle by Normandy's William the Conqueror, who took the throne.

THE SOLAR SYSTEM

LIGHTING UP

A comet is made mostly of frozen water, dust, and rock. This solid core is known as its nucleus. When a comet is in the distant Solar System, it is cool and dark. Yet, as it passes the orbit of Jupiter, a comet heats up enough to release a cloud of gas, known as a coma. As a comet reaches Earth's orbit, a tail of hot gas starts to grow. Then, as the comet nears the Sun, a second tail appears, made of dust from the nucleus.

Eventually, after thousands or millions of years, a comet runs out of gas and dust, so it can no longer release glowing tails. It becomes "extinct," just a small, dark lump of rock.

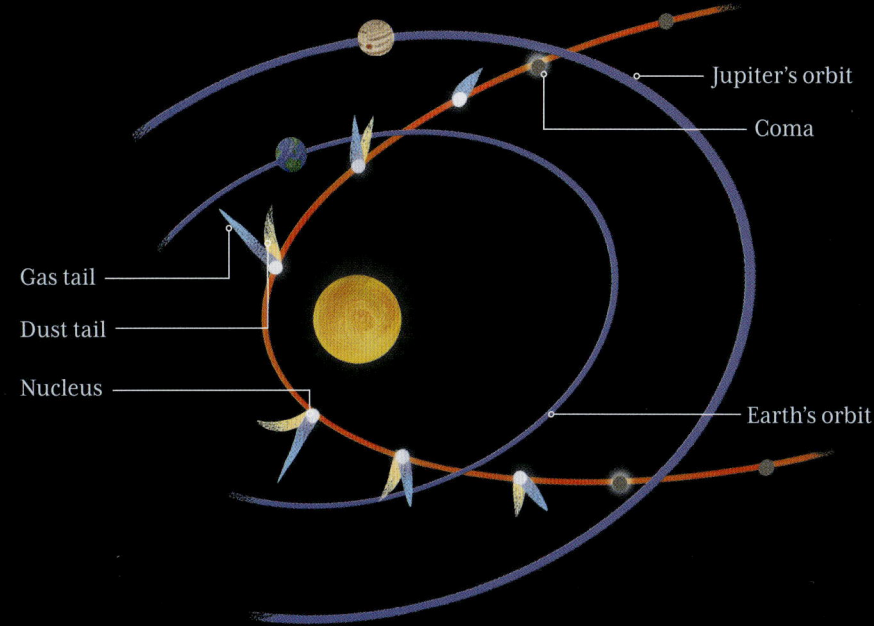

A comet's gas tail glows blue and is always blown away from the Sun. It may stretch for 150 million km (93 million km). The dust tail is golden and curves toward the path of the comet's orbit.

Halley's Comet Facts

OBJECT	Short-period comet
MASS	220 trillion kg (485 trillion lb)
SIZE	Nucleus 11 km (6.8 miles) across
ORBIT	75 years
LOCATION	Journeying between 88.7 million km (55 million miles) and 5.2 billion km (3.2 billion miles) from the Sun
LAST SEEN	1986
NEXT SEEN	2061

Edge of the Solar System

The Kuiper Belt is not the edge of the Solar System. Stretching beyond it is another region of spinning icy objects—the Scattered Disk. Yet even this cold, dark region is not yet the end. Billions of kilometers away are other mysterious objects held by our star's gravity.

Although trillions of objects orbit the Sun beyond Neptune, they are so far from us that not one of them was discovered until powerful telescopes were built in the 20th century. The first object discovered in this vast region was the Kuiper Belt's Pluto, in 1930. It was 66 years later, in 1996, that the first object in the Scattered Disk was seen, using telescopes at Hawaii's Mauna Kea Observatory.

Beyond the Scattered Disk are the detached objects, the first of them found in 2000. Detached objects are too far away to be pulled by the gravity of Neptune, making them seem "detached" from the rest of the Solar System, even though they still orbit the Sun. No one has yet spotted an object in the even more distant Oort Cloud. In fact, we do not know for sure that it exists. The possibility of this cloud of icy objects was suggested by Dutch astronomer Jan Oort in 1950. If the Oort Cloud does exist, its outer objects are the most distant things that feel—weakly—the pull of the Sun's gravity.

KUIPER BELT

Astronomers have now discovered thousands of Kuiper Belt objects (KBOs), but there may be a trillion or more still to be spotted, most of them smaller than 100 km (62 miles) wide. The combined mass of all the KBOs is probably no more than 1 percent of Earth's mass.

SCATTERED DISK

The billions of objects in the Scattered Disk probably used to orbit in the Kuiper Belt, but they were "scattered" by Neptune's gravity, giving them very tilted, elliptical (stretched out) orbits. When closest to the Sun, Scattered Disk objects are in the Kuiper Belt, but they may travel twice as far from the Sun as KBOs: up to 15 billion km (9.3 billion miles).

OORT CLOUD

The Oort Cloud may stretch from 300 billion to 30 trillion km (186 billion to 18.6 trillion miles) from the Sun. The inner cloud may be ring-shaped, while the trillions of objects in the outer cloud form a sphere as they have been scattered by the pull of other stars. Oort Cloud objects may be made of material from the edge of the disk that surrounded the newborn Sun.

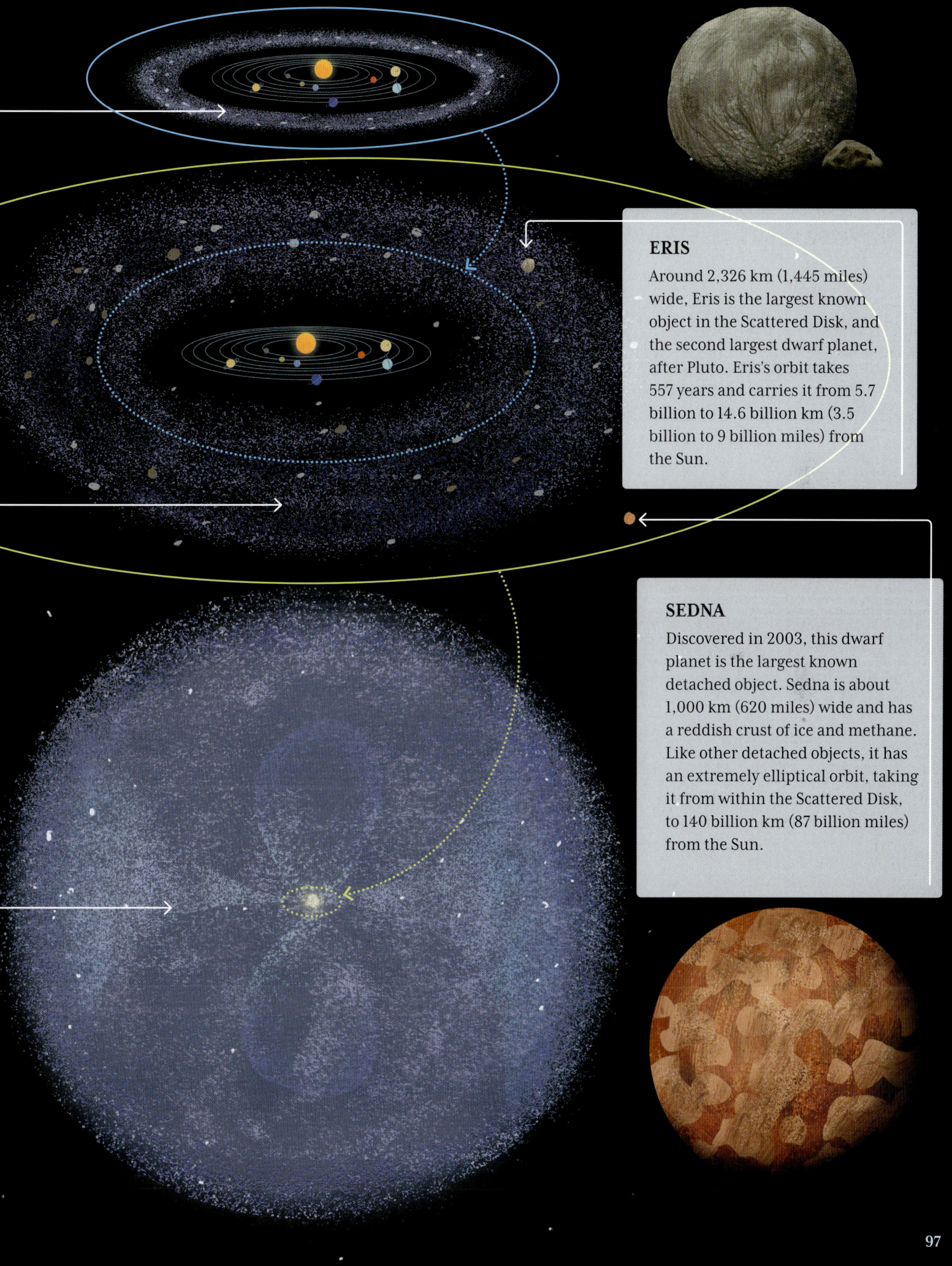

ERIS

Around 2,326 km (1,445 miles) wide, Eris is the largest known object in the Scattered Disk, and the second largest dwarf planet, after Pluto. Eris's orbit takes 557 years and carries it from 5.7 billion to 14.6 billion km (3.5 billion to 9 billion miles) from the Sun.

SEDNA

Discovered in 2003, this dwarf planet is the largest known detached object. Sedna is about 1,000 km (620 miles) wide and has a reddish crust of ice and methane. Like other detached objects, it has an extremely elliptical orbit, taking it from within the Scattered Disk, to 140 billion km (87 billion miles) from the Sun.

Earth and the Moon

No more than 100 million years after the Sun's birth, our planet formed in the spinning disk of dust and gas around the young star. Particles bumped and stuck together. The gravity of these particles pulled in other particles, and all the crashing made the growing clump super-hot, up to 10,000 °C (18,000 °F). By around 4.5 billion years ago, the clump was a planet-sized sphere of molten, mixed-together rock and metal—the brand-new Earth. Around 200 million years later, a smaller planet—which astronomers call Theia—was probably tugged or thrown into Earth. The crash shattered Theia and flung rubble into space. Pulled by Earth's gravity, the rubble formed an orbiting sphere of rock and metal—the Moon.

Since metal is heavier than rock, Earth's molten metal sank, while its liquid rock rose toward the surface. The metal formed our planet's core of iron and nickel. The core was wrapped by a thick layer of dense rock, known as the mantle. Lighter rock formed the planet's crust. Even today, Earth's mantle is so hot, up to 3,700 °C (6,690 °F), that some of its rock is molten. The metal in the outer core is still so hot, over 4,500 °C (8,130 °F), that it is liquid. The inner core is even hotter, around 5,400 °C (9,750 °F)—as hot as the Sun's surface. Yet in the inner core, the metal is squeezed so tightly it is solid.

Slowly, our planet became suitable for life. By 4.4 billion years ago, Earth had cooled enough for rain, which fell from its atmosphere, to fill oceans in dips in the crust. Earth was now the right temperature—and the right distance from the Sun—for all its water to neither freeze into ice nor boil into steam. It was in the oceans that, around 3.8 billion years ago, tiny living things appeared.

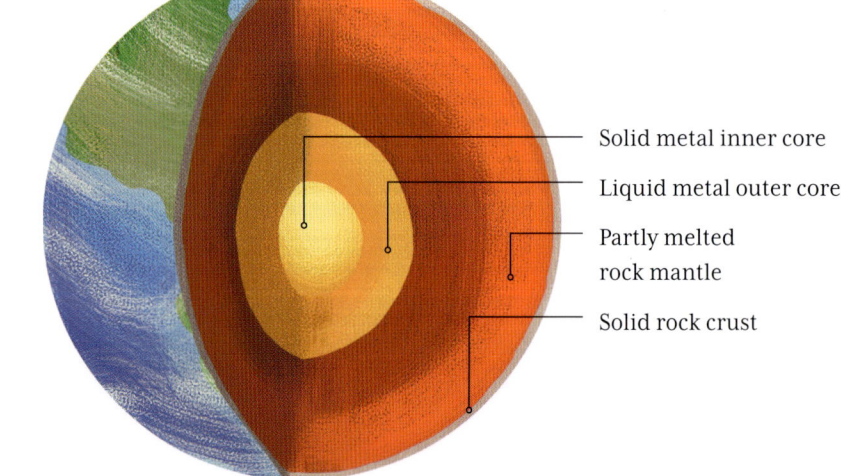

Earth's outer layer is called the crust. Today, our planet's surface has an average temperature of 15 °C (59 °F).

Solid metal inner core

Liquid metal outer core

Partly melted rock mantle

Solid rock crust

Astronomers cannot be sure, but many think the Moon formed when a Mars-sized planet, called Theia, crashed into Earth at around 14,000 km/h (8,700 miles per hour). Pieces of Earth and Theia came together to form the Moon.

Earth's Crust

Earth's crust is between 5 and 70 km (3 and 43 miles) thick. The crust is broken into jagged-edged pieces, called tectonic plates, which float on the hot rock beneath. The movement of these plates creates mountains and deep crack-like valleys, as well as earthquakes and volcanoes.

MOVING PLATES

Around 3 billion years ago, as Earth cooled, the crust and upper mantle cracked into around seven large plates and many smaller ones. We cannot usually see the edges of plates at the surface because they are covered by soil, water, or new rock. However, the plates move by up to 10 cm (4 in) per year, as the partly melted rock in the mantle flows very slowly, rising and falling due to convection (see page 51). The movement of tectonic plates has reshaped Earth's continents many times over.

The edges of plates are called boundaries. There are three main types of boundaries. At convergent boundaries, the plates are moving toward each other. One plate sinks below the other, which folds or shoves rock upward, creating mountain ranges. At divergent boundaries, the plates are moving apart. This can create deep valleys called rifts. At transform boundaries, plates are sliding past each other.

EARTHQUAKES

Earthquakes usually take place at plate boundaries. They can happen at any of the three boundary types, when the plates get stuck on each other as they move. Pressure builds until the rock suddenly cracks, shaking the ground. The shaking travels through the ground in waves, called seismic waves. Like ripples on a pond, these weaken as they spread outward.

The spot underground where the rock breaks is called the earthquake's hypocenter. The spot on the surface above the hypocenter is called the epicenter. Close to the epicenter, powerful earthquakes can damage buildings, roads, and power lines. Sometimes, if the epicenter is underwater, earthquakes make tall ocean waves called tsunamis.

VOLCANOES

Volcanoes are cracks in the crust where hot rock—called magma—escapes. Volcanoes often form at divergent and convergent boundaries. At divergent boundaries, magma wells up from the mantle between the two plates. At convergent boundaries, rock is melted, then surges to the surface. Volcanoes can also form in the middle of plates, over very hot areas in the mantle, called hotspots. Earth's largest volcano, Mauna Loa on the Island of Hawaii, formed over a hotspot in the Pacific Plate.

Once magma has erupted, it is called lava. Over time, many volcanoes take the shape of mountains as their lava cools into solid rock, eruption after eruption. Stratovolcanoes erupt thick lava that does not flow far before it cools, creating a tall cone shape. Shield volcanoes have runnier lava, which forms a flatter shape, like an ancient warrior's shield.

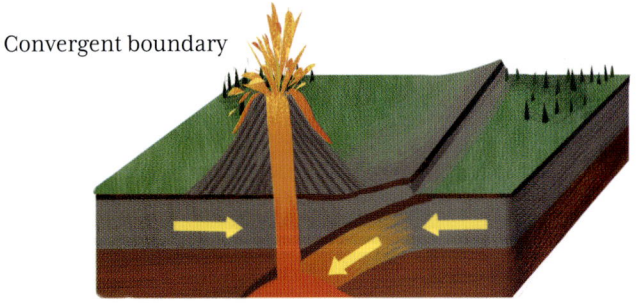

Convergent boundary

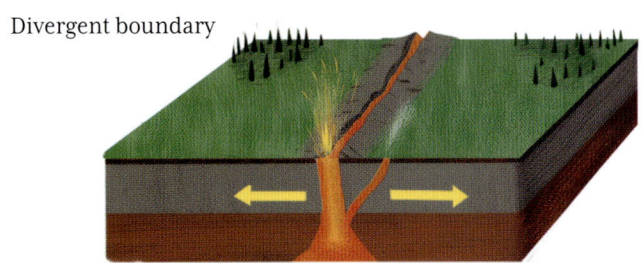

Divergent boundary

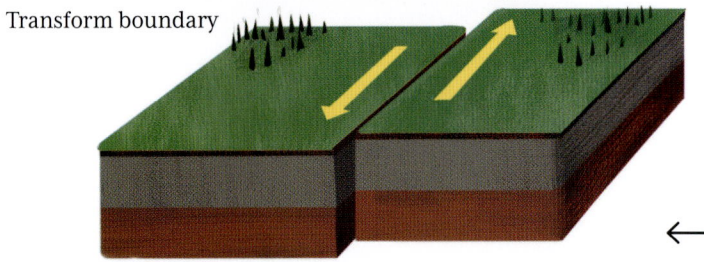

Transform boundary

There are three main types of boundaries between tectonic plates. In each type, the plates are moving differently in relation to each other.

EARTH AND THE MOON

Ash cloud

Crater

Lava flow

Mount Etna is an active stratovolcano on the Italian island of Sicily, which lies on a convergent boundary. An active volcano is either erupting or likely to erupt in the future; a dormant volcano may possibly erupt again; while an extinct volcano no longer has a magma supply so cannot re-erupt.

Side vent

Crust

Magma chamber

Scientist Profile

NAME Inge Lehmann
DATES 1888–1993
NATIONALITY Danish
BREAKTHROUGH
Lehmann studied how seismic waves travel through Earth. In 1936, her studies made her the first to realize that our planet must have a solid inner core within its liquid outer core.

Upper mantle

EARTH AND THE MOON

Earth's Atmosphere

There would be no life on Earth without its atmosphere, the blanket of gases held around our planet by its gravity. The atmosphere—also known as air, contains the gas oxygen and water. Earth's living things need oxygen and water to survive.

Air is around 78 percent nitrogen and 21 percent oxygen gas, with traces of gases such as argon. Plants and animals need to take in oxygen to make energy for living. Scientists divide the atmosphere into layers, each layer less packed with air than the one below, as the pull of Earth's gravity weakens. The lowest layer, called the troposphere, also holds lots of water, mostly in the form of a gas called water vapor. When this water falls as rain, it gives plants and animals the water needed to transport food through their bodies.

When the Sun's visible light (see page 42) reaches Earth's atmosphere, it is scattered by molecules of gas. Sunlight contains all the shades of the rainbow, from red to blue. Blue light is scattered more than the rest, because it travels as shorter waves. This makes the sky look blue during daytime, even though the gases in the atmosphere are invisible.

MESOSPHERE
This is where streaks of light, known as meteors or shooting stars, can be seen. When fragments from comets and asteroids enter the atmosphere, they crash into air molecules, getting so hot they usually burn up, creating bright streaks. If a rock is large enough to survive and hit the ground, it is called a meteorite.

TROPOSPHERE
As the Sun warms Earth's oceans and lakes, some water evaporates—it turns into water vapor and drifts into the troposphere. As the water vapor cools, some condenses into drops of liquid water, forming clouds. When the drops grow heavy, they fall as rain.

EXOSPHERE

Extending to 10,000 km (6,200 miles) above Earth's surface, this is where many human-made satellites orbit. The exosphere fades gradually into space, where there is almost nothing at all, just a little dust, gas, and high-energy particles from the Sun.

THERMOSPHERE

The thermosphere extends from 80 to 600 km (50 to 370 miles) above the surface. This is the region where auroras form (see page 106).

STRATOSPHERE

The stratosphere lies between 10 and 50 km (6 and 30 miles) above Earth's surface. Passenger planes often fly in the low stratosphere, above the clouds of the troposphere, where the air is relatively still.

EARTH AND THE MOON

Earth's Orbit

Every 365.25 days, Earth completes an orbit around the Sun, having journeyed 940 million km (584 million miles). Like all orbits, Earth's is not a perfect circle, but an oval called an ellipse. When closest to the Sun, Earth is 147 million km (91 million miles) away, while at the farthest it is 152 million km (94 million miles) away.

A YEAR ON EARTH

For thousands of years, humans have devised calendars to mark out the passing of time. Around the world, the most commonly used calendar is based on Earth's orbit around the Sun, with a year equal to one orbit. It is sometimes called the Gregorian calendar because it was introduced by Pope Gregory XIII, in 1582.

In most parts of the world, we can follow the course of Earth's journey around the Sun by watching the changing seasons through the year. Seasons are caused by the fact that Earth's axis is slightly tilted. When the northern hemisphere (half) of Earth is tilted toward the Sun, it has summer with hotter weather. At the same time, the southern hemisphere of Earth has winter, with colder weather. Places close to the equator see fewer seasonal changes, as they are hot all year.

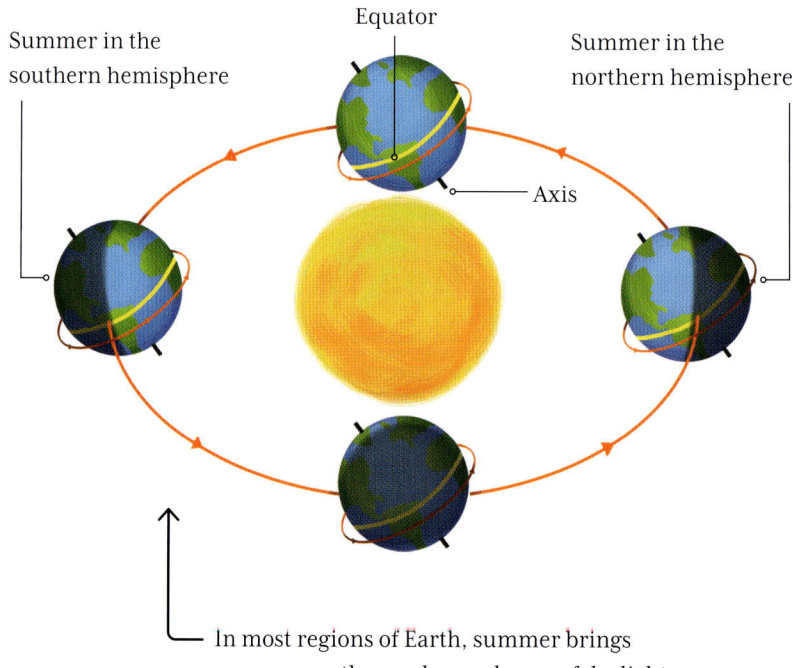

In most regions of Earth, summer brings warmer weather and more hours of daylight.

Spring

Summer

A DAY ON EARTH

As Earth orbits, it also rotates around its axis. Each rotation takes nearly exactly 24 hours—which we call a day. As Earth turns, the Sun appears to rise in the east, then set in the west. When one half of Earth is turned toward the Sun, it has daylight, while the other half has night.

Due to Earth's tilted axis, days and nights are not usually of equal length. When the northern hemisphere is tilted toward the Sun, it has longer days and shorter nights, while the southern hemisphere has longer nights. The poles see the most extreme pattern of darkness and light. During their winter, the poles are plunged into darkness for around 11 weeks.

CALENDAR CATCH-UP

Since Earth's orbit takes 365.25 days, it is impossible for the calendar—based on days of equal length—to keep pace with it. To correct this problem, we use a system of leap years. Most calendar years have 365 days, but every 4 years, we add an extra day—February 29—so the calendar year again matches up with the astronomical year. This system was introduced by the ancient Roman ruler Julius Caesar in 45 BCE, and was later adjusted by Pope Gregory.

Earth's Orbit Facts

TIME	365.25 days
DIRECTION	Counterclockwise
SPEED	107,208 km/h (66,616 miles per hour) on average
DISTANCE	940 million km (584 million miles) covered in each orbit
APHELION	Farthest distance from the Sun is 152.1 million km (94.5 million miles)
PERIHELION	Closest distance to the Sun is 147.1 million km (91.4 million km)

In Earth's temperate regions, which are midway between the poles and the equator, there are four seasons. The seasons can be observed through the changing temperature, which causes changes in many trees.

Fall or autumn

Winter

Earth's Auroras

Auroras are dancing lights in the sky that can be seen close to the North and South Poles. These beautiful light displays are most easily watched on dark, cloudless nights, far from the disturbance of city lights.

SOLAR WIND

Auroras are caused by the solar wind, a stream of electrically charged particles that flows constantly from the Sun. These particles include electrons, which are far smaller than a billionth of a millimeter across. When these high-energy particles meet Earth's atmosphere, they pass on energy to its gases. The molecules of gas begin to glow, with different gases glowing different shades. Oxygen usually glows green, but higher above Earth's surface, very excited oxygen can give off red light. Nitrogen tends to glow pink or purple.

All the other Solar System planets, apart from Mercury, experience auroras. Mercury has such a thin atmosphere that there are not enough gas molecules to be excited by the solar wind. Auroras have also been seen on the four largest moons of Jupiter, all of which have atmospheres. Auroras on other planets and moons are different shades, since their atmospheres contain different gases. On Saturn, for example, hydrogen glows red and purple.

EARTH'S MAGNETIC FIELD

Auroras can be seen only around Earth's poles because it is here that the planet's magnetic field is weakest. Due to its iron core, Earth is a giant magnet with a powerful magnetic field. Magnetism is a force that can be made by the flow of electrons through magnetic metals, such as iron. As liquid iron swirls in Earth's outer core, electrons flow, creating the magnetic field.

Earth's magnetic field protects it from the solar wind, which would otherwise strip away the atmosphere. Yet some charged particles manage to touch the atmosphere around the poles. Here they can become trapped between magnetic field lines, creating glowing arcs in the night sky. Charged particles can also be scattered into the atmosphere, creating widespread, patchy auroras.

Lines of magnetic force flow from one of Earth's poles to the other. This magnetic field diverts most of the particles of the solar wind.

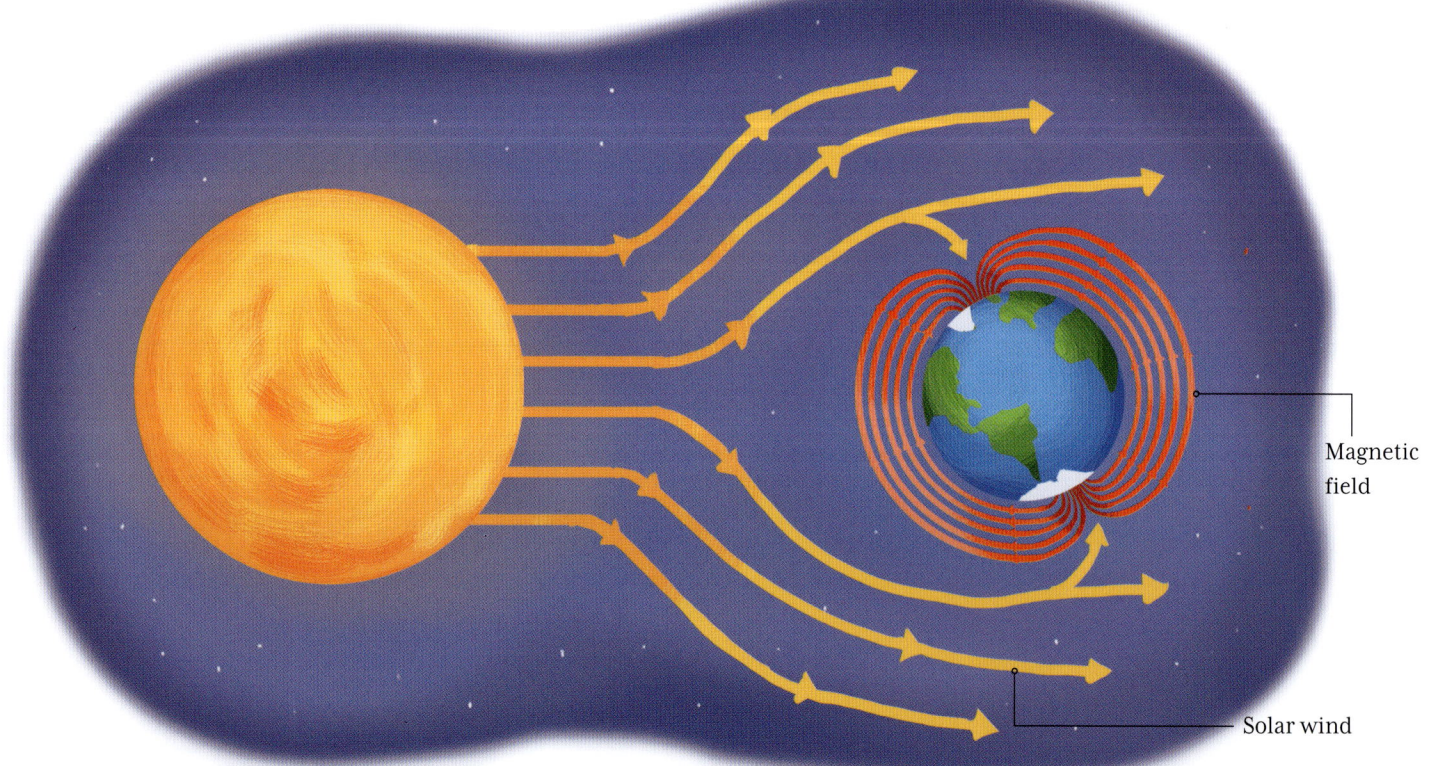

Magnetic field

Solar wind

Auroras can be seen on cloudless winter nights in places such as the far north of Norway, in northern Europe.

The Water Cycle

The water cycle is the constant movement of water through Earth's air, across its surface, and underground. As water moves, it changes state: from liquid water, to solid ice, to gassy water vapor. In total, all Earth's water adds up to 1.4 billion cubic km (336 million cubic miles).

AROUND AND AROUND

The water cycle is driven by the Sun, which heats water in oceans, lakes, rivers, and ponds. Surface water evaporates (see page 21), turning from a liquid to an invisible gas, called water vapor. Water also evaporates from plant leaves and soil.

Water vapor rises in warm air: Since warm air has more space between its molecules than cool air, it is less dense—so it floats upward. As air rises, it cools. Cool air can hold less water vapor than warm air, so some water vapor condenses (see page 21) into water droplets. We can see clusters of these droplets as clouds.

When water droplets grow too big and heavy to float, they fall as rain. In cold weather, water may fall as joined ice crystals, called snow. Rain, snow, hail, and sleet are all types of precipitation, which is any form of water that falls to the ground.

Back on Earth, water makes many journeys. It may freeze in ice sheets at the poles or on mountaintops. It may flow to the ocean in rivers that travel above- or underground. Water may collect in lakes, reservoirs, or swamps; or in underground rock or soil, where it is known as groundwater.

The water cycle is continuous: When water reaches Earth's surface, its cycle begins again.

ESSENTIAL CYCLE

As water evaporates, it leaves behind most of its impurities, such as salts. This is how the water cycle supplies land animals and plants with fresh, clean water, which they use to transport materials through their bodies. The water cycle also keeps oceans healthy, as the inflow of cool fresh water drives the mixing of ocean water—with cold water sinking and warm water rising—carrying nutrients and oxygen to all its living things.

In addition, the water cycle shapes Earth's surface. Over many years, rivers wear away rock and soil, carving wide valleys or narrow canyons. Bodies of ice, called glaciers, slide slowly down mountainsides, grinding out valleys with the boulders they carry.

Scientist Profile
NAME   Syukuro Manabe
BIRTH   1931
NATIONALITY Japanese-American
BREAKTHROUGH
He pioneered the use of computers to create models of Earth's atmosphere and study how changing conditions affect weather. In 1966, he warned the world about climate change (see page 110).

CLOUDS

Different types of clouds form at different heights in Earth's atmosphere. Among the highest are cirrus clouds, which form at up to 20 km (12.4 miles) high from ice crystals. The lowest, known as fog or mist, form at ground level when cold air is very full of water vapor.

Thick, dark clouds tend to bring rain or snow, while high, wispy clouds do not.

Cirrus: High, wispy clouds formed when warm, dry air rises.

Cirrocumulus: High, puffy clouds of ice crystals and water droplets.

Nimbostratus: Dark, thick layers of cloud that often bring heavy precipitation.

Cumulonimbus: Tall thunderclouds formed when hot, wet air rises fast.

Cumulus: Low, white puffy clouds that do not usually bring rain.

Stratus: Low featureless clouds that may bring light rain.

Climate Change

When scientists talk about climate change, they mean the changes in Earth's weather over the last 30 to 50 years. Climate change is caused by a rise in the temperature of Earth's air and oceans. That temperature rise, known as global warming, is caused by human activities.

Three main human activities are causing global warming and climate change: burning fossil fuels, cutting down forests, and farming methods. These activities release greenhouse gases into the atmosphere. Greenhouse gases—including carbon dioxide, methane, and nitrous oxide—trap the Sun's heat, a little like the glass in a greenhouse, making Earth warmer.

Greenhouse gases have always been in the atmosphere, but the extra quantities we have released since 1880 have made Earth 1 °C (1.9 °F) hotter. If we let greenhouse gas emissions continue to rise at the current rate, by 2100, Earth might be 5 °C (9 °F) warmer than in 1880. However, governments, businesses, and ordinary people are working to reduce emissions so we can slow down climate change.

BURNING FOSSIL FUELS
Humans burn coal, oil, and natural gas (see page 60) in power plants, factories, homes, and vehicles. This releases carbon dioxide, as well as smaller amounts of methane and nitrous oxide. Burning fossil fuels causes three-quarters of greenhouse gas emissions.

DEFORESTATION
In some regions, forests are cut down to make room for farms, towns, and factories. Trees soak up carbon dioxide (see page 151), so deforestation means less carbon dioxide is absorbed from the air. Burning trees releases the carbon dioxide they have stored.

FARMING METHODS
When cows and other grass-eating farm animals fart, they release methane, which they produce as they digest. In addition, some farmers spray human-made fertilizers onto crops to give them the nutrient nitrogen. When microorganisms in soil feed on the nitrogen, they release nitrous oxide.

EARTH AND THE MOON

WARMING OCEANS

Water expands as it gets warmer, so sea levels are rising. Since 1880, oceans have risen up the shore by 21 to 24 cm (8 to 9 in), which is putting low-lying islands at risk. Warming oceans are also affecting sea animals such as corals. Many corals take food from algae that live inside their body and make their own food from sunlight. When seawater gets too warm, stressed corals push out their algae, leaving themselves starving.

MELTING ICE

Earth is losing 1.2 trillion tonnes (1.3 trillion US tons) of ice each year, as rising temperatures melt ice on mountains and at the poles. This is shrinking the habitats of ice-dwelling animals (see page 204). It is also reducing the fresh water stored in glaciers, which are essential as a steady supply of drinking water for local people and animals. Melted land ice is trickling into oceans, worsening sea-level rise.

CHANGING WEATHER

Warmer air and oceans are speeding up the water cycle, which is—overall—increasing rainfall, storms, and flooding. However, some hot, dry regions are facing more droughts, which are long periods without rain. This is because, as evaporation speeds up, it dries out surface soil and plants, further reducing precipitation in these already dry places. Droughts raise the risk of wildfires, which spread quickly through dry vegetation.

Habitats

A habitat is the natural home of a living thing, where it is suited to the conditions, such as the level of heat, light, and water. Each habitat—from the rain forest to the desert—is home to different groups of plants, animals, fungi, protists, and microorganisms.

Stretching across the world are large land habitats, called biomes. From rain forest to polar ice, each biome has different conditions due to its climate. Climate is the usual weather in a region. Regions closer to the poles usually have colder, drier climates than those near the equator, where the Sun is more directly overhead. Different plants grow in different biomes, but in very cold or dry biomes, few or no plants grow. In warmer, wetter biomes, there are many plants, providing shelter and food for many other living things.

There are also different water biomes, divided into fresh water and salt water. These are divided yet more: Within the oceans, different communities of living things are found along coasts from on the cold, dark seafloor. Sunlit surface waters are home to many plants and other photosynthesizing life forms, which makes them the most biodiverse water biomes. Biodiversity ("variety of life") is a measure of the number of different species in an area.

POLAR ICE
In the far north and south of our planet, this biome is so cold and dry that no plants can grow. Few animals live here. Larger predatory birds and mammals—kept warm by thick layers of fur, feathers, or fat—hunt prey such as fish in the ocean.

TUNDRA
Found mainly in the far north, in a ring around the polar ice, tundra is a cold, dry biome where only small, tough plants can grow. Animals here have thick fur or feathers, while many fly or walk to warmer regions in winter.

CONIFEROUS FOREST
This biome is mainly in the north, bordering the southern edge of the tundra. Winters are long and cold, but the short summers give trees time to grow. Most trees are conifers, with small, tough, needle-like leaves that are not damaged by cold.

EARTH AND THE MOON

TEMPERATE FOREST
With plenty of rain and mild weather, many trees grow in this biome, which is halfway between the poles and equator. In colder parts of the biome, most trees are deciduous, which means they drop their wide, delicate leaves before winter.

GRASSLAND
Grassland is found in warm or hot regions with little rain, where only small plants such as grasses can survive. The biome is often home to herds of grass-eating mammals, such as zebras, as well as the animals that prey on them.

DESERT
This biome has very little rainfall, sometimes because it is far from the rain-bringing ocean. Some deserts are always hot, while others are hot on summer days and freezing during winter nights. The few animals that live here have evolved to survive with little water and to burrow or shelter from extreme heat or cold.

RAIN FOREST
Most rain forests are around the equator, in regions that are always hot and rainy. Trees and other plants grow thickly, most of them with broad, flat leaves that are kept year-round. Rain forests are the most biodiverse of all the biomes.

EARTH AND THE MOON

The Moon

Earth's Moon is the fifth largest in the Solar System, after three moons of Jupiter and one of Saturn. During its orbit around Earth, the Moon travels as far as 406,700 km (252,700 miles) and as close as 356,400 km (221,500 miles), when it appears 14 percent larger, earning the name "supermoon."

SEAS AND CRATERS

The dark areas that we can see on the Moon are often called seas (*maria* in Latin) because they were once believed to contain water. In fact, these areas are covered in dried lava that flowed from volcanoes billions of years ago. The lava cooled into the dark rock basalt, which is also common on Earth where volcanoes have erupted.

We can also see bright impact craters where asteroids and comets plunged into the Moon, mostly in the early years of the Solar System. The Moon has over 9,000 impact craters. Since the Moon has almost no atmosphere—and therefore no wind and no rain to wear away rock—these craters remain as deep as when they were first made. The largest crater, the South Pole–Aitken Basin, is around 2,500 km (1,600 miles) wide and 4.2 billion years old.

SAME OLD FACE

The Moon takes the same time to orbit Earth as it does to rotate around its axis—27.3 days. All the large moons in the Solar System also have equal orbits and rotations, a feature known as tidal locking.

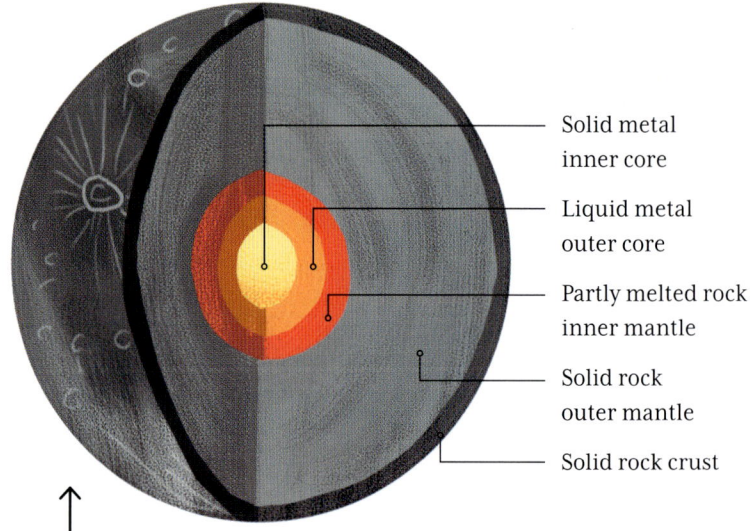

- Solid metal inner core
- Liquid metal outer core
- Partly melted rock inner mantle
- Solid rock outer mantle
- Solid rock crust

The Moon is made of similar materials to Earth. It has a small metal core, mostly iron with a little nickel, surrounded by a rocky mantle and crust. The crust's most common rocks are basalt and paler anorthosite.

This is because the pull of their planets' gravity slows their rotations to match their orbits.

Due to tidal locking, the Moon always has the same face turned toward Earth. (To understand why, roll a ball around yourself, while turning it so it finishes a rotation and an orbit together.) The face of the Moon that we see from Earth is often called the "near side." The first humans to see the "far side" were the three US astronauts onboard Apollo 8 in 1968.

OCEAN TIDES

Although the Moon's gravity is much weaker than Earth's, its effects can be seen on the world's oceans. The Moon pulls the oceans toward itself, creating bulges that make water rise up the shore, known as high tide. As Earth rotates, the water bulges move around the planet, making the tides rise and fall. When the Moon and Sun are lined up on the same side of Earth, their combined gravity creates extra-high tides.

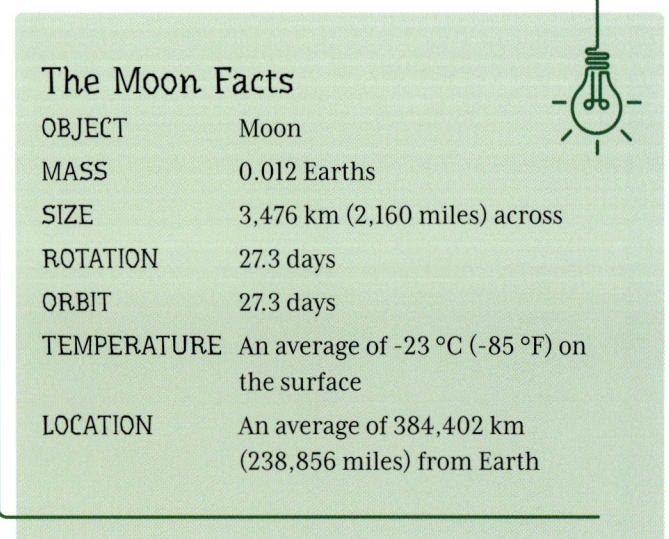

The Moon Facts

OBJECT	Moon
MASS	0.012 Earths
SIZE	3,476 km (2,160 miles) across
ROTATION	27.3 days
ORBIT	27.3 days
TEMPERATURE	An average of -23 °C (-85 °F) on the surface
LOCATION	An average of 384,402 km (238,856 miles) from Earth

The Moon has too little atmosphere to shield it from the Sun or hold in heat, so its surface ranges from a freezing -173 °C (-279 °F) at night to a boiling 117 °C (242 °F) during the day. With no atmosphere and no liquid water, the Moon is unsuitable for life.

EARTH AND THE MOON

Watching the Moon

If we watch the Moon, it appears to change as it journeys around Earth, while our planet also journeys around the Sun. These apparent changes in the Moon's shape are due to the fact we can only ever see the portion of the Moon that is lit by the Sun.

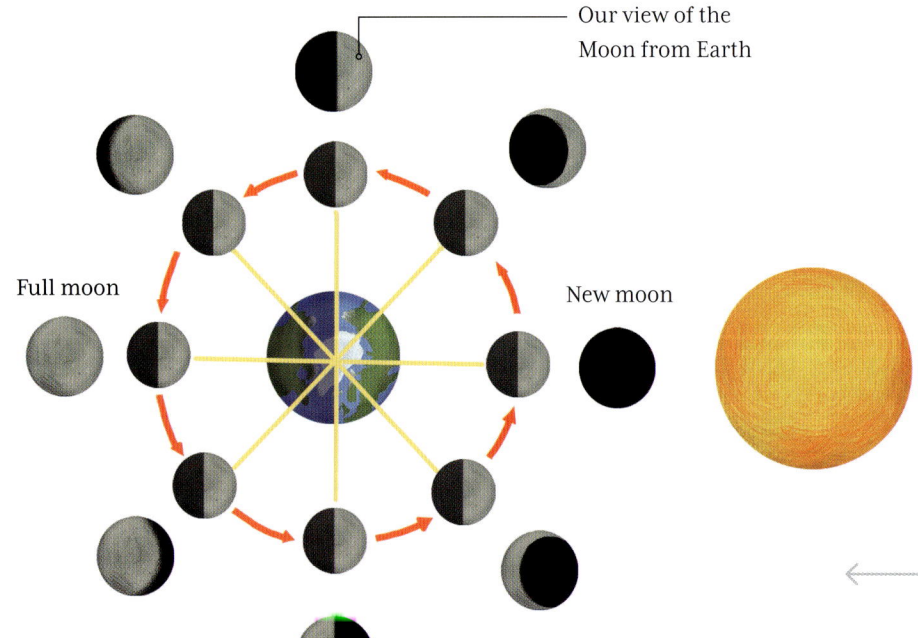

Our view of the Moon from Earth

Full moon

New moon

PHASES OF THE MOON

As the Moon orbits Earth, it appears to change from a new moon, when none of its face is visible, to a full moon, when we can see its whole near side. New moon is when the Moon lies between the Sun and Earth, so its lit side is not visible to us. Full moon takes place when the Moon is on the opposite side of Earth. Although the Moon's orbit takes 27.3 days, Earth's orbit around the Sun means it takes 29.5 days for the Moon to return to the same position in our sky and move through its phases.

ECLIPSES OF THE MOON

An eclipse of the Moon is when the Moon moves into Earth's shadow. This can happen at full moon if the Sun, Earth, and Moon are lined up. There is not an eclipse at every full moon because the tilts of the Moon's and Earth's orbits mean an exact line-up happens only up to four times a year. A total eclipse is when the Moon is in the central, darkest portion of Earth's shadow, while a penumbral eclipse is when it is in the outer part of the shadow.

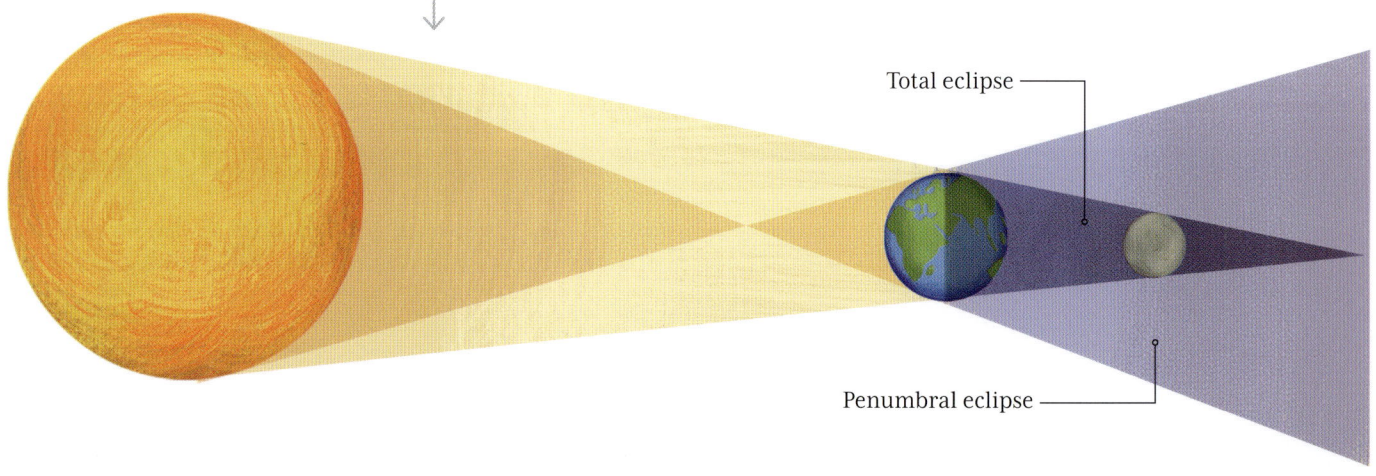

Total eclipse

Penumbral eclipse

EARTH AND THE MOON

Total eclipse
Partial eclipse

ECLIPSES OF THE SUN

A solar eclipse takes place when, as the Moon passes between the Sun and Earth, it partly or totally blocks the view of our star from a portion of Earth's surface. A total eclipse can be seen from somewhere on Earth around every 18 months, when the Sun, Moon, and Earth are exactly lined up and the Moon is close enough to Earth to fully block the view.

MAPPING THE MOON

People have watched the Moon since ancient times, but the first person to make a detailed map of the Moon's near side was the Polish astronomer Johannes Hevelius, in 1647. He spent several years observing and making measurements of the Moon's surface, using telescopes he built himself.

Landing on the Moon

The first people to walk on the Moon were US astronauts Neil Armstrong and Edwin "Buzz" Aldrin, on July 21, 1969, during the Apollo 11 mission. From launch to splashdown, the mission lasted 8 days, 3 hours, and 18 minutes.

The mission began when three astronauts—Armstrong, Aldrin, and Michael Collins—lifted off from Kennedy Space Center, in Florida, on July 16. Their Apollo space capsule was launched by a Saturn V rocket. After separating from the rocket, the capsule journeyed for 3 days until—by firing the engine to adjust course—it moved into orbit around the Moon. On July 20, Armstrong and Aldrin transferred from the capsule's command and service module into the lunar module, which Armstrong flew down to the Moon. Collins stayed in the command module to make sure the others could return safely.

Armstrong and Aldrin stayed on the Moon for just over 21 hours, but spent only 2 hours and 31 minutes walking on the surface. For the remainder of the time, they prepared and rested in the lunar module. At the end of their visit, they flew the lunar module back up to the command and service module, which the astronauts steered toward Earth. Once they had entered Earth orbit, the engine-carrying service module was separated from the command module, which splashed down in the Pacific Ocean on July 24. Floats stopped the module from sinking, while the astronauts were rescued by the US navy.

NEIL ARMSTRONG

Armstrong was the first to step onto the Moon, saying the famous words "One small step for [a] man, one giant leap for mankind." As the pair explored, Armstrong took most of the photos using a camera attached to his spacesuit.

STARS AND STRIPES

The astronauts planted a US flag, which fell over when the lunar module lifted off. Since there is little atmosphere—and no wind—on the Moon, the flag had a bar across the top so it looked as if it was fluttering in the photos.

EARTH AND THE MOON

LUNAR MODULE

The lunar module was nicknamed *Eagle*. A TV camera was mounted on it, so images of the astronauts' first steps were watched, almost live, by 600 million people. After *Eagle* had been flown back to the command and service module, it was left in Moon orbit.

TRANQUILITY BASE

When the lunar module landed in the Moon's Sea of Tranquility, the astronauts named the spot *Tranquility Base*. In 1970, three small craters to the north of the base were named Aldrin, Collins, and Armstrong.

EXPERIMENTS PACKAGE

A pack of scientific equipment included a device to measure moonquakes. Aldrin also hammered a metal tube into the Moon's surface to take a rock sample, while both men scooped dust into bags.

BUZZ ALDRIN

Aldrin experimented with methods of getting around in the Moon's low gravity (since it has less mass than Earth). He tried two-footed kangaroo hops but preferred bounding strides. Aldrin became the first to pee on the Moon, which he did into a bag inside his spacesuit.

Stars and Galaxies

Our star, called the Sun, is one of perhaps 1 septillion stars in the Universe. This number—a 1 followed by 24 zeros—can only be an estimate, as there are far, far too many stars to even begin to count. Just like the Sun, all stars are glowing spheres of gas so hot that it has turned to plasma—its atoms have torn apart, making them electrically charged. Although plasma is uncommon on Earth, in the Universe it is much more common than solids, liquids, or gases.

Most stars are part of a galaxy—a collection of stars, planets, gas, and dust, all held together by the force of gravity. On average, the stars in a galaxy may be around 5 light-years apart, with 1 light-year being the distance that light travels in a year—9.46 trillion km (5.88 trillion miles). Galaxies probably formed from immense, collapsing clouds of gas and dust, where many stars were pressed into life at once. Although stars cannot form in the near emptiness between galaxies, a minority of stars—although there are probably trillions of them altogether—lie between galaxies. Astronomers think these "intergalactic stars" formed inside a galaxy, but were tossed out, perhaps by a collision between galaxies.

The Sun is one of at least 100 billion stars in our galaxy, the Milky Way. In the whole Universe, there are perhaps 2 trillion galaxies of different shapes and sizes. Most galaxies are grouped together with other galaxies to form galaxy clusters, held together by their gravity, even though each galaxy may be more than a million light-years from the next. Galaxy clusters tend to be grouped into superclusters, containing perhaps 200,000 galaxies. There may be up to 10 million superclusters in the Universe.

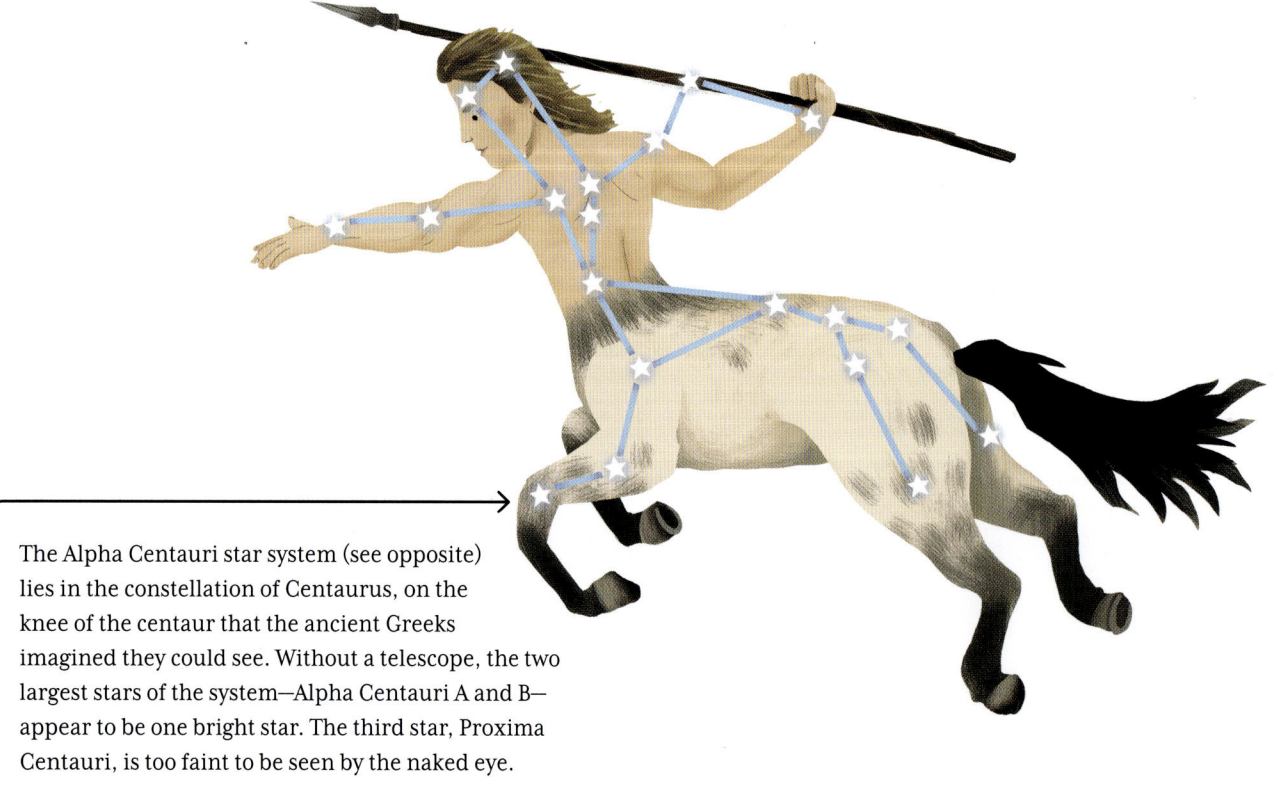

The Alpha Centauri star system (see opposite) lies in the constellation of Centaurus, on the knee of the centaur that the ancient Greeks imagined they could see. Without a telescope, the two largest stars of the system—Alpha Centauri A and B—appear to be one bright star. The third star, Proxima Centauri, is too faint to be seen by the naked eye.

Around 4.2 light-years away, the nearest star to the Sun is Proxima Centauri, a small reddish star known as a red dwarf. Proxima is part of a triple star system along with the stars Alpha Centauri A and B (top left). A star system is a small number of stars, within a galaxy, that orbit each other. Proxima Centauri is orbited by at least two planets.

STARS AND GALAXIES

Star Chart

When we look at the night sky, groups of stars seem to form the shapes of people, animals, or objects. These patterns are known as constellations. Astronomers agree on 88 official constellations. The stars in a constellation may be trillions of kilometers apart, but they appear close together when viewed from Earth.

PEGASUS
This large constellation takes its name from a winged horse of ancient Greek myths. Hundreds of years before the Greeks named the constellations, Babylonian astronomers saw a four-starred constellation here, called Iku ("field"). Today, those four bright stars are said to form an asterism, known as the Great Square. An asterism is a pattern of stars within one of the official constellations.

EQUULEUS
The name of this small, faint constellation means "little horse" in Latin. It is linked with the young horse Celeris, who in Greek myths was the child of the winged horse Pegasus. The Pegasus constellation lies nearby.

MILKY WAY GALAXY
Our galaxy can be seen as a pale streak of stars and dust as—from our location on Earth—we look at the side of its disk. This paleness earned the galaxy its "milky" name.

Northern hemisphere

Around 36 constellations can be seen in the northern hemisphere, from north of Earth's equator, for most of the year. About 52 constellations spend most of the year in the southern skies. Some constellations can be seen from the "other" hemisphere during all or part of the year. For example, the southern constellation Scorpius is visible from southern parts of the northern hemisphere during the summer months.

As our planet rotates over the course of a night, the constellations appear to move from east to west across the sky, just like the Sun appears to do during the day. As Earth orbits the Sun, the constellations also move slowly westward during the year. These changes are due to our changing viewpoint as we look into space.

AQUARIUS

Aquarius means "water-carrier" in Latin. More than 3,000 years ago, Babylonian astronomers thought these stars looked like their water god, Ea, as he poured water. The constellation is in part of the sky, known as the Sea due to its constellations linked with water, including Cetus ("whale"), Piscis Austrinus ("southern fish"), and Eridanus ("river").

OPHIUCHUS

The ancient Greeks saw Ophiuchus ("serpent-bearer") as a man wrestling a snake. His snake was seen in the nearby constellation Serpens ("serpent"). In fact, Ophiuchus divides Serpens in two—Caput ("head") and Cauda ("tail"). Both constellations are on the night sky's equator, crossing between the northern and southern hemispheres.

STARS AND GALAXIES

Star Types

Astronomers divide stars into types based on their size, temperature, and brightness. Usually, the heavier a star is, the hotter and brighter it is. Astronomers can identify a star's type by examining the light that it gives off.

STAR SIZES

From largest to smallest, the different sizes of stars have names, including hypergiant, supergiant, giant, and dwarf. The Sun is a dwarf, as are the majority of stars in the Universe. While the Sun is 1,390,000 km (864,000 miles) across, one of the largest known stars, the hypergiant UY Scuti, is 2,376,000,000 km (1,476,000,000 miles) wide. If it were placed in the middle of our Solar System, it would stretch past Jupiter.

Annie Jump Cannon used a magnifying glass to examine glass photographic plates. Since photography was then only in black and white, the plates did not actually show the different shades of starlight, but each star spectrum was broken up by black lines that made it possible to figure the shades out.

STARS AND GALAXIES

RAINBOW STARS

The light given off by stars is made up of all the shades of the rainbow—red, orange, yellow, green, blue, and violet—known as the spectrum (see pages 42–43). Yet stars with different temperatures give off different amounts of these shades. The hottest stars give off more light in the blue part of the spectrum. Cooler stars give off more yellow light, while even cooler stars are reddish. In fact, the human eye may not see these differences in shade clearly. For example, the Sun is classified as a yellow star, but our eyes see its light as white.

ANNIE'S STARS

Annie Jump Cannon was an astronomer who, in 1901, came up with a system for classifying stars—or placing them into different types. She worked at the Harvard College Observatory, in the United States, where the light from stars was split into its separate shades using a glass prism—like raindrops bend and split sunlight, creating a rainbow. The prism was placed in front of a telescope's eyepiece, then the resulting pattern was captured on a photographic plate.

Annie examined the plates to classify each star by its shade. She rearranged the existing star classification—in which stars were identified alphabetically—and suggested what is known as the Harvard system of star classification. The system uses the letters O, B, A, F, G, K, and M—with O the hottest and bluest, and M the coolest. Dying stars such as white dwarfs (see page 127) were not included in the classification. Today, Roman numerals have been added to the system to show brightness, also called luminosity. From brightest to darkest, these rankings are 0, I, II, III, IV, V, VI, and VII. For being a yellow star, the Sun is classified as G, while for being medium-bright it gets a V.

An O-type star has a surface temperature of over 29,700 °C (53,500 °F), while an M is less than 3,400 °C (6,150 °F).

Star Birth and Death

Stars are born in clouds of gas and dust. All stars eventually die. Over the course of one year in our Milky Way Galaxy, around seven stars are born, while at least one star dies. Some stars have short lives and violent deaths, while others live long and die quietly.

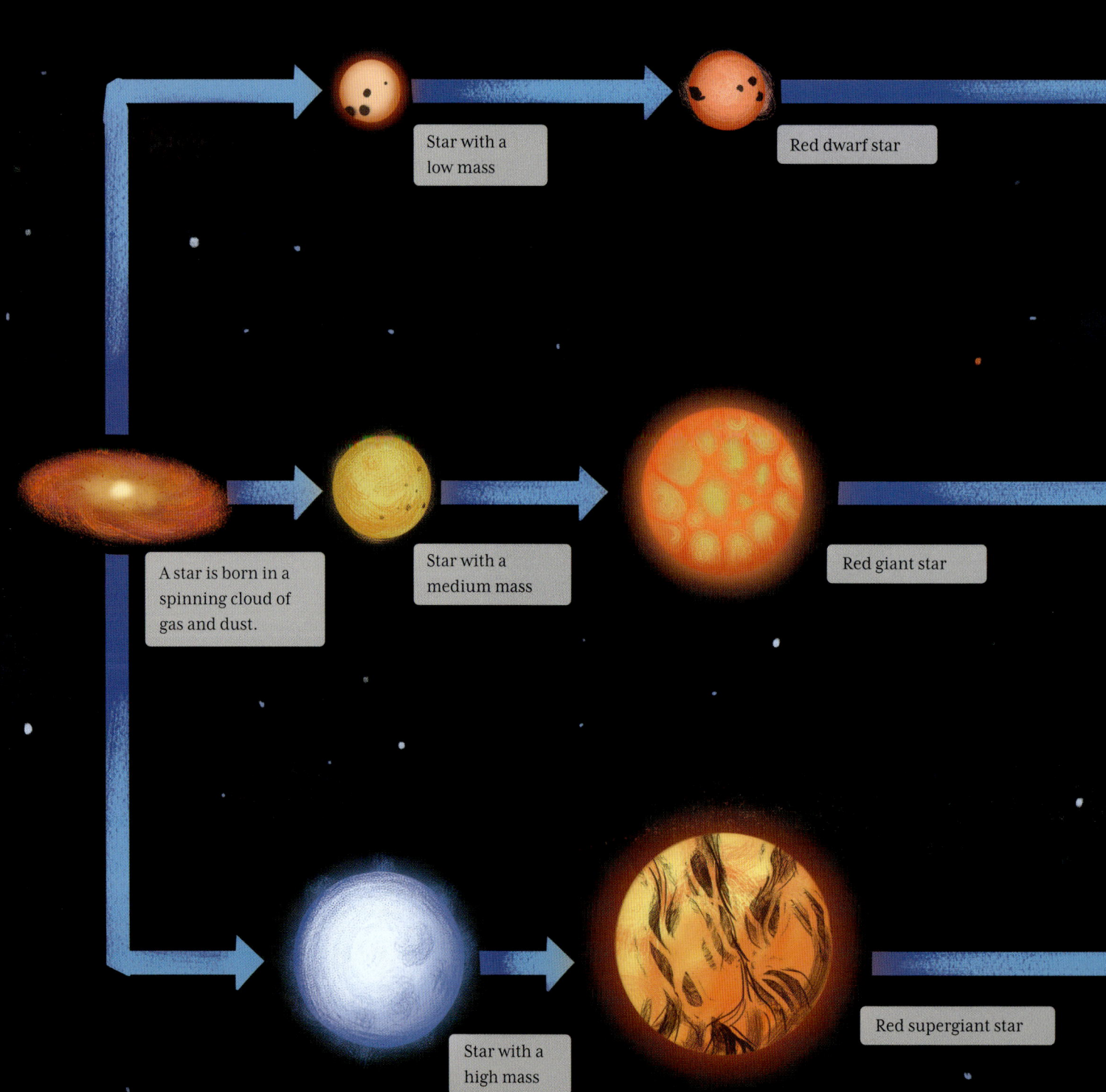

A star is born when a cloud of gas and dust collapses. At the core of the cloud, a tightly squeezed sphere of material grows. Here, atoms of hydrogen start to crash into each other, joining to become helium atoms. This releases energy, making the sphere glow as a newborn star. A star lives until it runs out of hydrogen, which is its fuel. Then the star begins to change—and eventually to die.

Although stars with a greater mass (or weight) contain more hydrogen, their greater mass also makes their gravity stronger—making hydrogen atoms crash together more quickly in their core. This means that massive stars use up their hydrogen fuel in perhaps a few million years. Massive stars die in an explosion known as a supernova. Smaller stars use their fuel more slowly, then die more peacefully. The smallest stars may live for trillions of years.

LOW-MASS STAR DEATH

If a star has less than half the mass of the Sun, it dies quietly. When it runs out of hydrogen, it slowly shrinks, cools, and fades, becoming a white dwarf. Around the size of Earth, a white dwarf is the "dead" remains of a star. Over billions of years, a white dwarf will probably grow so cool that it becomes a black dwarf. However, the Universe is not yet old enough for any black dwarfs to exist.

MEDIUM-MASS STAR DEATH

A Sun-sized star takes around 10 billion years to run out of hydrogen. Then it expands, becoming a red giant star. In the star's core, helium atoms crash together to become carbon and oxygen atoms. The intense heat from this process sends out a vast cloud of gas and dust, called a planetary nebula. After around 10,000 years, the cloud drifts away, leaving behind only a white dwarf, which may eventually fade into a black dwarf.

HIGH-MASS STAR DEATH

If a star is over 8 times more massive than the Sun, it expands into a red supergiant star when it runs out of hydrogen. Then, after it goes through its helium and other fuels, its core collapses, creating a huge explosion known as a supernova. Stars up to 25 times the Sun's mass collapse into a neutron star, while bigger stars collapse into a black hole (see page 128). Only around 10 km (6 miles) wide, a neutron star still has a mass greater than the Sun. Some spin super-fast and give out beams of energy, but they fade over billions of years.

Black Holes

A black hole is an area of space with very intense gravity. Anything that comes too close to a black hole cannot escape its pull. Black holes can form when massive stars die, but a mysterious black hole also lies at the heart of most galaxies.

PULLING SPACE AND TIME

Gravity is the force that pulls all objects toward each other. The bigger an object's mass, the stronger its gravity. If a huge mass is squeezed into a really small space—as happens when a massive star collapses—its gravity can stretch space itself, making a black hole. A black hole gains its name from the fact that even light cannot escape its pull, making it look black.

The region at the heart of a black hole is called a singularity. Anything that falls into the singularity—such as stars and dust—is crushed infinitely small, and its mass is added to the mass of the black hole. Strangely, the gravity of a singularity stretches time itself, so a clock close to a black hole would tick more slowly than a clock farther away.

FALLING INSIDE

The singularity is surrounded by a boundary known as the event horizon. Inside this boundary, the black hole looks black. If anything crosses the event horizon, it cannot escape because it would need to travel faster than the speed of light, which nothing can do. For an ordinary-sized black hole, the event horizon may be just 30 km (18.6 miles) from one side to the other.

The term "event horizon" comes from the fact that, if an event took place within the boundary (or horizon), information from that event could not reach anyone outside the boundary, making it impossible to know if the event took place.

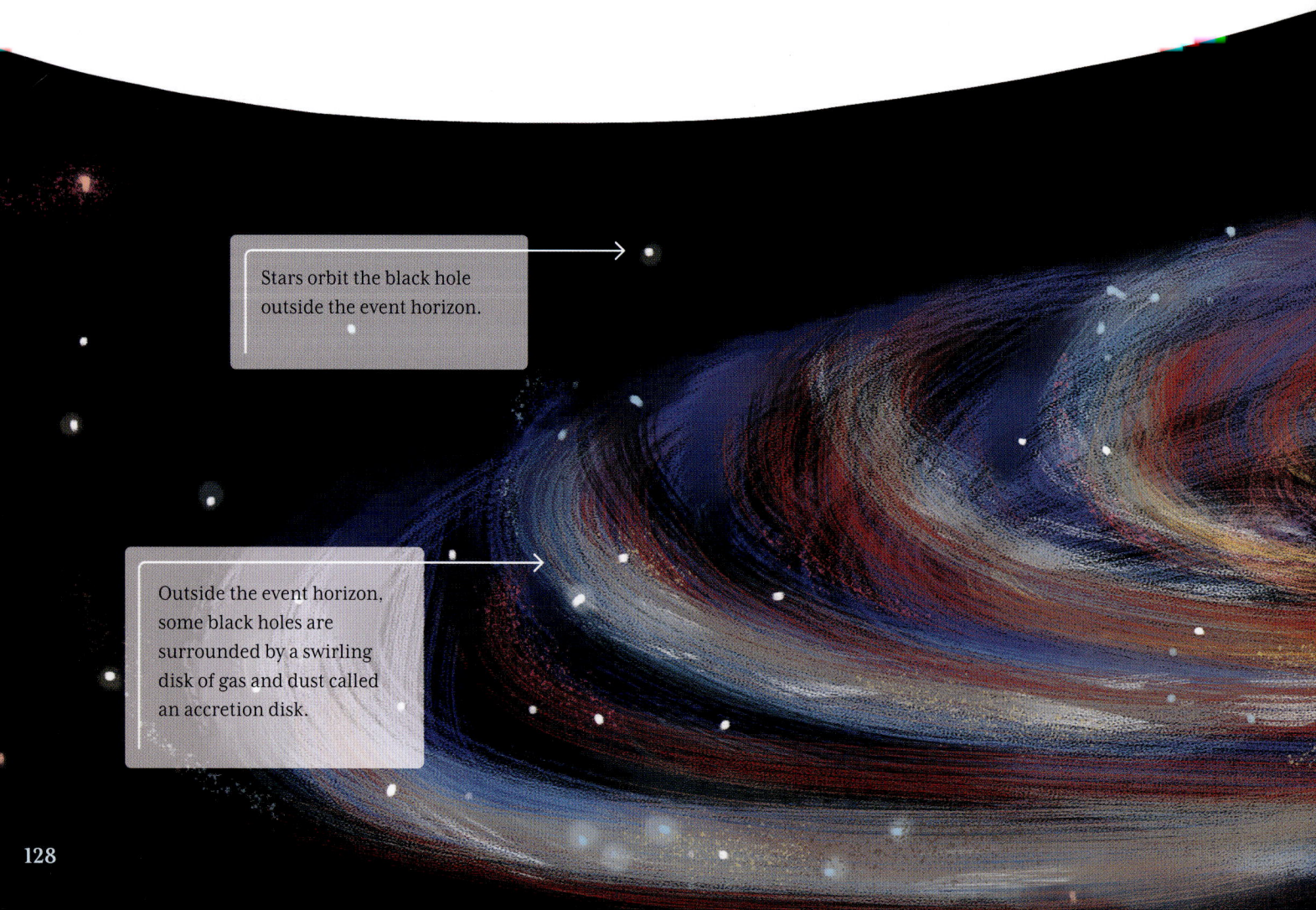

Stars orbit the black hole outside the event horizon.

Outside the event horizon, some black holes are surrounded by a swirling disk of gas and dust called an accretion disk.

STARS AND GALAXIES

GALAXY HEARTS

The black holes at the heart of most galaxies are called supermassive black holes because they are much bigger than ordinary black holes. They may have a mass billions of times that of the Sun. Astronomers are not sure how these black holes formed. Perhaps an ordinary-sized black hole grew larger as it sucked in material or joined with another black hole, then its gravity collected stars and dust around it, forming a galaxy. It is also possible that the supermassive black hole formed at the same time as the galaxy, as a cloud of gas and dust collapsed, forming multiple stars around a central black hole.

Sagittarius A* Facts

OBJECT	Supermassive black hole
MASS	4 million Suns
SIZE	24 million km (15 million miles) across the event horizon
TEMPERATURE	10 million °C (18 million °F) in the accretion disk
AGE	Possibly 13.6 billion years
LOCATION	26,000 light-years from Earth

The Sagittarius A* supermassive black hole lies at the middle of the Milky Way Galaxy, but it rarely pulls in gas or dust.

Exoplanets

The Sun is not the only star with planets in orbit around it. In fact, astronomers believe that most stars host one or more planets, giving them what is called a planetary system. Planets that orbit a star other than the Sun are known as exoplanets.

UNIVERSE OF PLANETS

Since the first exoplanet was spotted in 1992, astronomers have discovered more than 5,000 of them through their telescopes. They believe many trillions more may exist. Just like there are different types of planets in our Solar System, there are different types of exoplanets. There are rock and metal Earth-like planets, gas giants like Jupiter, and ice giants like Neptune. In addition, there are "hot Jupiters," which are gas giants that orbit very close to their star, as well as "super-Earths," which are similar to Earth, but much larger.

LOOKING FOR LIFE

Astronomers are excited by exoplanets because if one of the eight planets in our planetary system is home to life, it is possible an exoplanet is, too. Exoplanets are too far away to look for signs of life through a telescope. It would take more than 6,000 years for a space probe to reach the closest exoplanets, which orbit the nearest star, Proxima Centauri (see page 121). Instead, astronomers study the likely conditions on exoplanets to see if they could be habitable (or suitable for life).

The first factor to consider is the materials of the exoplanet. Since gas giants and ice giants have no solid surface, they probably cannot be home to life. Another factor is an exoplanet's distance from its star. Water is needed by all known living things. If a planet is too close to its star, water would boil away. If it is too far away, all water would freeze. Between these extremes is a habitable zone. Astronomers also look at the nature of each star. If, for example, a star has bursts of energy, it could make its planets uninhabitable. Considering all these factors, astronomers estimate there are 11 billion habitable exoplanets in the Milky Way Galaxy alone.

TOI-700 d Facts

OBJECT	Exoplanet
MASS	Around 1.7 Earths
SIZE	Around 15,160 km (9,420 miles) across
MOONS	None known
ROTATION	Possibly 37 days
ORBIT	37 days
TEMPERATURE	Possibly 22 °C (72 °F) on the surface
LOCATION	An average 24.4 million km (15.2 million miles) from TOI-700

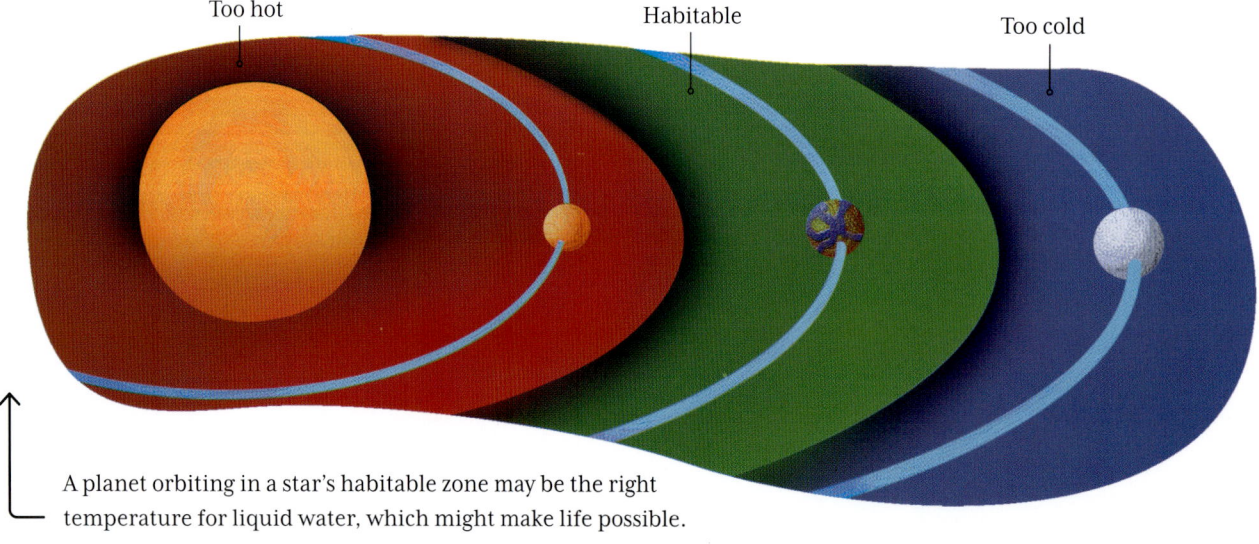

Too hot — Habitable — Too cold

A planet orbiting in a star's habitable zone may be the right temperature for liquid water, which might make life possible.

Around 101 light-years from Earth, the red dwarf star TOI-700 is orbited by four exoplanets. In order of distance from the star, they are TOI-700 b, c, e, and d. TOI-700 d is an Earth-like planet in the habitable zone. This illustration imagines it has oceans, although we cannot know that for sure.

Galaxies

The smallest galaxies, known as dwarf galaxies, have a few hundred stars. The largest, called supergiant galaxies, contain 100 trillion stars, all held together by gravity and all spinning around the galaxy's central point. Galaxies have three main shapes—spirals, ellipticals, and irregular.

SPIRAL GALAXIES

Around two-thirds of galaxies have a spiral shape. These galaxies are spinning disks with curving arms of thicker stars, gas, and dust stretching from their core. At the core is a bulge of stars that may be roughly circular (pictured) or stretched into a bar (see page 134).

ELLIPTICAL GALAXIES

These galaxies are the shape of a flattened ball. Although some elliptical galaxies are small, the Universe's largest galaxies are elliptical. While spiral galaxies contain many young stars, ellipticals have many old stars. Ellipticals probably formed over time, as smaller spiral galaxies joined together.

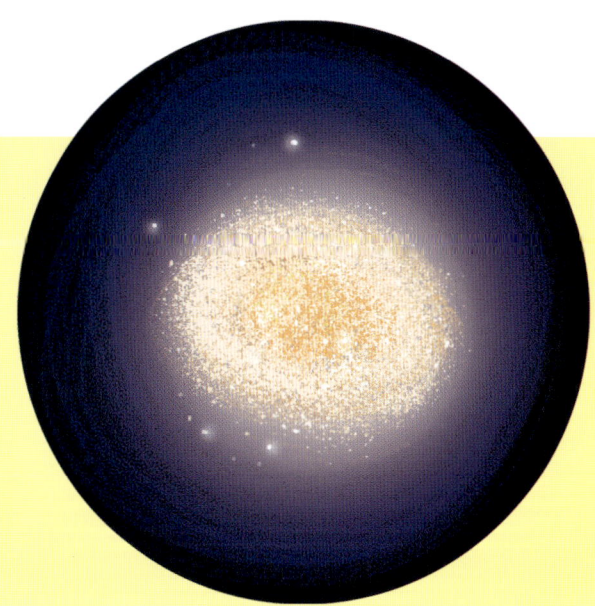

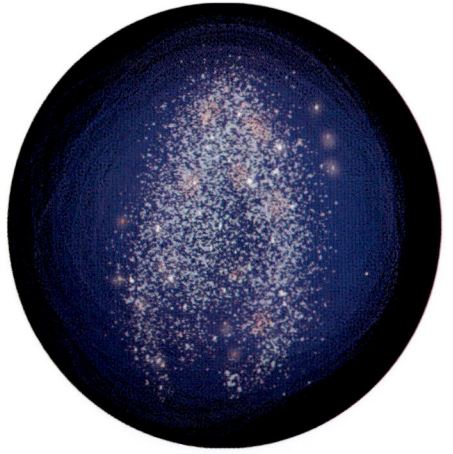 

IRREGULAR GALAXIES

A quarter of galaxies are neither spiral nor elliptical. These irregular galaxies may look "messy" (left) or have a strange shape, such as a ring (right). Irregular galaxies are usually dwarfs and may have been deformed by the gravity of a larger galaxy. A ring shape could have been made when a small galaxy crashed through the middle of a larger one.

VERA RUBIN

Vera Rubin was an American astronomer who studied galaxies and concluded in 1978, that there must be more matter in them than what could be seen. This invisible matter is called dark matter. Like ordinary matter—from dogs to dust and stars—dark matter has gravity. By studying the speed of stars spinning around the core of their galaxy, Rubin figured out there must be lots of dark matter in a galaxy, creating lots of extra gravity.

A blazar is an active galactic nucleus with jets that point at Earth, making it look super-bright.

Black hole
Accretion disk
Jet

Black hole
Accretion disk
Jet

A quasar is an active galactic nucleus with jets that point away from us.

ACTIVE GALACTIC NUCLEI

There are old galaxies and young galaxies. Some young galaxies have a very bright central area called an active galactic nucleus. Most galaxies have a supermassive black hole at their heart, but these younger galaxies have black holes that pull in lots of material. As this material circles the black hole, it gets so hot it emits jets of powerful energy. The black holes at the hearts of old galaxies are much quieter because they have run out of nearby material to suck inside.

3C 273 Facts

OBJECT	Blazar at the middle of a giant elliptical galaxy
MASS	886 million Suns
JETS	200,000 light-years long
BRIGHTNESS	4 trillion times brighter than the Sun
TEMPERATURE	10 trillion °C (18 trillion °F)
LOCATION	2.4 billion light-years from Earth

The Milky Way

The Milky Way is a spiral galaxy with a central bar of stars. Our galaxy is around 100,000 light-years across, but only about 2,000 light-years thick. It has at least 100 billion stars, perhaps as many as 400 billion. The galaxy takes around 230 million years to rotate once about its central point.

From our position in the Milky Way's disk, it is difficult to know the exact shape of the galaxy's curving arms. Yet astronomers have pieced together evidence by observing other galaxies and measuring the movements of the stars in our own. By looking at the night sky, we can tell that we do not live in an elliptical galaxy. If we did, we would see the stars and dust of our galaxy spread across the sky, rather than in a narrow band.

The Milky Way probably started to form not long after the Universe's very first stars, around 13.7 billion years ago. The oldest stars in the Milky Way date from this time, while its youngest stars probably formed within the last year. Over the billions of years since our galaxy's birth, it has grown by merging with other galaxies. Today, it continues to grow by pulling in material from the 59 smaller galaxies in orbit around it, known as satellite galaxies. The biggest of these satellites is the Large Magellanic Cloud, around 32,200 light-years across and 160,000 light-years away.

THE SOLAR SYSTEM

The Sun is around 28,000 light-years from the middle of the Milky Way, in the Orion-Cygnus arm. This minor arm lies inside the major Perseus arm and may be a branch of it.

PERSEUS ARM

The Perseus arm begins from the end of the central bar that is farthest from our Solar System. It is named after the Perseus constellation of stars as it can be seen in this direction when viewed from Earth.

NORMA ARM

This minor arm of the Milky Way stretches from its central bar. It is named for the southern constellation of Norma, through which it seems to pass.

GLOBULAR CLUSTER

A globular cluster is a roughly ball-shaped group of stars, held together by gravity. These clusters are found within the Milky Way's disk and beyond it, in the more loosely scattered stars of the galactic halo.

CENTRAL BAR

The galaxy's bar cuts across its central region, with a bulge of old yellow stars at its middle. It is here that the supermassive black hole Sagittarius A* is found.

SCUTUM-CENTAURUS ARM

This major arm begins from the nearest end of the Milky Way's central bar. Like the galaxy's other arms, it is thick with stars, gas, and dust. New stars form among its dense clouds.

The Local Group and Beyond

The Milky Way is one of at least 80 galaxies in a galaxy cluster called the Local Group. The Local Group is one of over 100 clusters in the Virgo Supercluster. Our supercluster is part of the Pisces–Cetus Supercluster Complex, a vast wall of superclusters known as a galaxy filament.

If the distance from the Milky Way to the next large galaxy seems vast, the distance to the next galaxy cluster or the next supercluster—around 300 million light-years—becomes dizzying. In fact, there are some distances so vast that we can never even know them. We cannot know the size of the whole Universe. We do not know if it continues forever or not. When astronomers discuss the size of the Universe, they talk about the "observable Universe." This is the ball-shaped portion of it that can be seen from Earth, because its light (which our eyes and telescopes detect) has had time to reach us since the Big Bang.

Since it is 13.8 billion years since the Big Bang, we might think that the observable Universe would extend for only 13.8 billion light-years in every direction. However, the objects that gave off light 13.8 billion years ago have since moved farther away from us due to the growth of the Universe—and they are now 46.5 billion light-years away. This means that the distance across the observable Universe—with Earth at its middle—is twice that—93 billion light-years.

LOCAL GROUP

Around 10 million light-years across, the Local Group contains two collections of galaxies—the Milky Way and its satellite galaxies, and the Andromeda Galaxy and its satellites. The mass of the whole cluster is around 2 trillion Suns.

VIRGO SUPERCLUSTER

The Local Group is about 65 million light-years from the middle of the Virgo Supercluster. Some astronomers think this supercluster may be part of an even larger supercluster, known as Laniakea.

THE OBSERVABLE UNIVERSE

Superclusters are grouped together into yet larger structures called filaments, with nearly empty space—known as voids—between them. This gives the observable Universe an almost sponge-like appearance.

STARS AND GALAXIES

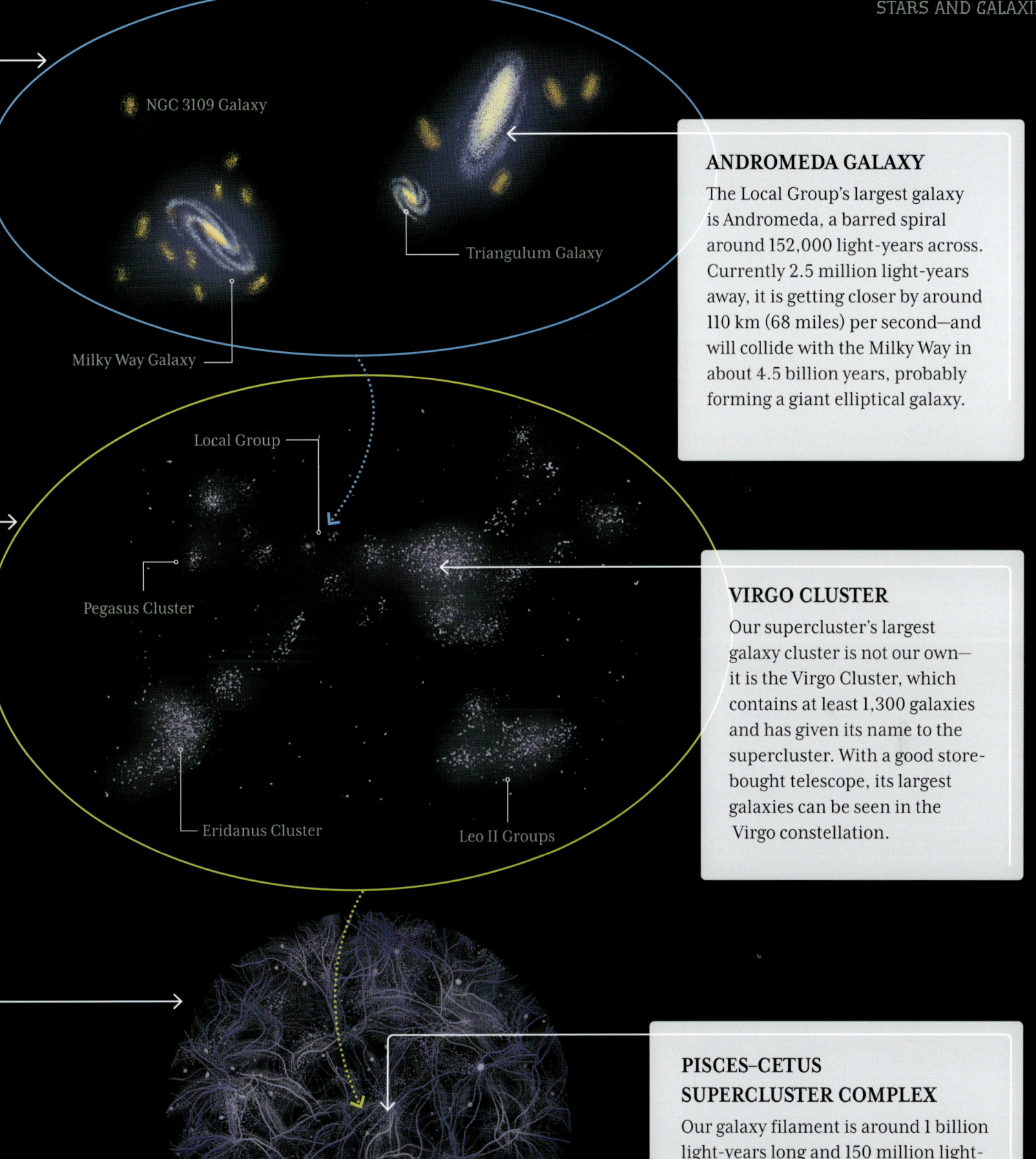

- NGC 3109 Galaxy
- Triangulum Galaxy
- Milky Way Galaxy
- Local Group
- Pegasus Cluster
- Eridanus Cluster
- Leo II Groups

ANDROMEDA GALAXY

The Local Group's largest galaxy is Andromeda, a barred spiral around 152,000 light-years across. Currently 2.5 million light-years away, it is getting closer by around 110 km (68 miles) per second—and will collide with the Milky Way in about 4.5 billion years, probably forming a giant elliptical galaxy.

VIRGO CLUSTER

Our supercluster's largest galaxy cluster is not our own— it is the Virgo Cluster, which contains at least 1,300 galaxies and has given its name to the supercluster. With a good store-bought telescope, its largest galaxies can be seen in the Virgo constellation.

PISCES–CETUS SUPERCLUSTER COMPLEX

Our galaxy filament is around 1 billion light-years long and 150 million light-years wide. The Virgo Supercluster makes up only one-thousandth of the filament's mass.

STARS AND GALAXIES

The Universe

Around 13.8 billion years ago, the Universe began with an event that astronomers call the Big Bang. We do not know if anything existed before the Big Bang, but we do know that, in the first moment of the Big Bang, the Universe started to expand from a tiny point—and it has been getting bigger ever since.

At first, the Universe was an incredibly hot, tightly packed point that astronomers now call the "singularity." As the Universe expanded from the singularity, it cooled. After 1 second, the Universe was 200 trillion km (124 trillion miles) wide and 10 billion °C (18 billion °F). Today, the Universe that we can see (known as the observable Universe) is 900 sextillion km (560 sextillion miles) wide. Its average temperature is -270 °C (-454 °F).

In its first moments, the Universe contained no matter. Matter is anything, from people to stardust, that has mass (weight). But less than a second after the Big Bang, the first matter came into being—tiny particles. After thousands of years, these particles came together to form the first atoms, which are the building blocks for all ordinary matter in the Universe. Over the next millions and billions of years, stars, galaxies, and planets formed.

380,000 YEARS

Protons, neutrons, and electrons come together to make the first atoms. Atoms have a nucleus (middle) containing protons and neutrons, circled by electrons. The earliest atoms are the lightest and simplest atoms—hydrogen and helium. Now the Universe has clouds of hydrogen and helium atoms, which form floating gases.

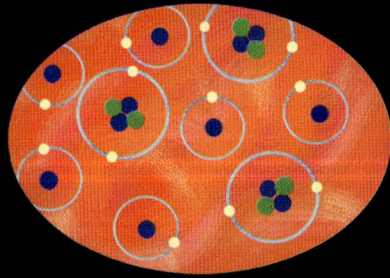

0.0001 SECONDS

As the Universe cools, the conditions become right for the first matter to form. Tiny particles appear, far too small to be seen by the human eye. The particles include protons, neutrons, and electrons.

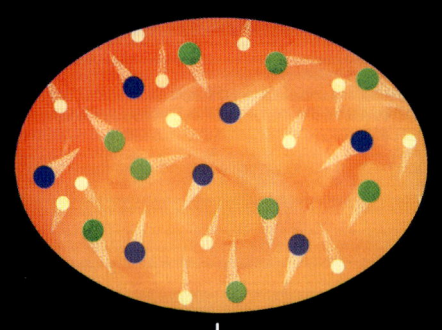

0 SECONDS

Space and time come into being with an explosion too powerful to imagine. In the first fractions of a second, the Universe doubles in size again and again, then its growth slows.

STARS AND GALAXIES

100 MILLION YEARS
Gravity pulls clouds of hydrogen and helium gas together, making the first stars. Inside stars—as they die or explode—atoms combine to make other, heavier types of atoms, from oxygen to iron.

200 MILLION YEARS
The first small galaxies form as gravity pulls stars, gas, and dust together. Over time, gravity pulls galaxies toward each other, making larger galaxies and clusters of galaxies.

9.2 BILLION YEARS
Our Solar System forms around a new star in a 9-billion-year-old galaxy called the Milky Way. Around 600 million years later, tiny life forms appear on one planet in the Solar System—Earth.

Life

Life began on our planet around 3.8 billion years ago, when tiny, simple living things appeared in the oceans. Over millions of years, these living things changed. Some remained small and simple; some developed stems and leaves; and a few grew brains, beaks, and wings. This slow process, called evolution, has resulted in at least 8 million species on our planet today, from immense whales to microscopic bacteria. A species—such as humans or Scots pine trees—is a group of living things that look similar and breed together to make more of their kind.

Despite their differences, all living things share characteristics. All are made of tiny building blocks called cells, although some are made of just one cell, and others—such as humans—are made of trillions. Unlike a rock or a shoe, all living things are sensitive to changes in their surroundings, such as light and touch. They can all control the conditions inside themselves, from the beating of their heart to the movement of water through their roots and stems. All living things grow and develop, from a tadpole to a frog, a seed to a tree, a tiny bacterium to a larger one. They can also move at some stage in their life, whether that is the slow growth movements of plants or the speedy running of a cheetah.

All living things need food, which they use for energy. However, their methods of getting food are very different: Animals eat other living things, plants make their own food, and fungi—such as mushrooms—soak up food from their surroundings. Finally, all living things can reproduce, although they do it in many ways. While meerkats give birth to small baby meerkats, bacteria divide into two, and fungi release tiny spores, which develop into new fungi.

The earliest animals evolved in the oceans more than 700 million years ago. They were simple, soft-bodied, and—like today's insects and jellyfish—they were invertebrates, which do not have a backbone.

After studying the giant tortoises of the Pacific Ocean's Galápagos Islands, the British scientist Charles Darwin (1809–82) figured out important ideas about how and why animals evolve. He noticed that tortoises living on islands with tall shrubs and cacti had evolved longer necks and arched shells so they could reach food.

Cells

All living things are made of cells. Most cells are too small to be seen by the human eye, with the tiniest 0.00002 cm (0.000008 in) across. One of the largest cells, up to 30 cm (12 in) long, belongs to a protist known as a seaweed. There are two types of cells: prokaryotic and eukaryotic.

PROKARYOTIC CELLS

Prokaryotic cells were the first form of life on Earth. Those first prokaryotes were unicellular organisms, which means they were living things made of just one cell. Today's prokaryotes belong to two groups—bacteria and archaea—which are both unicellular and too tiny to be seen without a microscope. Prokaryotic cells are smaller and simpler than eukaryotic cells. Unlike eukaryotic cells, they do not have a central structure called a nucleus, where deoxyribonucleic acid (DNA; see page 144) is stored.

> **Scientist Profile**
> NAME: Robert Hooke
> DATES: 1635–1733
> NATIONALITY: English
> BREAKTHROUGH
> In 1665, he discovered cells when examining plants through a microscope. He named them "cells" from the Latin word *cellula*, meaning "small room."

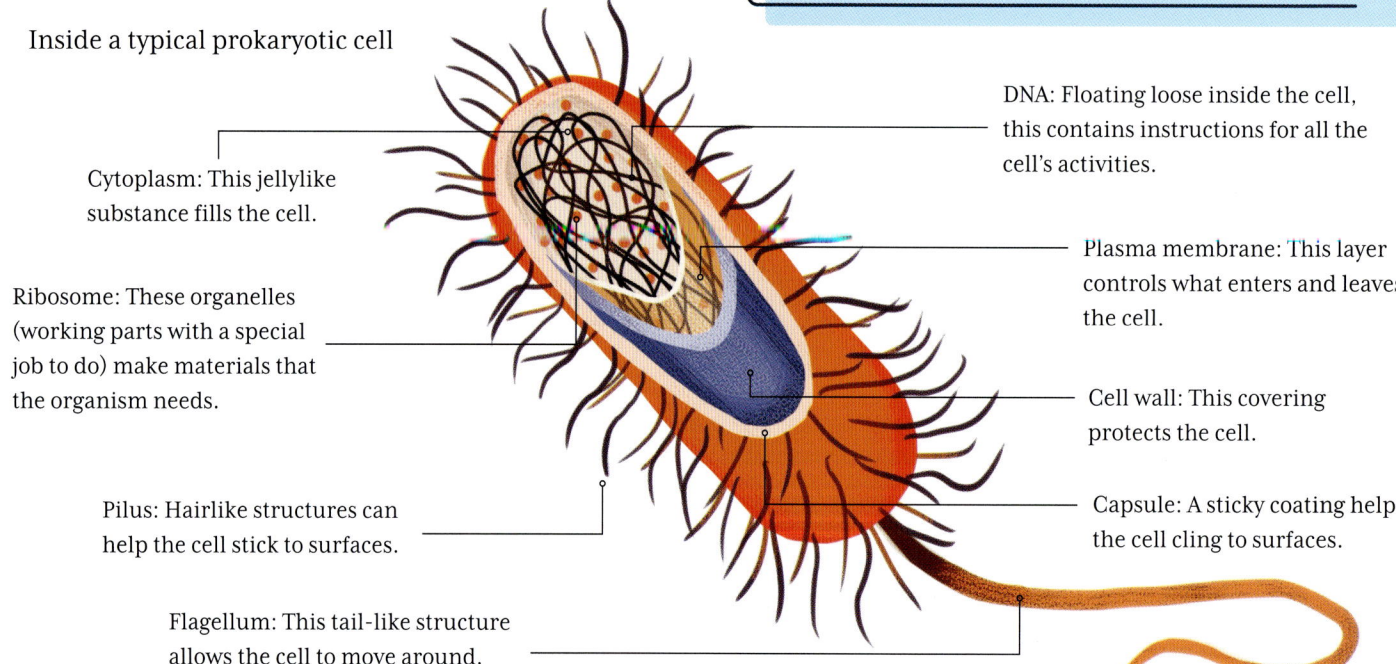

Inside a typical prokaryotic cell

Cytoplasm: This jellylike substance fills the cell.

Ribosome: These organelles (working parts with a special job to do) make materials that the organism needs.

Pilus: Hairlike structures can help the cell stick to surfaces.

Flagellum: This tail-like structure allows the cell to move around.

DNA: Floating loose inside the cell, this contains instructions for all the cell's activities.

Plasma membrane: This layer controls what enters and leaves the cell.

Cell wall: This covering protects the cell.

Capsule: A sticky coating helps the cell cling to surfaces.

PROKARYOTES

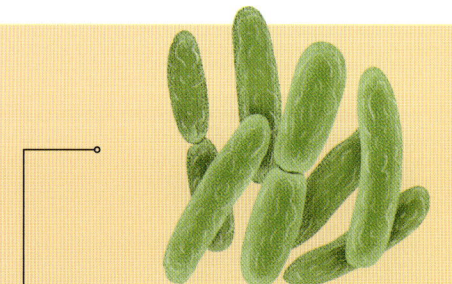

Bacteria: These unicellular microorganisms are found on land, in water, and inside other living things, where some cause disease.

Archaea: Made of different materials from bacteria, these unicellular organisms live nearly everywhere on Earth, including extreme environments such as deep underground.

EUKARYOTIC CELLS

The first eukaryotic cells evolved from prokaryotic cells around 2.5 billion years ago. Four groups of living things are made of eukaryotic cells: animals, plants, fungi, and protists. Some are multicellular, which means they are made of many cells, while others are single-celled. In organisms with many cells, all the cells are not identical in shape and function, since they specialize to make different structures, such as skin or hair. In addition, the cells of animals, plants, fungi, and protists have different characteristics to support their different lives. However, most eukaryotic cells share some basic parts, including a nucleus and organelles with their own particular jobs.

Inside a typical animal cell

Nucleus: This structure stores the cell's DNA.

Nucleolus: Ribosomes are made here.

Ribosome: These organelles make materials needed by the body.

Endoplasmic reticulum: This organelle makes materials.

Microtubule: These stiff, hollow rods help with the movement of materials inside the cell.

Cell membrane: This covering controls what materials enter and leave the cell.

Cytoplasm: This jellylike substance fills the cell.

Mitochondrion: These organelles make energy for the cell's work, using oxygen (taken from water or air by the animal) and glucose sugar (taken from food).

Lysosome: These organelles break down worn-out cell parts.

Golgi apparatus: This organelle packages materials made by the endoplasmic reticulum, then sends them to other organelles or out through the cell membrane.

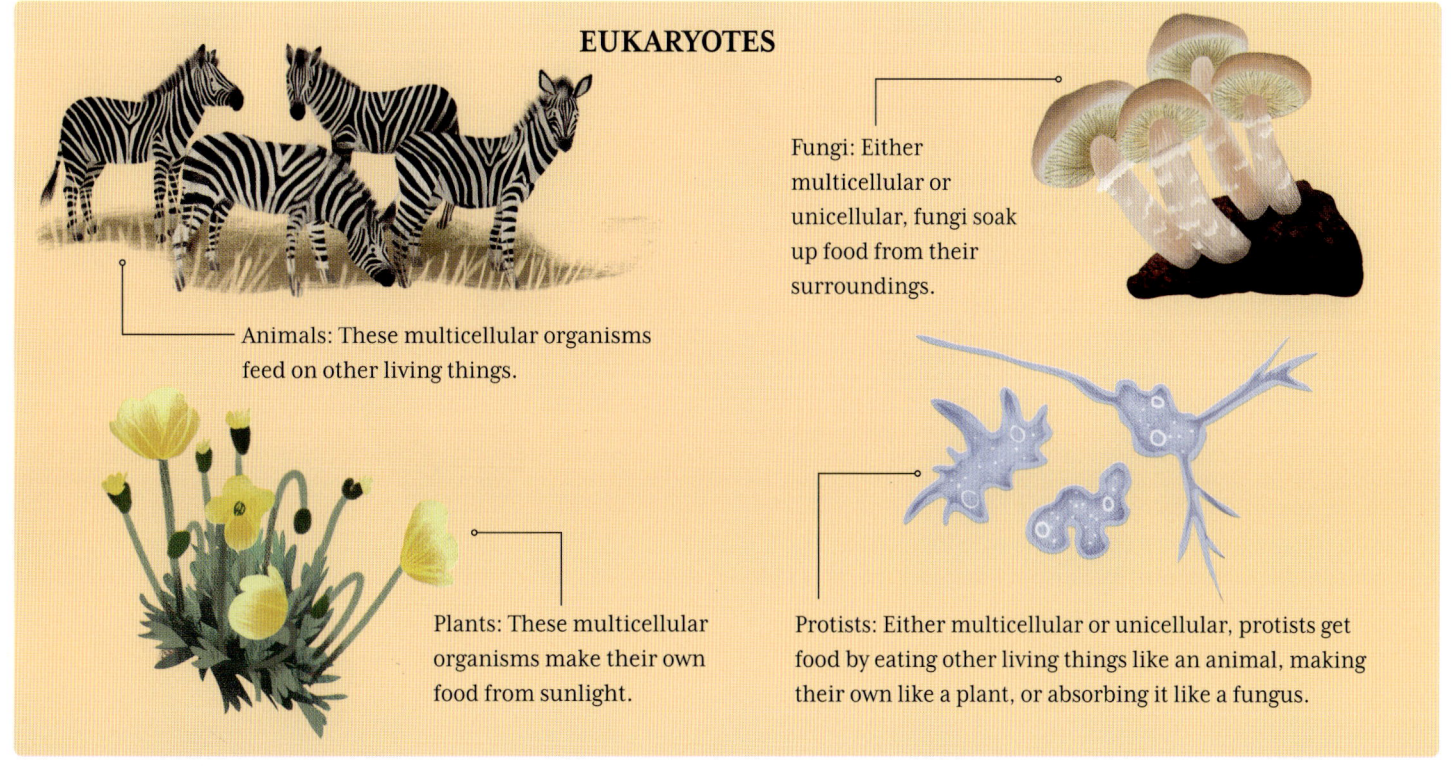

EUKARYOTES

Animals: These multicellular organisms feed on other living things.

Fungi: Either multicellular or unicellular, fungi soak up food from their surroundings.

Plants: These multicellular organisms make their own food from sunlight.

Protists: Either multicellular or unicellular, protists get food by eating other living things like an animal, making their own like a plant, or absorbing it like a fungus.

DNA

Strands of deoxyribonucleic acid (DNA) are in the cells of every living thing. DNA contains the recipe for each organism, with instructions for its appearance and the workings of its body. If the DNA strands in one human cell were stretched out, they would be 2 m (6.6 ft) long.

DOUBLE HELIX

DNA strands are the shape of a twisted ladder, known as a double helix. The rungs of the ladder are made of four chemicals: adenine, thymine, cytosine, and guanine. Each rung contains two chemicals: Adenine always forms rungs by pairing with thymine, and cytosine always pairs with guanine. Each short section of DNA—containing different patterns of rungs—holds a separate instruction, known as a gene.

This is easier to understand if you think of DNA as a language, with the four chemicals as its letters. Different combinations of "letters" spell out different "words," which are an individual gene. Human DNA contains 20,000 to 25,000 genes, each gene giving a particular instruction for which materials your cells make, how your organs work, or how you look.

Cells frequently split in two to make a new cell, so that the organism can grow bigger, repair itself, or reproduce. When a cell divides, a new copy of its DNA is needed. This is achieved easily, because of the way DNA's rungs are constructed. Just before a cell divides, its DNA splits down the middle of the ladder, creating two new strands that are then completed by adding the matching chemical to make each rung: Adenine joins thymine, and cytosine joins guanine.

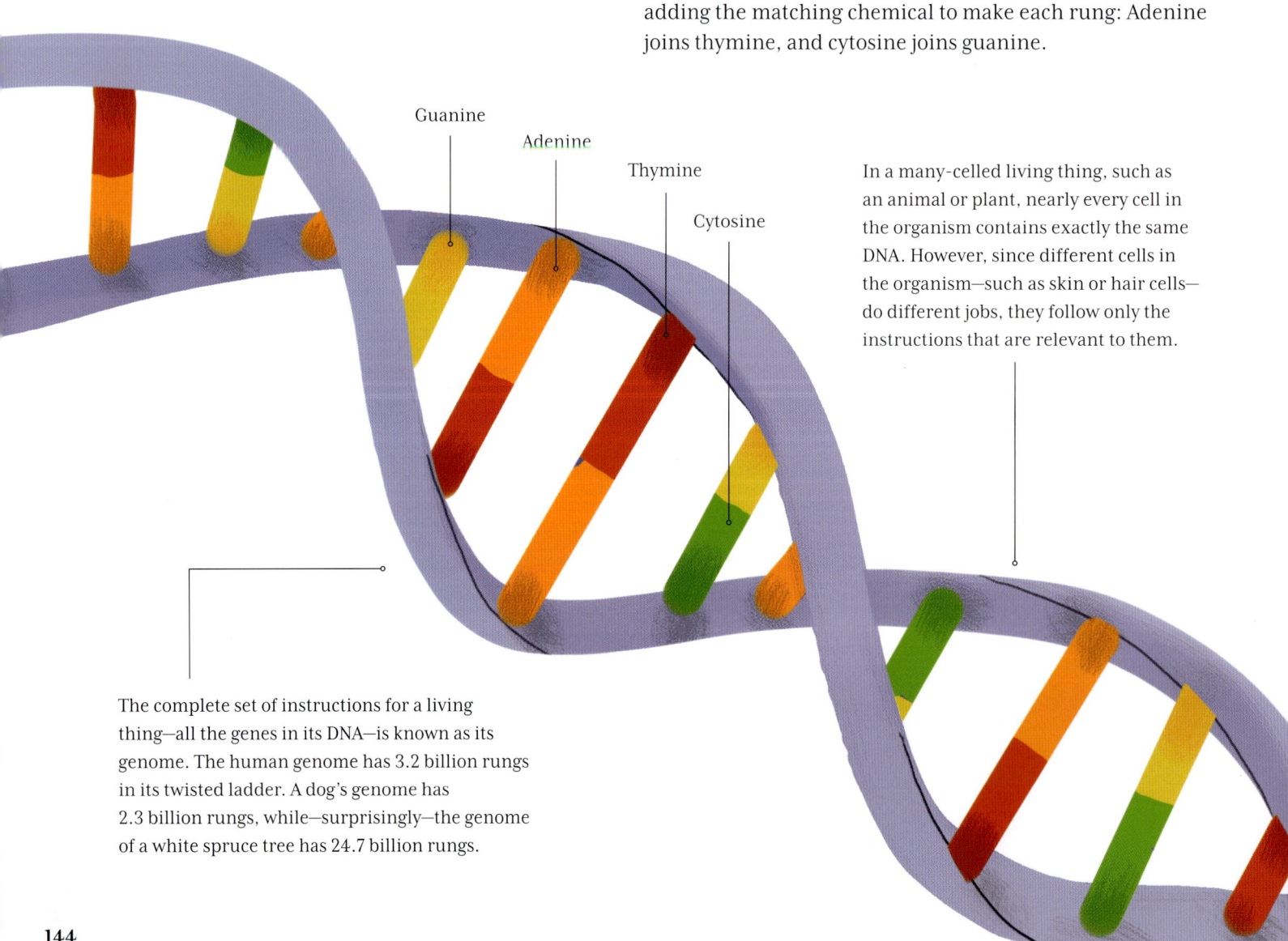

In a many-celled living thing, such as an animal or plant, nearly every cell in the organism contains exactly the same DNA. However, since different cells in the organism—such as skin or hair cells—do different jobs, they follow only the instructions that are relevant to them.

The complete set of instructions for a living thing—all the genes in its DNA—is known as its genome. The human genome has 3.2 billion rungs in its twisted ladder. A dog's genome has 2.3 billion rungs, while—surprisingly—the genome of a white spruce tree has 24.7 billion rungs.

CHROMOSOMES

Most of the time, DNA is loosely coiled inside a cell's nucleus, but before a cell divides, each strand of DNA coils more tightly into a finger-like structure, called a chromosome, to prevent tangling. Different living things have different numbers of chromosomes: Bacteria have just 1 chromosome, while humans have 23 pairs of chromosomes (46 in total).

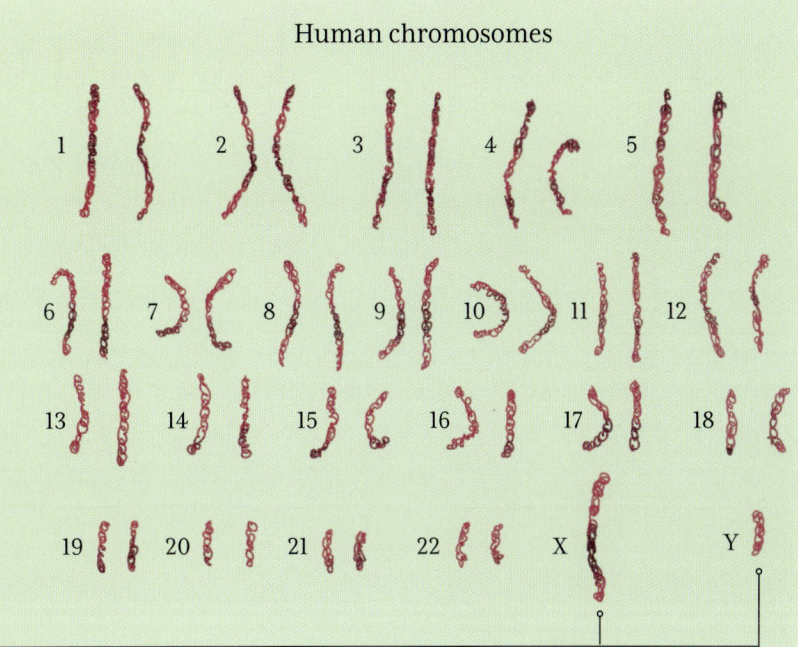
Human chromosomes

The 23rd pair of chromosomes determines the sex a baby is born with: Two big "X" chromosomes mean your birth sex is female, while an "X" and a small "Y" chromosome make your birth sex male.

INHERITANCE

Most animals—as well as many plants and some fungi and protists—reproduce sexually, which is when a cell from a male joins with a cell from a female in the same species. In these living things, their chromosomes are in pairs, half of each pair from the mother, half from the father. This is how characteristics, such as height and hair color, are passed on in DNA from both parents.

Single-celled organisms usually reproduce asexually, without the help of another organism. For example, many bacteria and archaea simply divide themselves into two. Their offspring are copies of themselves, with just one set of chromosomes.

Scientist Profile

NAME   Gregor Mendel
DATES   1822–84
NATIONALITY German-Czech
BREAKTHROUGH
By studying pea plants, he figured out rules about inheritance in plants and animals. Some characteristics, such as round peas—or brown eyes in humans—are "dominant," so they are more likely to appear in offspring if either parent has that characteristic. Other characteristics, such as wrinkled peas—or blue eyes in humans—are "recessive," so may not appear in offspring.

Evolution

Evolution is the process through which living things change, generation by generation. This process has allowed living things to adapt to all Earth's habitats, from seafloors to deserts to mountaintops.

Evolution allows living things to adapt to their environment, so that they are suited to finding food and shelter. Over thousands or millions of years, it allowed living things to move into new habitats, where there was less competition for resources. It allowed some to move from the ocean onto land, then later to evolve wings so they could fly or to evolve large paws so they could burrow underground.

Evolution can take place because parents pass on characteristics to their offspring through their DNA. In any species, there are slight differences in characteristics, so one giant tortoise may have a longer neck than the rest. Sometimes, a difference is so useful—such as a longer neck that allows a tortoise to reach more food—that the tortoise has a better chance of surviving to adulthood than other tortoises. That tortoise passes on its long neck to its babies, which pass on their long necks. Over time, long-necked tortoises become common, while short necks die out. This process is called natural selection.

When a species has been through lots of changes, scientists call it a new species. As habitats change and new competitors evolve, other species become extinct.

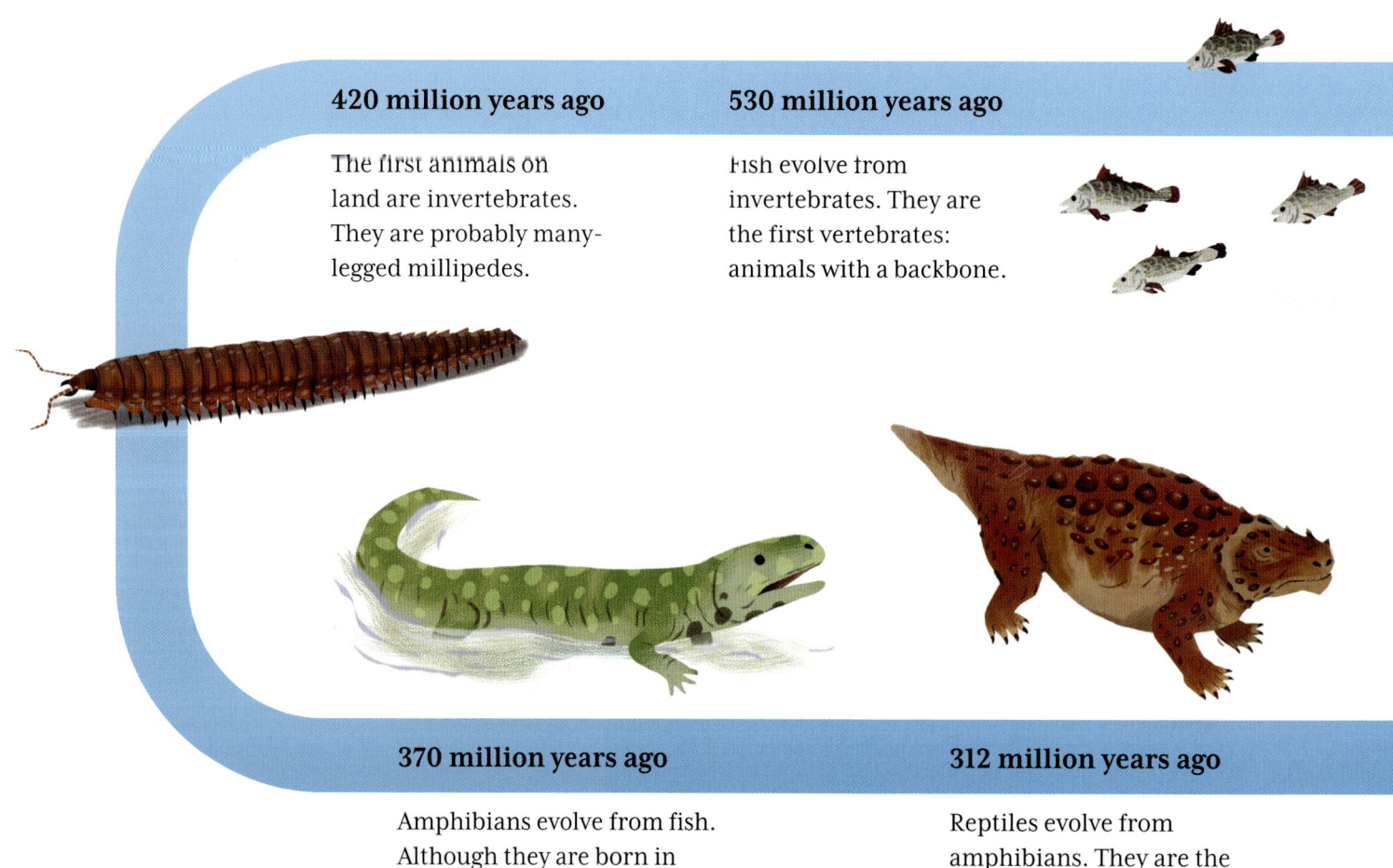

420 million years ago

The first animals on land are invertebrates. They are probably many-legged millipedes.

530 million years ago

Fish evolve from invertebrates. They are the first vertebrates: animals with a backbone.

370 million years ago

Amphibians evolve from fish. Although they are born in water, amphibians are the first vertebrate animals to spend time on land.

312 million years ago

Reptiles evolve from amphibians. They are the first vertebrates to spend their whole lives on land.

LIFE

4.5 billion years ago

Earth forms in a cloud of dust around the young Sun.

3.8 billion years ago

Prokaryotic cells appear in the oceans.

2.5 billion years ago

Simple eukaryotes evolve from prokaryotes.

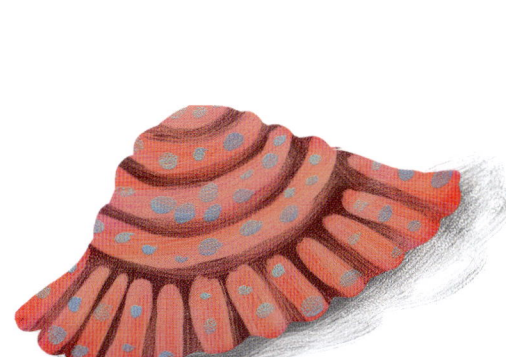

700 million years ago

Animals evolve from ocean-living protists that live in groups called colonies. These first animals are invertebrates: animals without a backbone.

700 million years ago

Plants evolve from ocean-living seaweeds, which are plantlike protists.

1 billion years ago

Fungi evolve in the oceans.

233 million years ago

A group of reptiles called dinosaurs evolves. They walk with their legs directly beneath their body, so they can take bigger, faster strides.

225 million years ago

Mammals evolve, with hair and larger brains than other animals.

72 million years ago

Birds evolve from a group of small, feathered dinosaurs.

Microorganisms

There are many millions of species of microorganisms, many of them yet to be discovered. Microorganisms are living things that can be seen only with a microscope. They belong to all groups of living things, but most are bacteria, archaea, protists, or fungi. Scientists often include viruses among microorganisms, although they are not true living things.

LACTOBACILLUS ACIDOPHILUS

Humans have millions of these bacteria in their intestines, where they get energy by soaking up passing food. Most babies get their first lactobacilli from their mother before they even take their first breath. These bacteria are helpful to humans, as they help us digest food.

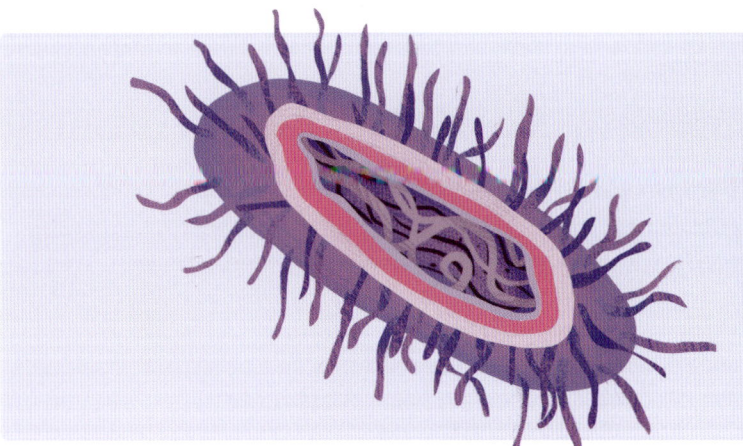

MYCOBACTERIUM TUBERCULOSIS

This bacterium (pictured in cutaway) can infect human lungs, leading to the disease tuberculosis. Spread from person to person by sneezes and coughs, tuberculosis causes coughing, fever, and possibly death. Today, it is prevented by vaccinations and treated by antibiotics (medications that kill bacteria).

Scientist Profile

NAME Elizabeth Bugie
DATES 1920–2001
NATIONALITY American
BREAKTHROUGH
In 1943, she helped develop the medication streptomycin, the first antibiotic that could kill *Mycobacterium tuberculosis*. Streptomycin is itself made by the bacterium *Streptomyces griseus*, which lives in soil.

SULFOLOBUS SOLFATARICUS

Like many other archaea, *Sulfolobus* lives in an extreme environment: hot springs where the water is heated by a volcano to 80 °C (176 °F), far too hot for most living things. *Sulfolobus* uses a chemical reaction (see page 22) to turn sulfur in the water into energy for itself.

AMOEBA PROTEUS

This protist lives in fresh water. It moves and feeds by changing its shape: It stretches out armlike portions of itself to swim and to trap smaller organisms. These are enclosed by the *Amoeba*, then broken down.

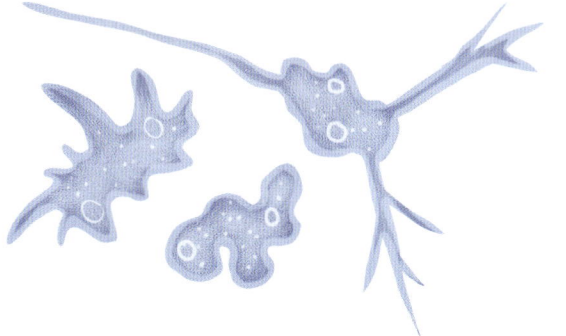

RHINOVIRUS

If this virus gets inside a human's nose or mouth, it can cause a cold. Around 0.000002 cm (0.0000008 in) across, it is spread from person to person by coughs and sneezes. Viruses are not true living things, because they do not grow, move, feed, or respond to the world around them. They are also not made of cells. However, they do contain DNA or a similar molecule called RNA, surrounded by a protective coat. They do reproduce, but only inside a cell belonging to a living thing. Once inside, the virus's RNA instructs the cell to make more viruses. This damages the cell, which can cause disease.

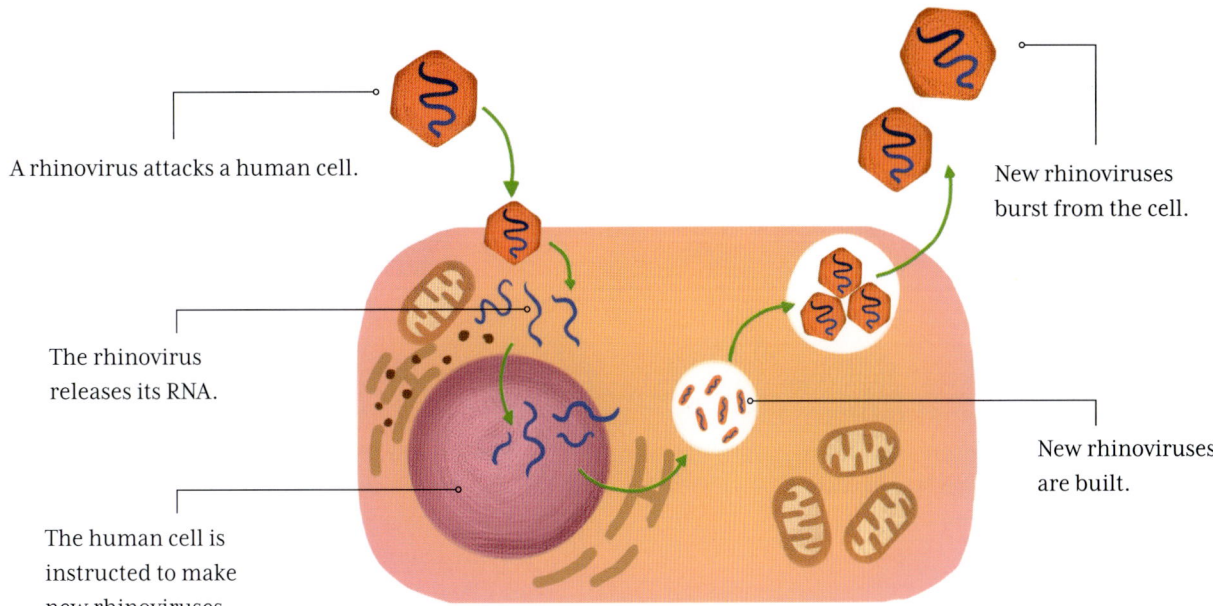

A rhinovirus attacks a human cell.

The rhinovirus releases its RNA.

The human cell is instructed to make new rhinoviruses.

New rhinoviruses are built.

New rhinoviruses burst from the cell.

Plants

There are around 385,000 species of plants, ranging in size from duckweed—only 1 mm (0.04 in) across—to the giant sequoia tree, which grows 95 m (311 ft) tall. Most plants are green and have roots, stems, and leaves. All plants make their own food.

DIFFERENT PLANTS

As long as plants have enough sunlight, warmth, and water, they can grow in habitats from shallow oceans to mountaintops. They have evolved a range of different characteristics to suit different conditions. For example, desert plants, such as cacti, have evolved thick stems where they store water, so they can survive dry periods. Mountain plants grow low to the ground for protection from cold and the drying wind. There are four main groups of plants, all of them found in a wide range of habitats:

Flowering plants: There are more than 350,000 species of flowering small plants, shrubs, and trees (which have a thick, woody stem). Flowering plants have roots, stems, and leaves that are usually broad and flat. They grow flowers that make seeds containing new baby plants.

Coniferous plants: There are around 1,000 species of conifers and their relatives, which are mainly shrubs and trees. They have roots, stems, and leaves shaped like needles or scales. They grow male and female cones. Male cones make pollen, which is carried by the wind or insects to female cones, which then make seeds.

Ferns: There are around 13,000 species of ferns, which range from small to tree-sized. They have roots, stems, and leaves called fronds, which are often divided into feathery leaflets. Instead of making seeds, ferns release tinier, simpler spores, which will develop into new plants.

Rootless plants: There are around 20,000 species of rootless and stemless plants, such as mosses, which are usually small and low-growing. They attach to surfaces and soak up water using hairlike threads called rhizoids. They release spores to make new plants.

MAKING FOOD

Plants make food using a process called photosynthesis. To do this, they need three ingredients: water, carbon dioxide, and sunlight. Most plants take in water from the soil through their roots. Land plants soak up carbon dioxide gas from the air, but water-living plants can take it from water.

Plants soak up sunlight using a green chemical called chlorophyll, which is why most plants look green. Sunlight is energy released by the Sun. Plants use this energy to carry out a chemical reaction (see page 22), which changes water and carbon dioxide into glucose sugar. This sugar travels throughout the plant in tiny tubes, so that every cell can make energy from it.

ESSENTIAL PLANTS

Plants provide shelter and food for other living things. Dead and rotting plants are fed on by bacteria, fungi, and animals such as earthworms. Many other animals—from rabbits to giraffes—feed on living plants. By changing sunlight into glucose, plants create a type of energy that animals can eat. Plant-eating animals pass on some of that energy to the meat-eating animals that feed on them.

In addition, when plants photosynthesize, they release oxygen as a waste product. Before plants—and some bacteria and protists—started to photosynthesize, there was no oxygen in Earth's atmosphere. All animals, and most other living things, need oxygen to survive.

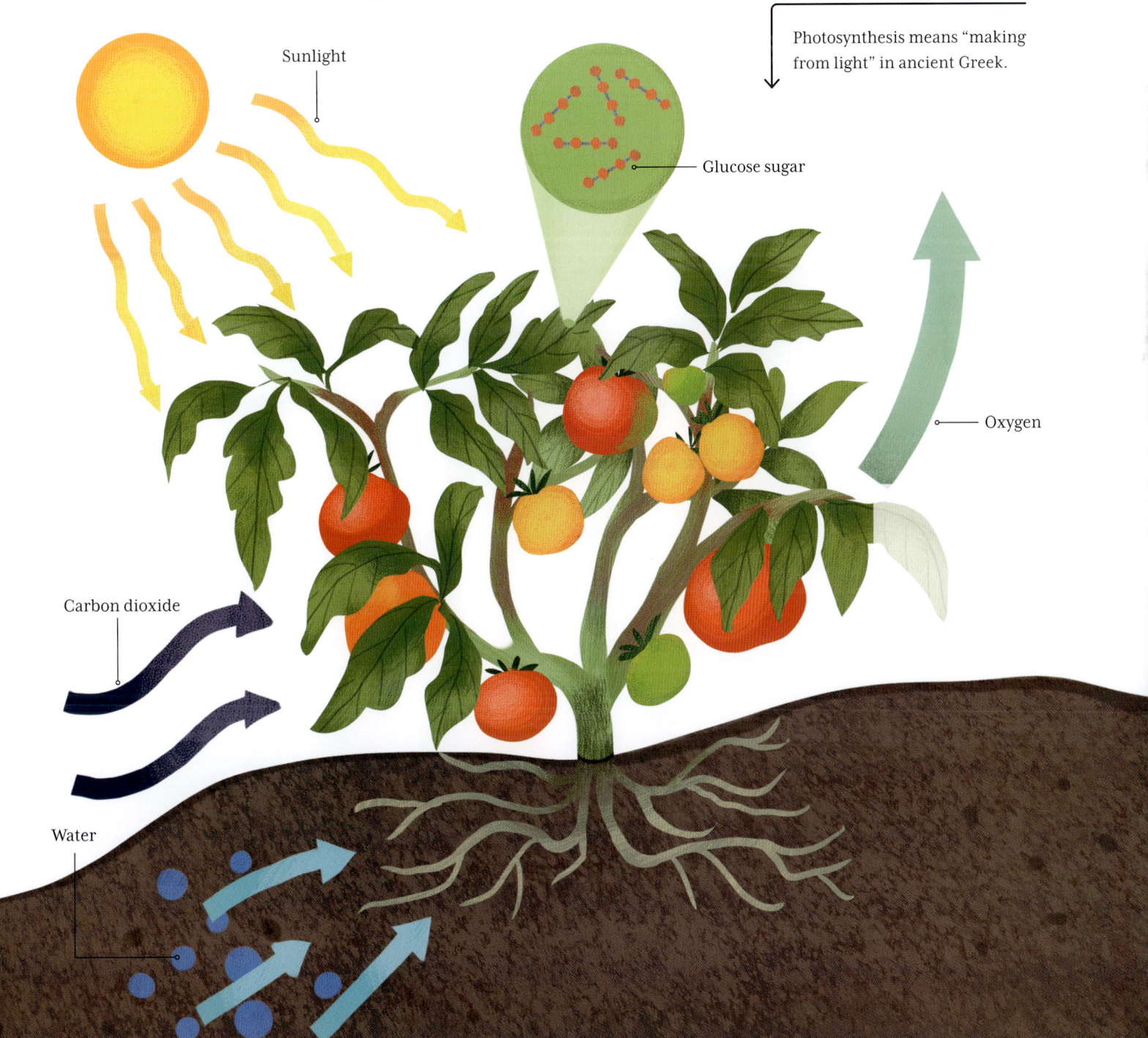

Photosynthesis means "making from light" in ancient Greek.

LIFE

Flowers

Flowers are produced by flowering plants so they can make seeds, which grow into new baby plants. The first step on this journey is pollination, which is when a flower receives a yellow powder called pollen.

FLOWERS

Each flower usually has male and female parts. The male parts, called stamens, make pollen. The female parts include the stigma and ovary, which contains ovules. The stigma is sticky, so it collects pollen easily—usually when it is delivered from the male parts of a different flower. Bits of pollen then travel from the stigma to the ovary. When an ovule receives pollen, it turns into a seed.

POLLINATION

Many flowers are pollinated by animals, including birds, bats, and insects such as bees, wasps, and butterflies. Flowers attract pollinators with their smell or by making a sweet liquid, called nectar. As pollinators visit flower after flower, they carry pollen on their hairy or feathery bodies. Some flowers are pollinated when wind or water carry pollen from another plant.

- Stamen
- Stigma
- Ovary
- Ovule
- Petal
- Sepal

FRUIT

As ovules grow into seeds, the ovary develops into a fruit. Some fruits are soft and fleshy, while some, known as nuts, are dry with a hard shell. Others, such as the tiny, tufted fruits of a dandelion, look nothing like the fruit bought in stores!

SPREADING SEEDS

The purpose of fruit is to spread seeds, so that new plants do not grow in the shadow of their parent. Many fleshy fruits are eaten by animals, which poop the hard seeds a few hours or days later. Some dry fruits are spiky, so they stick to animal fur. Others float on rivers or drift on the wind.

GERMINATION

The moment when a seed starts to sprout is known as germination: A root grows downward, and a shoot grows upward. A seed contains a baby plant and food for the baby, enclosed in a hard coat. The coat cracks—allowing the seed to grow—only when conditions are ideal, with enough water and warmth.

Fungi

Fungi range in size from tiny yeasts to massive, mushroom-sprouting mycelia. Like plants, fungi cannot walk, crawl, or swim from place to place. Unlike plants, they cannot make food: They soak it up from their surroundings. Around 148,000 species of fungi have been named.

Gills

ARMILLARIA OSTOYAE

The biggest living thing may be an *Armillaria ostoyae* in a forest in the United States' Oregon: It spreads over 9.1 sq km (3.5 sq miles). Most of the fungus is underground, where it forms a mass of rootlike threads called a mycelium. Its mushrooms sprout above ground in fall (autumn), when their gills release spores. These are blown away, then grow into new fungi.

BAKER'S YEAST

Around 0.0007 cm (0.0003 in) wide, this single-celled fungus is used by bakers. The yeast soak up sugar in dough, then release the gas carbon dioxide, which makes bread fluffy. These fungi reproduce by budding: A new, identical cell grows from a parent cell.

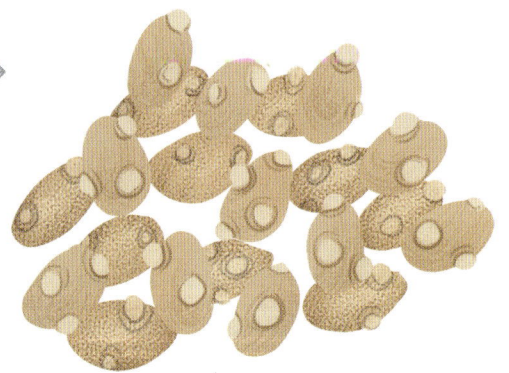

TURKEY TAIL

Named for its mushroom's similarity to a wild turkey's tail, this fungus grows in the logs or stumps of trees. It digests damp wood, making it rot. Wood-rotting fungi are vital in forests, since they return nutrients (materials needed for life and growth) in trees to the soil, where they can be used by new plants.

LIFE

ZOMBIE-ANT FUNGUS

Found in tropical forests, this fungus lives inside carpenter ants. The fungus soaks up nutrients inside the ant, then sprouts a mushroom. This releases spores that land on more ants and soak their way inside using chemicals.

FLY AGARIC

This fungus soaks up nutrients from rotting plants in woodland soil. It produces mushrooms that are poisonous to humans. The mushrooms can make spores on their own, without contact from another fungus. If the threads of the fungus's mycelium touch another mycelium, it can also reproduce sexually.

PENICILLIUM RUBENS

This fungus often grows as "mold" on fruits and vegetables. Like all fungi, it releases chemicals called enzymes onto the material it is growing on. The enzymes break down the material, which is then absorbed by the fungus.

Scientist Profile

NAME Alexander Fleming
DATES 1881–1955
NATIONALITY Scottish
BREAKTHROUGH
In 1928, he discovered that *Penicillium rubens* releases chemicals that kill bacteria which cause infections in humans, including of the eyes, throat, and lungs. This discovery led to the creation of penicillin, the first effective antibiotic medication.

The Human Body

An average-sized adult is made of around 30 trillion cells—that is a 3 followed by 13 zeros. Cells are the human body's smallest working parts, most of them too tiny to be seen without a microscope. Your body contains around 200 different types of cells, each with a different shape and its own particular work. For example, long brain cells called neurons pass on messages. Blob-shaped stomach cells called chief cells make chemicals that break down food.

Cells group together with similar cells to make tissues, something like the way bricks build a wall. For example, muscle cells form muscles, and skin cells form skin. Different types of tissues join together to form organs. Organs are body parts with a particular job to do. The stomach is an organ with the job of mushing the food you eat, while the heart has the job of pumping blood around your body. You have around 78 organs, ranging in size from your brain's tiny pineal gland—weighing around 0.1 g (0.004 oz)—to your skin, which weighs up to 3.6 kg (8 lb).

Your cells contain even smaller parts including mitochondria. These tiny factories make energy so the cell can do its work. Mitochondria use two main ingredients to make energy: glucose sugar from the food you eat, and oxygen from the air you breathe. Organs including your lungs, heart, and stomach are always busy making sure all your cells have a constant supply of these ingredients. Your body's most important organ, the brain, watches over the work of these organs—and over every other organ in your body.

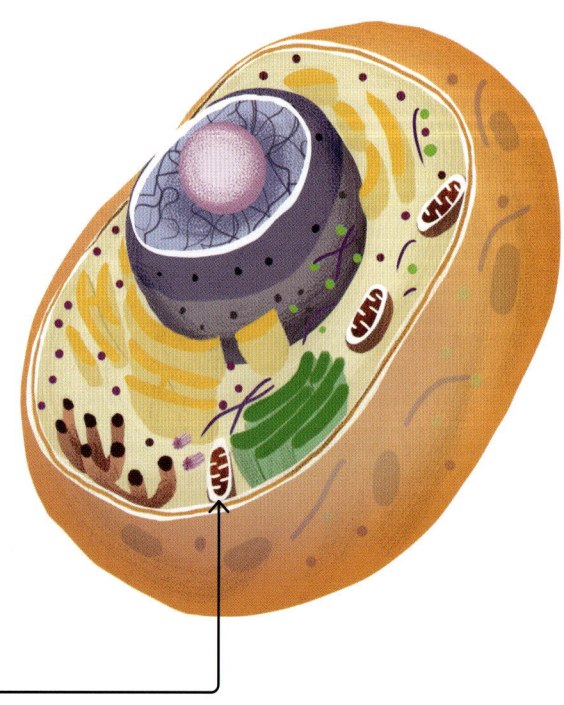

Mitochondria make energy to power a cell's work. Different cells carry out different work, such as making or transporting materials, and—in the case of muscle cells—shortening, so that you can move!

Medicine is the study of the human body, diseases, and how to treat them. In 1864, Rebecca Lee Crumpler was the first African American woman to become a doctor of medicine. She is using an early stethoscope, which helps a person hear sounds inside the body, such as the heartbeat and breathing.

THE HUMAN BODY

Organ Systems

Your 78 organs are in 11 organ systems. An organ system is a group of organs that work together to do complicated tasks. Your organ systems work with each other to keep your body healthy.

RESPIRATORY SYSTEM

This system carries out the work of breathing: Taking in oxygen so it can be used by cells, then getting rid of a waste gas called carbon dioxide (see page 166).

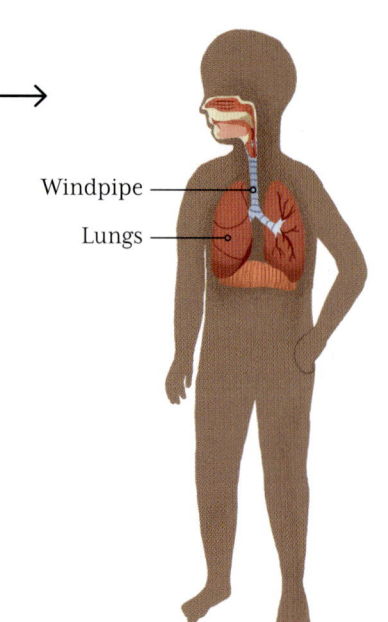

Windpipe
Lungs

DIGESTIVE SYSTEM

The digestive system breaks down food into smaller, useful parts—called nutrients—that can be used by cells (see page 168).

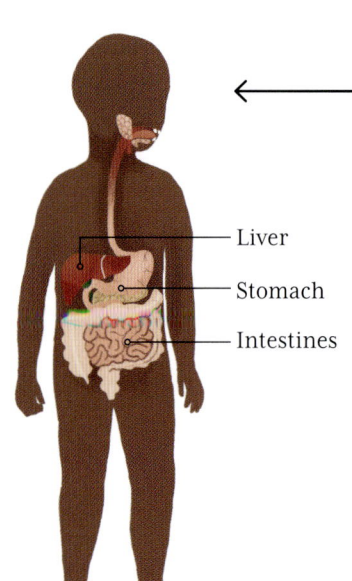

Liver
Stomach
Intestines

CIRCULATORY SYSTEM

This system's heaviest organ is the heart, which pumps blood around the body through tubes called blood vessels (see page 167). Blood carries oxygen, nutrients, and hormones to where they are needed, as well as carrying away waste made by cells and organs.

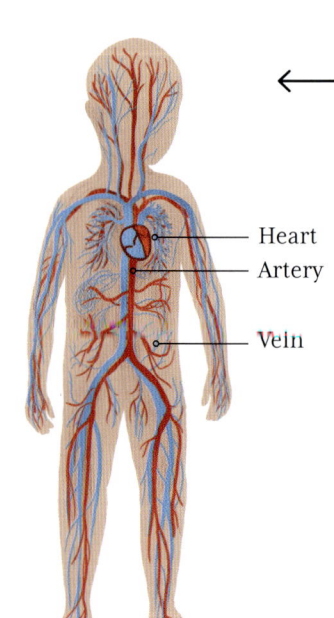

Heart
Artery
Vein

URINARY SYSTEM

The urinary system gets rid of waste made by cells and organs. The kidneys filter waste and water out of the blood, creating a liquid called urine (pee). Urine is stored in a bag-like organ called the bladder until you use the toilet.

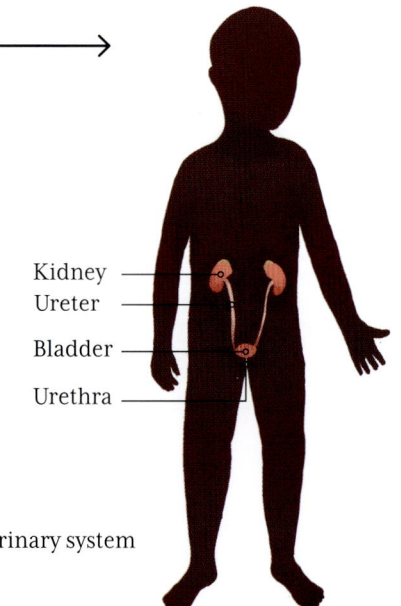

Kidney
Ureter
Bladder
Urethra

Female urinary system

ENDOCRINE SYSTEM

This system is made up of organs, called glands, that make hormones. These chemicals carry messages through the blood, instructing particular organs to change their activities. For example, growth hormone, made in the pituitary gland, tells your bones and muscles to grow during childhood.

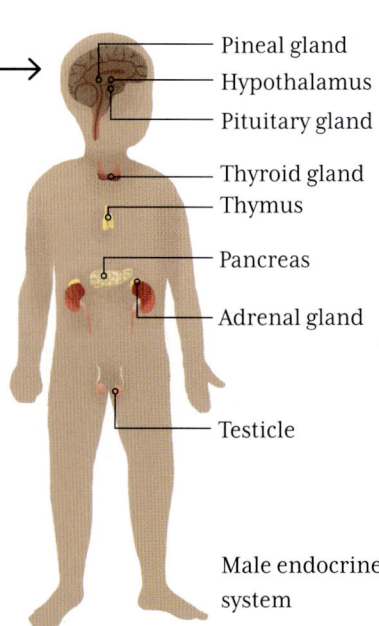

Pineal gland
Hypothalamus
Pituitary gland
Thyroid gland
Thymus
Pancreas
Adrenal gland
Testicle

Male endocrine system

THE HUMAN BODY

LYMPHATIC SYSTEM

The lymphatic system makes and releases lymphocytes (a type of white blood cell), which target and kill invaders such as viruses and bacteria. The system also collects excess liquid from your tissues and returns it to the blood to keep your fluid levels healthy.

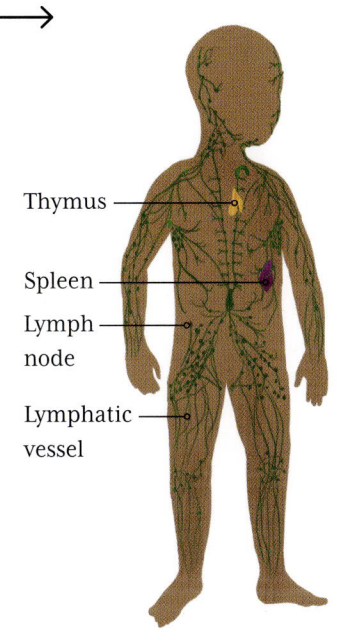

Thymus
Spleen
Lymph node
Lymphatic vessel

INTEGUMENTARY SYSTEM

Your skin, hair, and nails form this system, which helps protect you from infection and from getting too hot, cold, wet, or dry. The skin's sweat glands cool you down as sweat uses your body heat to evaporate (see page 21).

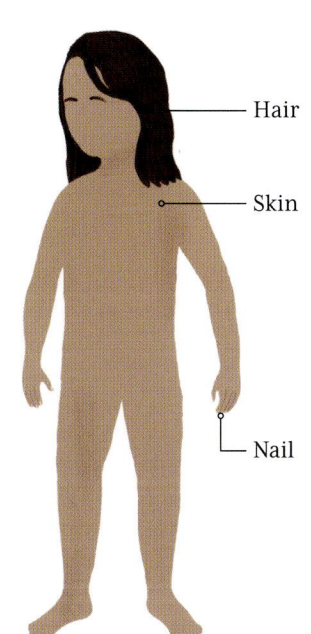

Hair
Skin
Nail

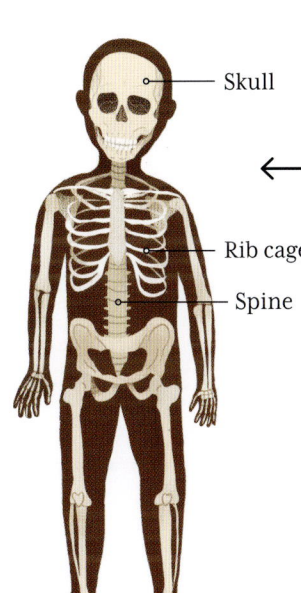

Skull
Rib cage
Spine

SKELETAL SYSTEM

The skeletal system is made up of your bones, which form a strong frame that gives your body shape, protects your organs, and helps you move (see page 160).

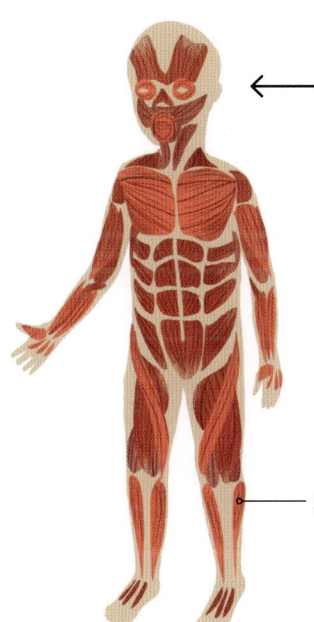

MUSCULAR SYSTEM

You have three types of muscle: Skeletal muscle allows your bones to move (see page 161); heart muscle makes your heart beat; and smooth muscle is found in the walls of organs.

Skeletal muscle

REPRODUCTIVE SYSTEM

This system allows adults to make babies (see page 170). Female reproductive organs include the ovaries and uterus, while male organs include the testicles and penis.

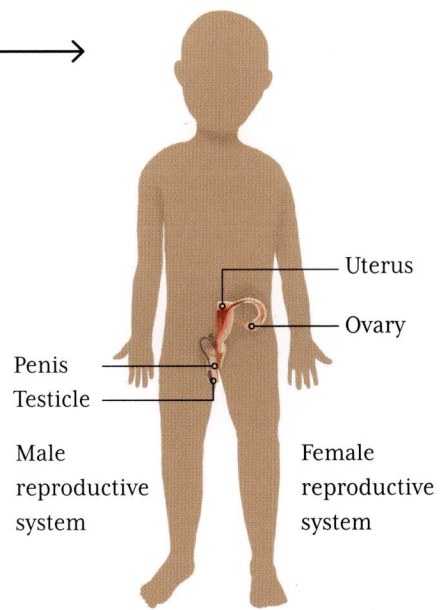

Uterus
Ovary
Penis
Testicle
Male reproductive system
Female reproductive system

NERVOUS SYSTEM

The nervous system is made up of the brain, sense organs including the eyes and ears, and nerves, along which messages travel between the brain and body. This system controls the body's activities, lets you respond to the world, and allows you to think and learn.

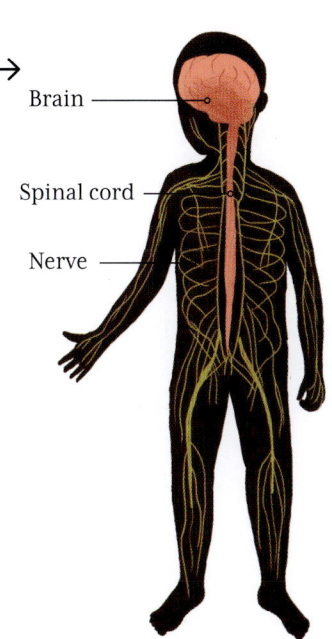

Brain
Spinal cord
Nerve

159

THE HUMAN BODY

Bones and Muscles

Most adults have around 206 bones and over 650 skeletal muscles. The longest bone is the femur (thigh bone), and the longest muscle is the thigh's sartorius, both of them over 50 cm (20 in) long in tall adults. Your bones and muscles work together so you can run and jump.

BONE TYPES

Bones with different jobs have different sizes and shapes. In your arms and legs are long bones that give the body strength and balance. Small, cube-shaped bones in your wrists and ankles allow a wide range of movements. Flat, plate-like bones in the skull and ribcage protect your organs.

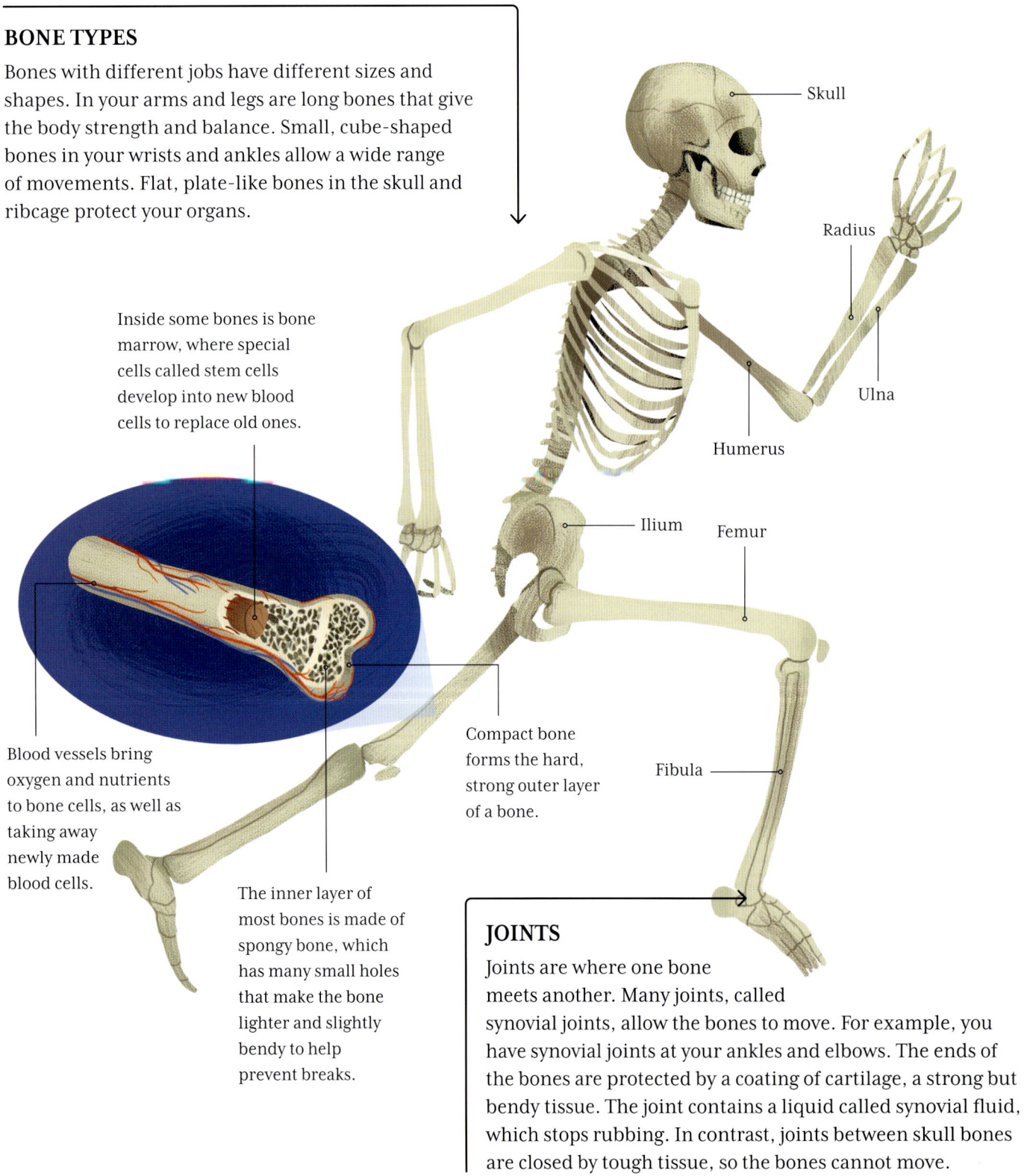

Inside some bones is bone marrow, where special cells called stem cells develop into new blood cells to replace old ones.

Blood vessels bring oxygen and nutrients to bone cells, as well as taking away newly made blood cells.

The inner layer of most bones is made of spongy bone, which has many small holes that make the bone lighter and slightly bendy to help prevent breaks.

Compact bone forms the hard, strong outer layer of a bone.

Skull · Radius · Ulna · Humerus · Ilium · Femur · Fibula

JOINTS

Joints are where one bone meets another. Many joints, called synovial joints, allow the bones to move. For example, you have synovial joints at your ankles and elbows. The ends of the bones are protected by a coating of cartilage, a strong but bendy tissue. The joint contains a liquid called synovial fluid, which stops rubbing. In contrast, joints between skull bones are closed by tough tissue, so the bones cannot move.

THE HUMAN BODY

MUSCLE MOVES

Skeletal muscles pull on your bones so you can move. A muscle gets the instruction to pull from the brain: The command travels in the form of an electrical signal, from the brain, down the spinal cord, and along nerves to the muscle. Muscles can only contract, making them shorter, which means they can only pull bones, not push them. For this reason, muscles usually work in pairs, with one pulling a bone one direction and the other pulling it the opposite way.

Scientist Profile
NAME Luigi Galvani
DATES 1737–98
NATIONALITY Italian
BREAKTHROUGH
In 1780, he discovered that the legs of a dead frog would twitch when touched with an electric spark. This began the study of bioelectricity, which is the electricity made by animal cells to send messages, such as from the brain of a frog to its leg muscles.

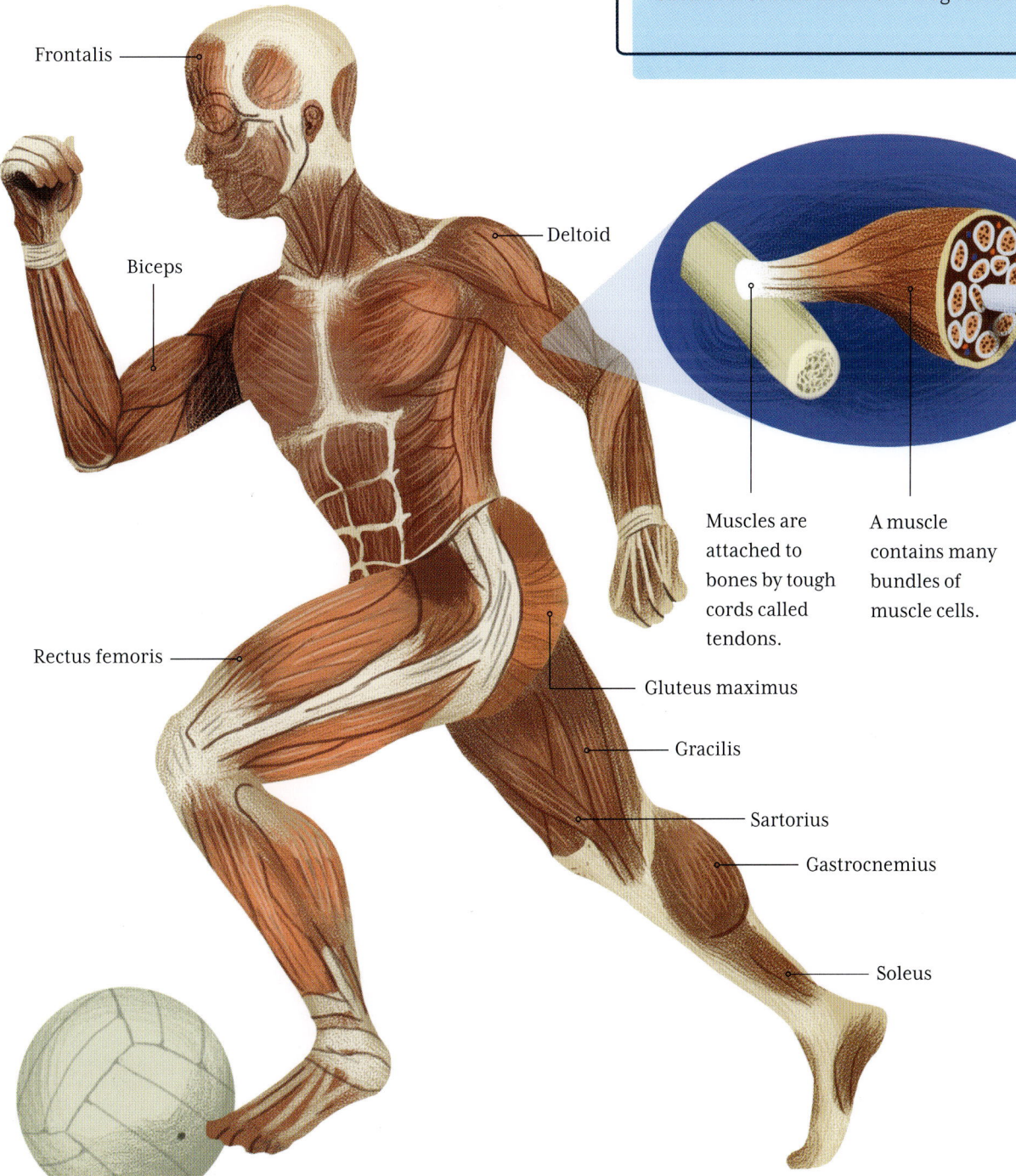

Frontalis
Biceps
Deltoid
Rectus femoris
Gluteus maximus
Gracilis
Sartorius
Gastrocnemius
Soleus

Muscles are attached to bones by tough cords called tendons.

A muscle contains many bundles of muscle cells.

A muscle cell is long, threadlike, and has the ability to shorten.

161

THE HUMAN BODY

The Brain

An adult's brain weighs around 1.3 kg (2.9 lb), about as much as a pineapple. The brain has two main areas of work: conscious thoughts and unconscious activities, which you are unaware of—but keep you healthy.

Your brain has three main parts: cerebrum, cerebellum, and brainstem. The surface layer of the cerebrum is where most of your conscious thoughts—your decision to read a book or wave to a friend—take place. These thoughts are created by billions of tiny brain cells, called neurons, sending electrical signals to each other. The cerebellum and brainstem are in charge of most unconscious activities.

The cerebrum is in left and right halves, called hemispheres, connected to each other by nerves. The left and right hemispheres are almost mirror images of each other. The left hemisphere controls the right side of your body, while the right hemisphere controls the left side. Both sides work together on most tasks. Each hemisphere is divided into four regions, called lobes, by deep wrinkles. Each of the four lobes focuses on particular areas of work.

FRONTAL LOBE

The frontal lobe of the cerebrum is focused on planning, making decisions, and solving problems. It also helps you control how you talk and behave with other people.

TEMPORAL LOBE

The cerebrum's temporal lobe processes information from the nose and ears. It helps you to understand what people say and to enjoy music.

162

THE HUMAN BODY

PARIETAL LOBE
The cerebrum's parietal lobe helps you understand what you touch and taste. It also helps you know where your body is in relation to other people and objects.

OCCIPITAL LOBE
This lobe of the cerebrum helps you understand signals from your eyes. It allows you to identify objects that you see and to recognize people's faces.

CEREBELLUM
Without you noticing, the cerebellum co-ordinates your movements so, for example, you can walk without falling over. The cerebrum sends muscles the commands to move, but the cerebellum adjusts the commands as it gets information from the body about the position of your legs and arms.

BRAINSTEM
The brainstem keeps your heart beating and your lungs breathing, speeding them up if your muscles need more energy when you are running. It also makes you aware of your surroundings when you are awake, then helps you lose awareness as you drift off to sleep.

THE HUMAN BODY

Senses

You have five main senses, which give your brain information about the world around you. Your sense organs include your eyes for sight, ears for hearing, nose for smell, mouth and nose for taste, and skin for touch.

SIGHT

Sunlight (or light from a lamp) bounces off objects and into your eyes. First, light travels through the eye's see-through coating: the cornea. Then it enters a hole, called the pupil, and travels through a lens. The curved shapes of the cornea and lens bend the light to make a focused image of the object on the retina, at the back of the eye. The retina has 95 million light-sensitive cells: Each one turns its section of the image into an electrical signal, which travels along a nerve to the brain.

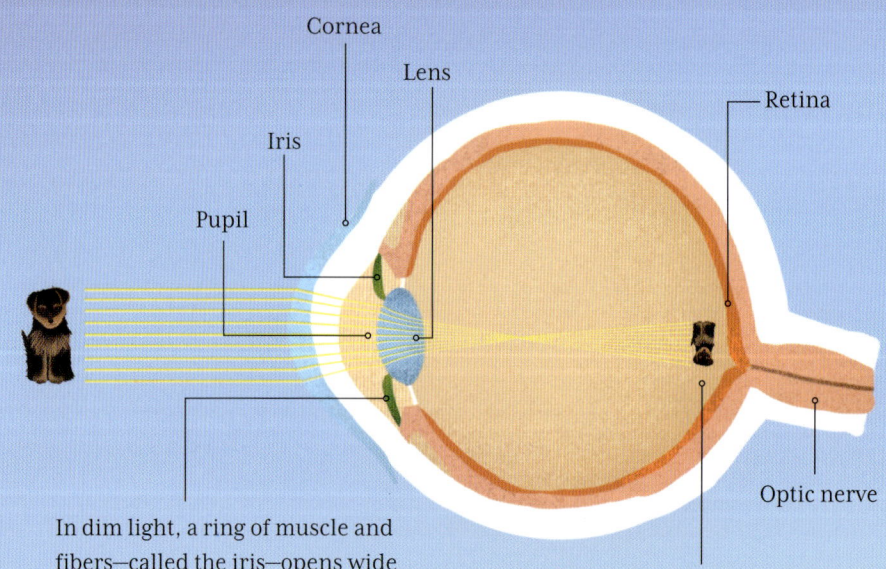

In dim light, a ring of muscle and fibers—called the iris—opens wide to let more light into the pupil. In bright light, the iris closes partly so the eye is not dazzled.

The cornea and lens bend light so the image on the retina is upside down, but the brain corrects it.

TOUCH

Your skin contains different types of sensitive cells, which respond to touch, pain, heat, or cold. The cells send electrical signals along nerves to the brain. If you prick your finger, the signal travels along your arm at up to 2 m (6.6 ft) per second.

THE HUMAN BODY

HEARING

Sounds are made by vibrations: shaking often too small to see. When you bang a drum, its skin vibrates. When you speak, breathed-out air shakes bands of tissue—called vocal cords—in your throat's voice box (see page 166).

The vibration makes surrounding air molecules vibrate. Then these molecules pass on their shaking to surrounding molecules, creating a "sound wave" that travels through the air in all directions.

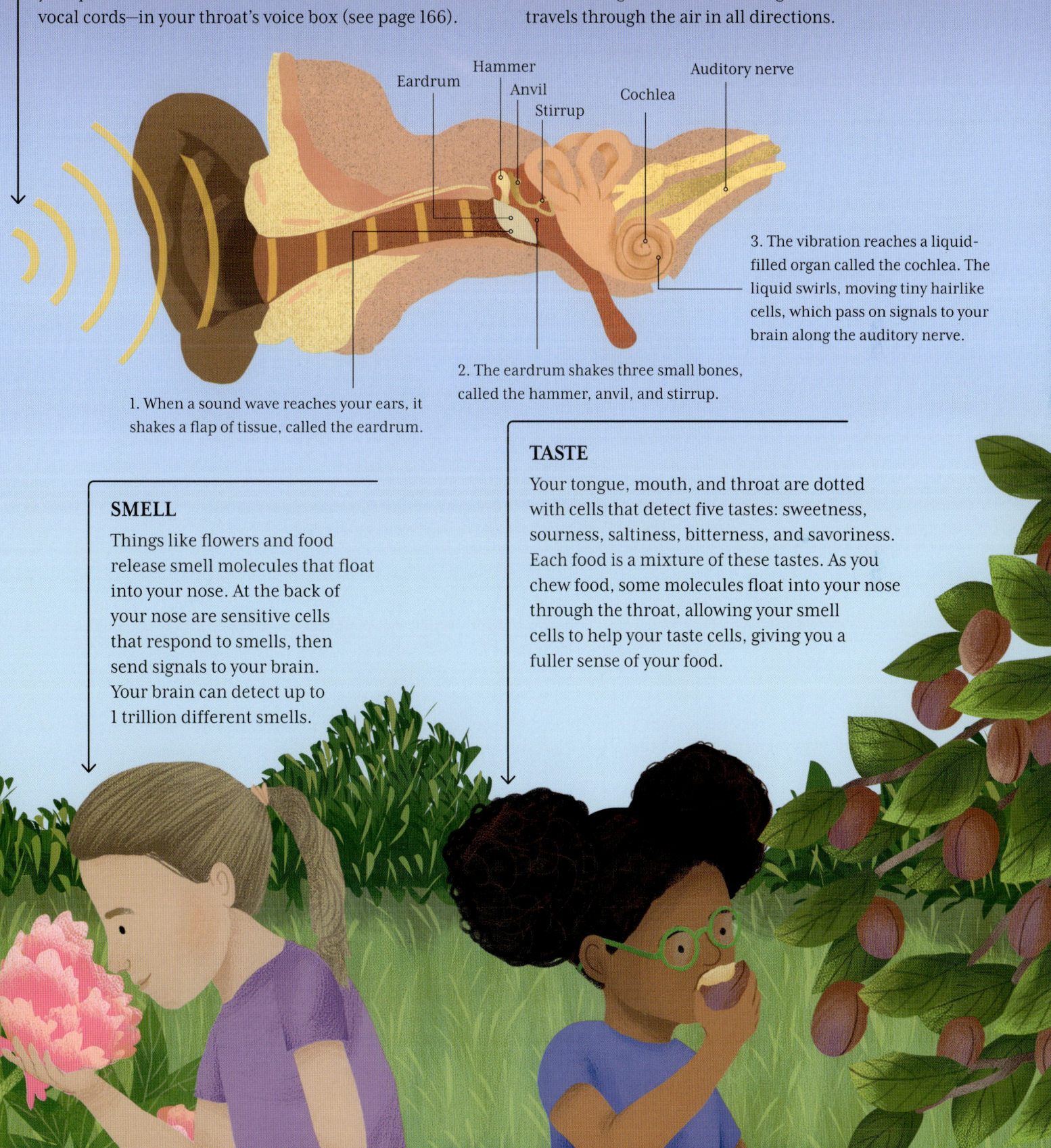

Eardrum | Hammer | Anvil | Stirrup | Cochlea | Auditory nerve

1. When a sound wave reaches your ears, it shakes a flap of tissue, called the eardrum.

2. The eardrum shakes three small bones, called the hammer, anvil, and stirrup.

3. The vibration reaches a liquid-filled organ called the cochlea. The liquid swirls, moving tiny hairlike cells, which pass on signals to your brain along the auditory nerve.

SMELL

Things like flowers and food release smell molecules that float into your nose. At the back of your nose are sensitive cells that respond to smells, then send signals to your brain. Your brain can detect up to 1 trillion different smells.

TASTE

Your tongue, mouth, and throat are dotted with cells that detect five tastes: sweetness, sourness, saltiness, bitterness, and savoriness. Each food is a mixture of these tastes. As you chew food, some molecules float into your nose through the throat, allowing your smell cells to help your taste cells, giving you a fuller sense of your food.

THE HUMAN BODY

Lungs and Heart

Your lungs are the largest organ in the respiratory system, while your heart is the chief organ of the circulatory system. The lungs are in charge of breathing in oxygen, while the heart makes sure oxygen is delivered to every cell in your body.

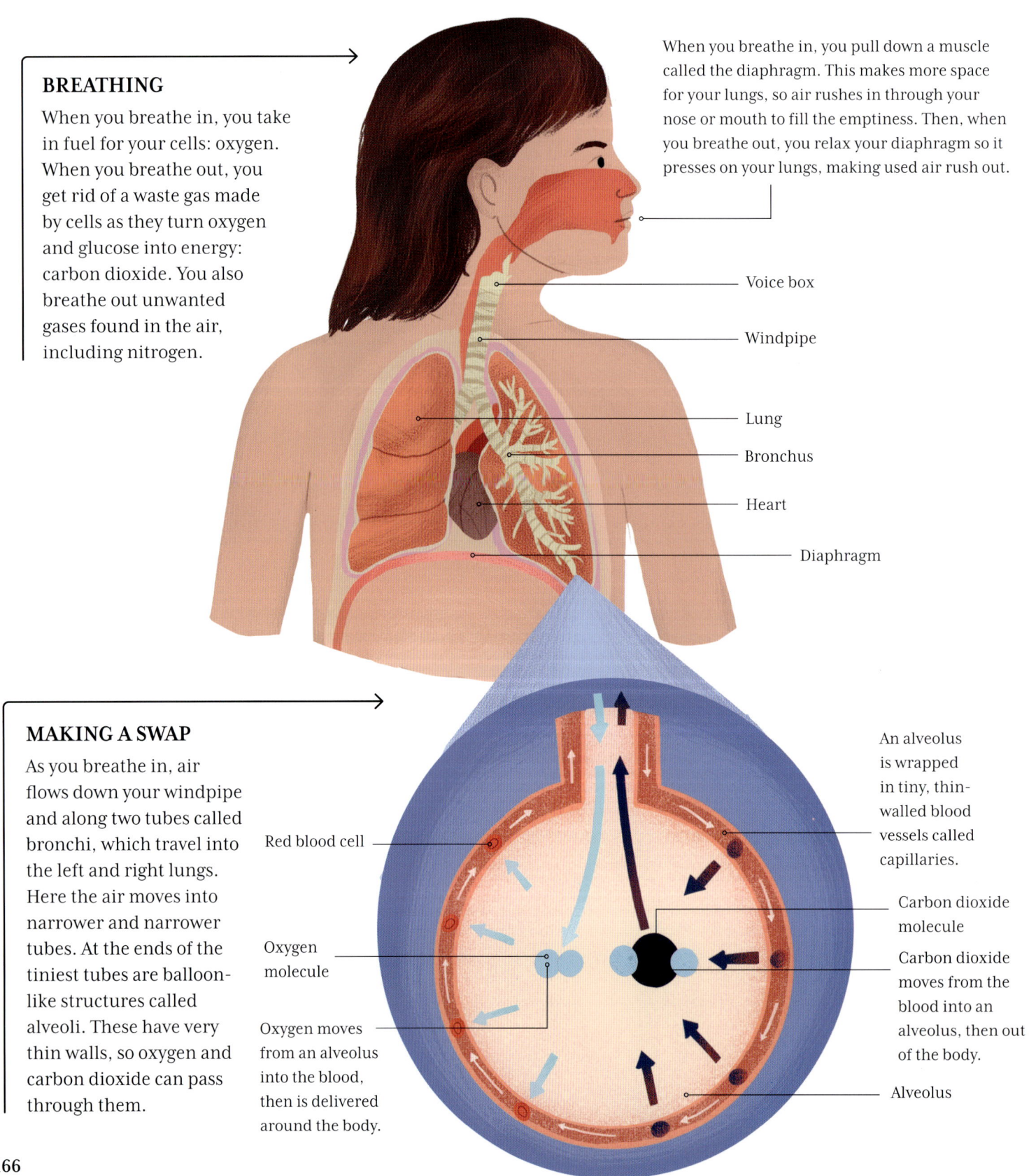

BREATHING

When you breathe in, you take in fuel for your cells: oxygen. When you breathe out, you get rid of a waste gas made by cells as they turn oxygen and glucose into energy: carbon dioxide. You also breathe out unwanted gases found in the air, including nitrogen.

When you breathe in, you pull down a muscle called the diaphragm. This makes more space for your lungs, so air rushes in through your nose or mouth to fill the emptiness. Then, when you breathe out, you relax your diaphragm so it presses on your lungs, making used air rush out.

- Voice box
- Windpipe
- Lung
- Bronchus
- Heart
- Diaphragm

MAKING A SWAP

As you breathe in, air flows down your windpipe and along two tubes called bronchi, which travel into the left and right lungs. Here the air moves into narrower and narrower tubes. At the ends of the tiniest tubes are balloon-like structures called alveoli. These have very thin walls, so oxygen and carbon dioxide can pass through them.

- Red blood cell
- Oxygen molecule
- Oxygen moves from an alveolus into the blood, then is delivered around the body.

An alveolus is wrapped in tiny, thin-walled blood vessels called capillaries.

- Carbon dioxide molecule
- Carbon dioxide moves from the blood into an alveolus, then out of the body.
- Alveolus

THE HUMAN BODY

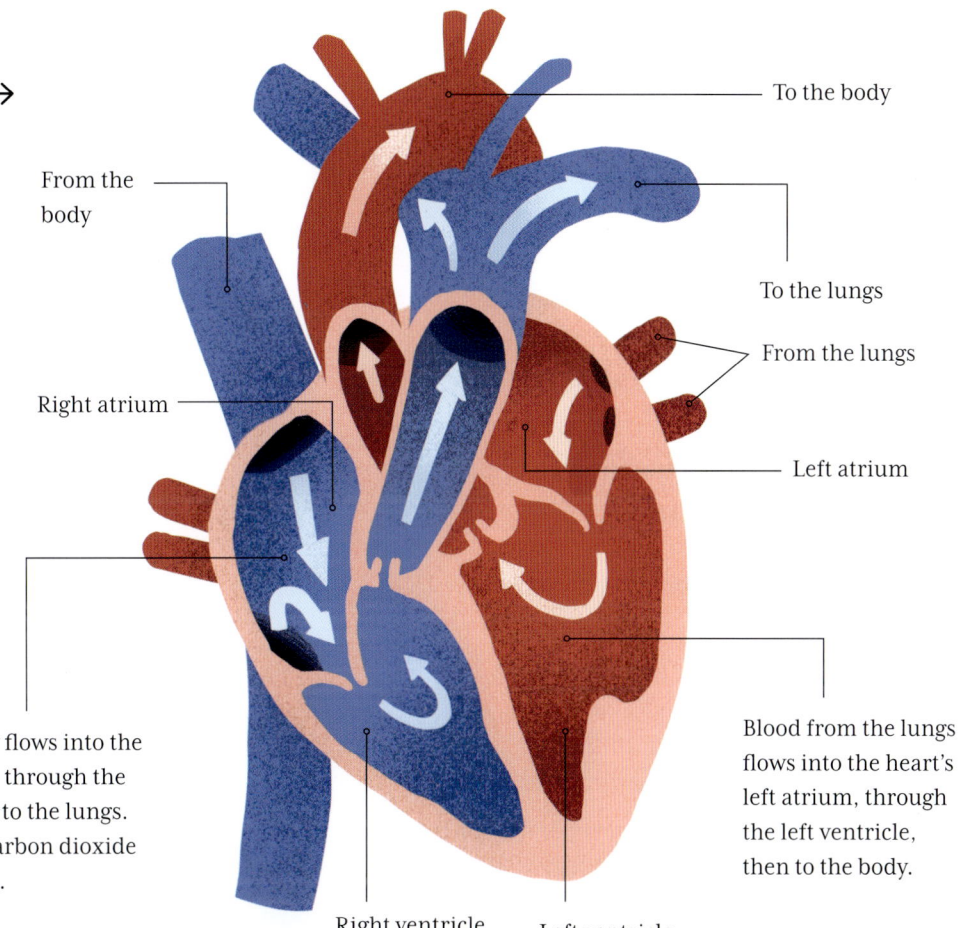

BEATING HEART

About the size of your fist, your heart is a pump that squeezes and relaxes, over and over again. When it squeezes, it shoots blood through your blood vessels at up to 90 cm (3 ft) per second. Blood vessels that carry blood away from the heart are called arteries. Blood vessels that carry blood from the body to the heart are called veins.

Blood from the body flows into the heart's right atrium, through the right ventricle, then to the lungs. There it gets rid of carbon dioxide and picks up oxygen.

Blood from the lungs flows into the heart's left atrium, through the left ventricle, then to the body.

- From the body
- To the body
- To the lungs
- From the lungs
- Right atrium
- Left atrium
- Right ventricle
- Left ventricle

IN YOUR BLOOD

Your blood is made of a pale-yellow liquid called plasma, in which are floating lots of red blood cells, white blood cells, platelets, nutrients from food, and waste.

Red blood cells carry oxygen to cells, where they pick up carbon dioxide to take to the lungs.

White blood cells help your body fight infection.

Platelets clump together if you cut yourself, making a scab and stopping your bleeding.

Scientist Profile

NAME Christiaan Barnard
DATES 1922–2001
NATIONALITY South African
BREAKTHROUGH
In 1967, he carried out the first heart transplant: During surgery, a heart from a person who had just died was placed in the body of a patient with a diseased heart.

THE HUMAN BODY

Digestive System

This organ system digests the food you eat: It breaks it down into basic parts, which can be transported and used by the body. The bits of food that your body cannot digest are expelled—as poop! It takes 1 to 3 days for food to travel from your mouth to the toilet.

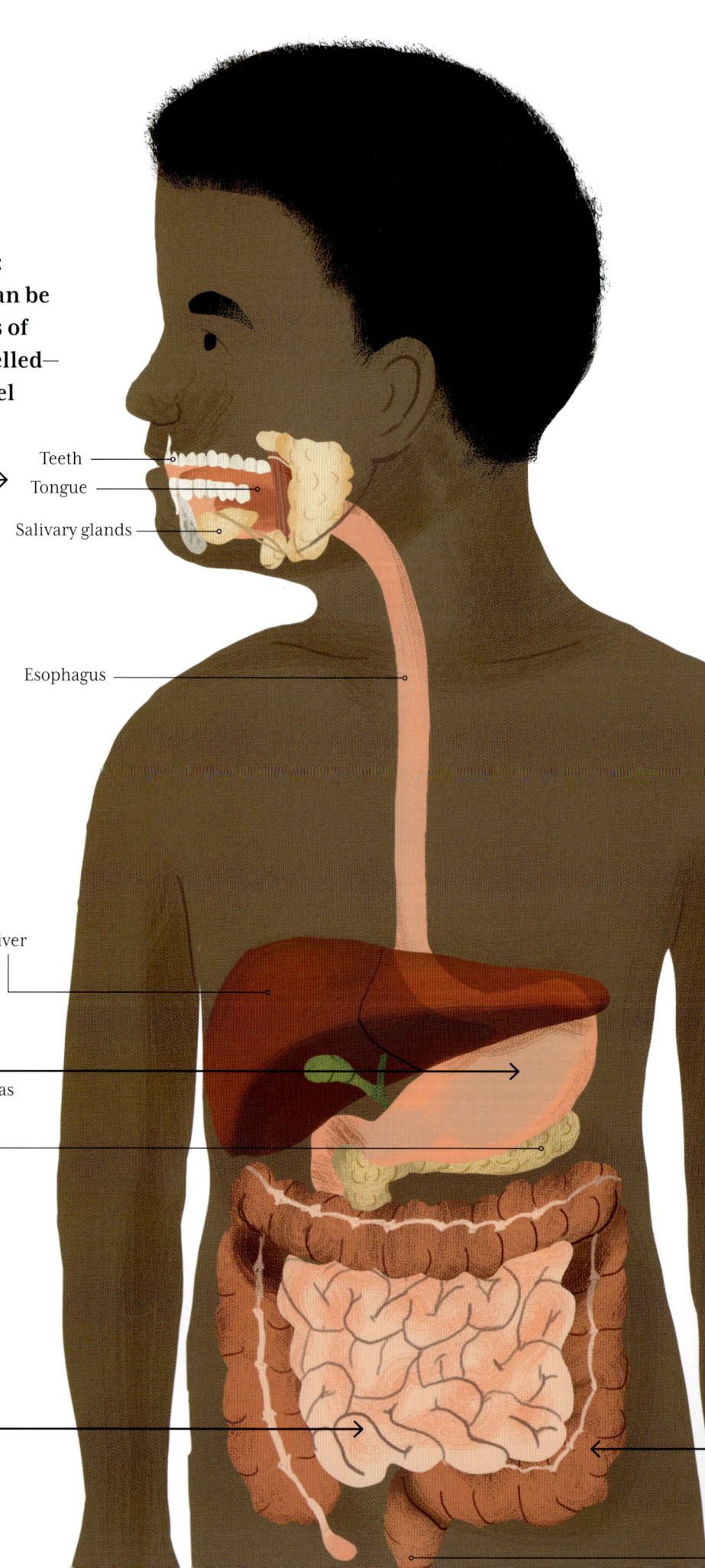

Teeth
Tongue
Salivary glands
Esophagus
Liver
Pancreas

MOUTH

Food is sliced by your sharp front teeth and ground by your flat back teeth. Salivary glands release saliva (spit) to soften food. As you swallow, your tongue moves food toward your throat, and you close a flap called the epiglottis to block the entrance to your windpipe (see page 166).

STOMACH

Swallowed food enters a tube called the esophagus, which squeezes food toward the stomach. Your stomach is a muscly bag, which tightens and relaxes to churn food. The stomach's walls make acid, which kills some bacteria, and chemicals called enzymes that break food up.

SMALL INTESTINE

When food is soupy, it trickles through a ring of muscle into the small intestine. Named for its narrowness, this intestine is around 2.5 cm (1 in) wide but 4 m (13 ft) long in an adult. Here food is broken down by a green liquid called bile, made by the liver, and more enzymes, made by the pancreas. As the intestine squeezes food along, its walls soak up nutrients and pass them into the blood.

THE HUMAN BODY

FOODS YOU NEED

If you are eating a variety of foods, including plenty of vegetables and fruits, your body is probably getting everything it needs to be healthy. A varied diet includes three types of foods: carbohydrate, protein, and fat. Enzymes in your digestive system break down these foods into essential nutrients.

Healthy fat is found in vegetable oils, nuts, seeds, and fish. It is broken into fatty acids and glycerol, which help your body store energy and make materials.

Healthy carbohydrate is found in whole grains (foods containing entire seeds, such as brown rice and whole wheat bread), vegetables, fruits, and beans. It is broken down into glucose, which is used by cells to make energy.

Healthy protein is found in fish, poultry, beans, nuts, cheese, and eggs. It is turned into amino acids, which are used for building new cells.

LARGE INTESTINE

The large intestine is around 7.5 cm (3 in) wide and 1.5 m (4.9 ft) long. Its walls soak up some water and the last nutrients. The large intestine's final section is called the rectum: This is where poop is stored until you go to the toilet.

Rectum

Scientist Profile
NAME   Marie Maynard Daly
DATES   1921–2003
NATIONALITY: American
BREAKTHROUGH
She discovered the effects of eating saturated fats, which are found in animal-based foods such as red meat and eggs. The body needs fats to build healthy cells, but in very large amounts saturated fats can cause arteries to clog up, causing heart problems in older people.

169

THE HUMAN BODY

A New Life

Your story began when you were a single cell, just 0.01 cm (0.004 in) across. Over the next nine months, maybe a little more or less, you developed into a beautiful newborn baby. A newborn has around 26 billion cells and is about 50 cm (20 in) long.

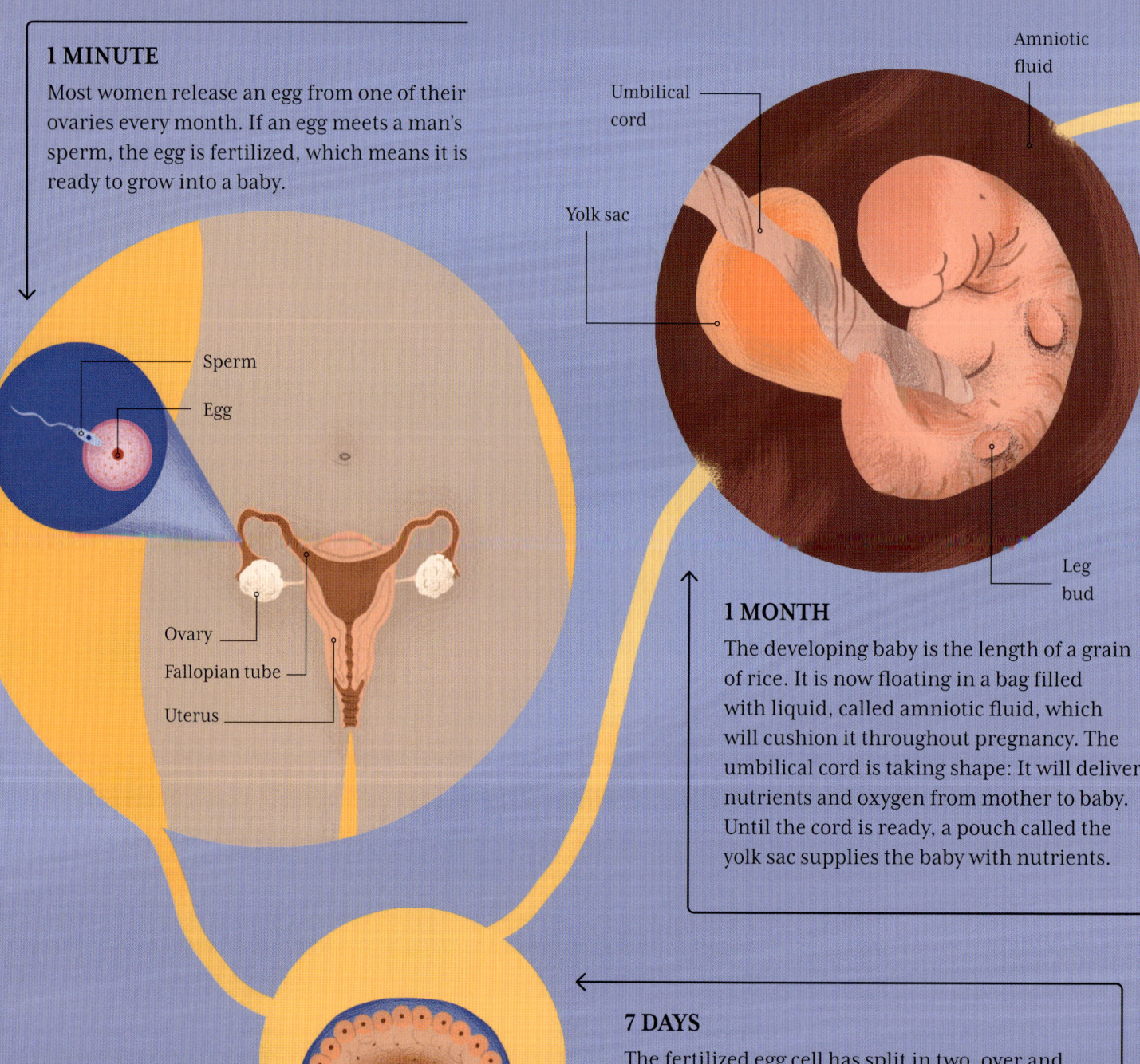

1 MINUTE
Most women release an egg from one of their ovaries every month. If an egg meets a man's sperm, the egg is fertilized, which means it is ready to grow into a baby.

1 MONTH
The developing baby is the length of a grain of rice. It is now floating in a bag filled with liquid, called amniotic fluid, which will cushion it throughout pregnancy. The umbilical cord is taking shape: It will deliver nutrients and oxygen from mother to baby. Until the cord is ready, a pouch called the yolk sac supplies the baby with nutrients.

7 DAYS
The fertilized egg cell has split in two, over and over again, making around 120 cells. An inner group of cells will develop into the baby, while an outer group will make the structures that protect it during pregnancy. The cluster of cells has journeyed down the fallopian tube and into a stretchy organ called the uterus. It has burrowed into the uterus wall so it can soak up nutrients.

THE HUMAN BODY

The average pregnancy lasts around nine months, but not every pregnancy is average. Pregnancies with twins—or triplets or more—are usually slightly shorter. Identical twins happen when a single egg develops into two similar-looking babies with nearly the same DNA (see page 144). Non-identical twins happen when a woman releases two eggs in one month, and each is fertilized.

Some parents need help from a doctor to get started with having a baby. The doctor may use a technique called in vitro fertilization (IVF), which is when the egg is fertilized with sperm in a laboratory, then placed in the woman's uterus to develop. Since the first IVF baby in 1978, more than 12 million heathy babies have been born using this method.

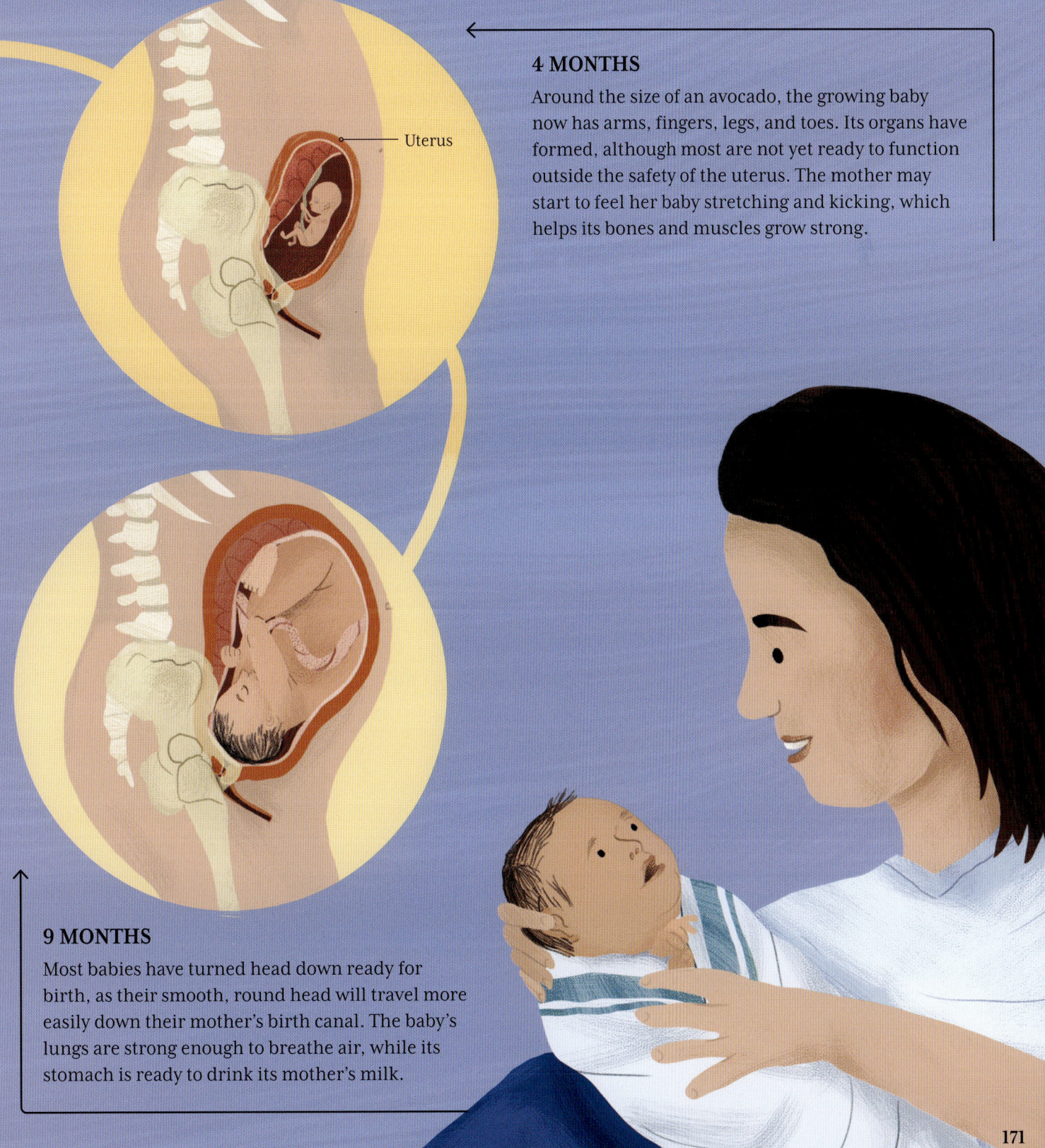

Uterus

4 MONTHS

Around the size of an avocado, the growing baby now has arms, fingers, legs, and toes. Its organs have formed, although most are not yet ready to function outside the safety of the uterus. The mother may start to feel her baby stretching and kicking, which helps its bones and muscles grow strong.

9 MONTHS

Most babies have turned head down ready for birth, as their smooth, round head will travel more easily down their mother's birth canal. The baby's lungs are strong enough to breathe air, while its stomach is ready to drink its mother's milk.

Animals

Amazing animals live in all our planet's habitats, from rain forests to deserts and cities to coral reefs. Scientists estimate that there are at least 20 quintillion (2 followed by 19 zeros) animals alive today. These animals belong to more than 1.5 million different species. Among the most common species are tiny ocean-living animals such as the Antarctic krill, which numbers in at least the trillions. Among the rarest species are the many animals at risk of extinction, such as the Bornean orangutan and axolotl. These animals have been endangered by—and can be protected by—the activities of the planet's smartest species: humans.

Around two-thirds of animals are meat-eaters, feeding on other animals—from insects to fish and mammals—at least part of the time. The world's deadliest killer is probably the largest animal of all, the 29.9-m (98-ft) long blue whale. It feeds on krill, consuming around 40 million in a single day and as many as 1 trillion in its 80-year life. The remaining third of animals feed on plants or living things such as seaweed or mushrooms. The world's biggest land animal, the 3.96-m (13-ft) tall African bush elephant, is a plant-eater. The elephant's great size protects it from predators and—since it has no need to run fast, hide, or leap to catch prey—does not prevent it from finding food.

Many insects, from bees to fruit flies, live for only the time taken to mature, mate, and lay eggs, which may be as little as 50 days. Yet many larger animals live for years, decades, or even centuries. Perhaps the longest lived is the slow-swimming, slow-growing Greenland shark, which may survive for up to 500 years. A tiny jellyfish, known as the immortal jellyfish, could live for longer, as it can regenerate itself by changing back into its immature form when it is old or sick. Yet it is likely to be eaten by a predator long before it reaches 500 years old. Like all the world's amazing animals, large and small, it is locked in a constant battle to feed, mate, and survive another day.

The axolotl is an amphibian that lives only in lakes and ditches around Mexico City, in Mexico. Fewer than 1,000 wild axolotls remain due to the water being polluted by human waste and chemicals from farms and factories.

Found in African grasslands and forests, the African bush elephant lives for 60 to 70 years, while the smaller giraffe and zebra live for around 25 years.

Animal Groups

Animals share some key characteristics. All animals must feed on other living things. They need the gas oxygen, which is used as fuel for turning food into energy. Animals must also take in water, which transports materials around the body. During at least part of an animal's life, it can move.

Scientists have divided animals into six groups, based on their shared characteristics: fish, amphibians, reptiles, birds, mammals, and invertebrates. Within these groups, animals are divided into smaller and smaller groups of more and more similar animals, such as classes, orders, families, and species.

A species is a group of animals that look and behave alike and can mate together to produce young. For example, humans are a species with the scientific name *Homo sapiens* (meaning "wise human" in Latin). Humans are in the family of great apes, in the order of primates, in the class of mammals.

BIRDS

Birds have a lightweight skeleton, feathers, and wings. Most, but not all, birds can fly. Birds have a toothless beak made of bone and keratin, the same material found in feathers, claws, scales, and hair. They have lungs for breathing air and lay hard-shelled eggs on land. See pages 222–227.

AMPHIBIANS

Amphibians usually hatch from a jelly-like egg in fresh water, where they soak up oxygen using gills. After going through changes known as metamorphosis, most amphibians develop lungs for taking oxygen from air and start to live on land. Amphibians have thin skin protected by a slippery liquid called mucus. See pages 194–195.

FISH

Fish are water-living animals that soak up oxygen from water using body parts called gills. Their skin is usually protected by small, hard plates called scales. Most fish have body parts called fins, which help with swimming. The majority of fish lay jelly-like eggs in water, but a few give birth to live babies. See pages 188–191.

REPTILES

Reptiles have lungs for breathing air. Some live in water but swim regularly to the surface to breathe. They have skin protected by scales or by larger, bonier plates called scutes. Most reptiles lay tough-shelled eggs on land, but some give birth to live young. See pages 198–203.

MAMMALS

Mammals grow hair during at least part of their life. Nearly all give birth to live young, which they feed on milk. Mammals have lungs (see page 166), so those that live in water return to the surface to breathe air. Mammals usually have four limbs, which may be adapted to walking, jumping, climbing, flying, or swimming. See pages 204–219.

INVERTEBRATES

Invertebrates—which make up 97 percent of all animals—do not have a backbone. They have many different body types and methods of taking oxygen from air or water. Common groups include insects such as butterflies and beetles, which have a hard covering, a three-part body, and six legs; cnidarians such as jellyfish and corals, which have stinging tentacles; and mollusks such as octopus and snails, which have a soft body that may be covered by a shell. See pages 178–187.

ANIMALS

Victory Beach

New Zealand's Victory Beach is named for the steamship *Victory*, which ran aground here in 1861. Visited by several endangered animals, the sandy beach is backed by dunes where pikao sedge and marram grass grow, while seaweeds such as bull kelp are washed ashore.

Victory Beach is a mating ground for birds and mammals, such as penguins and sea lions, that spend much of their life at sea but must return to land to lay eggs or give birth. Some shorebirds make the beach their permanent home. These birds have long legs for wading through shallow water and webbed feet so they do not sink into soft sand.

Many invertebrates here are burrowers, which gives protection from being washed away by waves or attacked by predators such as birds. These invertebrates usually have a regular pattern of burrowing and emerging to feed that matches the rising and falling of the tides.

PIED STILT

Named for its long, stilt-like legs, this bird feeds in shallow water, using its long, pointed beak to dig into sand for invertebrates. It nests on the ground among sand, pebbles, or grasses, where its eggs are camouflaged by yellow-brown blotchy shells.

ROYAL SPOONBILL

Also known by the Maori name *kotuku ngutupapa*, this long-legged wading bird feeds by swinging its partly open, spoon-shaped beak from side to side in shallow water. When it feels fish, shellfish, or crabs, it snaps them up.

ANIMALS

NEW ZEALAND SEA LION
This sea lion is endangered due to habitat loss and past hunting. Females come ashore to give birth, then walk their pups up to 2 km (1.2 miles) to inland forests to protect them from storms. Unlike seals, sea lions can walk on all fours by turning their back flippers forward.

YELLOW-EYED PENGUIN
This New Zealand penguin is endangered due to predators, such as cats, which were brought to the islands by humans. Unlike Antarctic penguins, which nest in large colonies, a pair of yellow-eyed penguins nests out of sight of others.

LUGWORM
The lugworm makes the worm-shaped coils of sand often seen on beaches. These coils are formed by the burrowing lugworm swallowing sand—to catch the tiny animals and waste it contains—and then pooping it out.

SANDHOPPER
Up to 2 cm (0.8 in) long, this jumping invertebrate spends the daytime buried in damp sand or in seaweed washed up on shore. It comes out at night to feed on decaying seaweed.

Beetles

These insects have two pairs of wings: a flexible interior pair used for flight and a tough exterior pair for protection. There are around 400,000 species of beetles, making up a quarter of all animal species. Many beetles play vital roles in their habitat, by helping to spread seeds and break down waste.

SILKY HIDDEN-HEAD LEAF BEETLE

This beetle feeds on wildflower pollen, particularly from yellow umbellifer flowers. Males are golden-green, and females are bronze. Their shining exoskeletons, which glint different shades from different angles, are believed to attract a mate and distract predators.

MINOTAUR BEETLE

After mating, this European dung beetle digs a tunnel up to 1.5 m (4.9 ft) deep, where it stores the dung (poop) of rabbits and other plant-eaters. The female lays eggs by the dung, which is eaten by the young larvae after hatching. By burying plant-eater dung, this beetle spreads seeds and returns plant nutrients to the soil, which helps new plants grow.

OHLONE TIGER BEETLE

Found only in the coastal grasslands of Santa Cruz County, California, in the United States, this beetle hunts for small prey in the patches of bare soil between tufts of grass. Its long legs help it run fast, while its large jaws—known as mandibles—grab wriggling prey.

PIE-DISH BEETLE

Found in the dry grasslands and shrublands of Australia, this beetle is named for its flattened body shape and the broad rims on its body and outer wings. These rims protect the beetle's head, legs, and underside from attack by predators such as spiders.

GIANT CARRION BEETLE

This North American beetle feeds on carrion (dead animals). A male and female carrion beetle bury a dead animal, such as a bird or rodent, then the female lays eggs beside the body, so that her larvae will have food after hatching. Adult carrion beetles bury themselves in soil to survive the winter cold.

ZAMBESI SCARAB BEETLE

This nocturnal dung beetle uses its sense of smell to find antelope dung, then rolls the dung quickly away, digs a burrow, and feasts on it. The beetle can roll its dung in a perfectly straight line across the savanna by navigating using patterns in moonlight that are invisible to human eyes.

Beetle Facts

ORDER	Beetles
CLASS	Insects
SIZE	0.03–13.5 cm (0.01–5.3 in) long
RANGE	Most land and freshwater habitats in the Americas, Europe, Africa, Asia, and Australasia
DIET	Plants, dung, carrion, and small invertebrates

ANIMALS

Cape Honeybee

This honeybee lives in the fynbos shrubland of South Africa's Western Cape. It plays a crucial role by pollinating many of the region's flowering plants. The fynbos is home to nearly 6,000 species of plants that are found nowhere else on Earth.

BUSY BEE

Like other honeybees, the Cape honeybee feeds on the pollen and nectar of flowering plants. As it feeds, pollen collects on its hair and is carried from one flower to another—allowing the plants to reproduce. The Cape honeybee lives in a hive with up to 80,000 other bees, known as a colony. Most bees in a colony are female worker bees, while a few hundred are male drone bees. Each colony has a larger queen bee.

Collector worker bees use a straw-like mouthpart, known as a proboscis, to suck nectar from flowers. After returning to the hive, the collectors give the nectar to house worker bees, which turn it into honey by drying it. As collector bees visit flowers, their hairy legs get covered with pollen, which collects in dips on their back legs known as pollen baskets. Worker bees eat as much pollen and nectar as they need, then store the rest in the hive.

LIFE IN A HIVE

Usually found in a hollow tree trunk, a honeybee hive is constructed from beeswax, which is made by glands on a worker bee's abdomen. The hive contains many hexagonal cells, in which the queen lays eggs. These hatch into wingless, legless larvae, which are fed a mix of pollen and nectar, called beebread, by nurse worker bees. After a week, the nurse bees close the cells, and the larvae pupate, a life stage when they change into adult bees.

Male drone bees live only long enough to mate with the queen. Worker bees live for a few months, while the queen may live for 3 or 4 years. When the queen grows old, nurse worker bees create a new queen by feeding some female larvae lots of a rich food made in glands on their head, called royal jelly. During winter, the colony stays in its hive and feeds on stored honey.

Cape Honeybee Facts

SUBSPECIES	*Apis mellifera capensis*
FAMILY	Bees
CLASS	Insects
SIZE	1–2 cm (0.4–0.8 in) long
RANGE	Southwestern South Africa in shrubland and farmland
DIET	Nectar and pollen

Some cells in a hive are used for housing eggs, larvae, and pupae, while others are used for storing pollen and honey.

ANIMALS

A honeybee has two sets of wings, which are attached to each other by tiny hooks. At the tip of its abdomen, a female bee has an adapted egg-laying organ, called an ovipositor, which can inject venom to give a "sting."

Crabs

There are around 4,500 species of crabs, which are decapod ("ten-footed") invertebrates. Crabs have a hard shell called an exoskeleton. They have eight walking legs, plus two front legs that end in pincers. Usually living in or around water, crabs can often be seen on shorelines.

RED ROCK CRAB

An inhabitant of rocky seashores, a female red rock crab carries her eggs on her body, stuck beneath her tail flap. When the spiny larvae hatch, she releases them into the ocean. After the larvae grow into young adults, they swim ashore. Young adults are black, keeping them camouflaged among rocks. As they grow, they shed their shell whenever it becomes too small, revealing a new, brighter shell beneath.

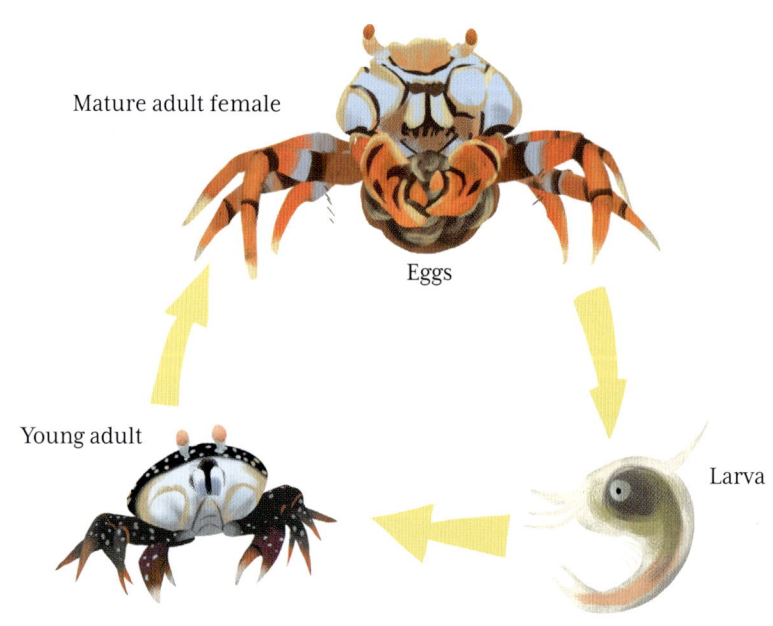

NORTHERN KELP CRAB

The northern kelp crab lives in the intertidal zone, in the area of shore that is above water at low tide and under water at high tide. It feeds on kelp and other seaweeds. Its shell has hook-shaped bristles, on which it sticks kelp so it can eat when it chooses.

VELVET SWIMMING CRAB

Named for its covering of short hairs, which looks like velvet, this crab can be recognized by its red eyes. It lives in tide pools and shallow water, where it swims using its flattened, paddle-like back legs. With its strong, sharp pincers, it seizes prey such as fish and prawns.

ANIMALS

ELEGANT FIDDLER CRAB
Male fiddler crabs have one pincer much larger than the other. The large pincer is used for fighting with other males. Females choose a mate with a big pincer that he can wave vigorously. These are signs that he is healthy and will dig a large burrow where the female can lay eggs.

HALLOWEEN CRAB
The Halloween crab digs a burrow among mangroves, sand dunes, or coastal rain forest in Central America. At night, it emerges to hunt for leaves to eat, climbing tree trunks to grasp twigs in its claws. It carries food back to its burrow, so it can eat in safety.

ATLANTIC GHOST CRAB
This well-camouflaged crab lives in a burrow that it digs with its pincers on a sandy seashore. It swivels its stalked eyes to keep a lookout. The crab enters the water only to release its larvae or moisten its gills. Like all crabs, it breathes through gills, which must be damp to soak up oxygen.

Crab Facts
INFRAORDER Crabs
ORDER Decapods
SIZE 0.01–3.7 m (0.03–12.1 ft) long
RANGE All oceans plus land and fresh water of all continents except Antarctica
DIET Algae, plants, invertebrates, fish, and waste

ANIMALS

Californian Chaparral

Shrubland known as chaparral covers around 121,000 sq km (47,000 sq miles) of California and Oregon, in the United States, and northern Mexico. The word "chaparral" comes from the Spanish for scrub oak, a small shrubby oak that reaches 1 to 2 m (3.3 to 6.6 ft) tall.

Despite cities and farms, wide stretches of California's coastal hills are chaparral. The summer here is very dry, with temperatures often higher than 37 °C (99 °F). Today, global warming is causing even drier summers, which lead to more wildfires, putting this habitat at risk.

Most chaparral plants, such as yuccas and creosote bushes, have hard leaves that can protect the water taken from their wide, deep roots. Chaparral animals have evolved to survive on little water, with many getting much of their water from eating plants.

GREATER ROADRUNNER
A member of the cuckoo order of birds, the strong-footed roadrunner walks more than it flies, reaching a speed of 32 km/h (20 miles per hour) as it runs after prey. It often eats lizards, venomous snakes, and tarantulas.

BLAINVILLE'S HORNED LIZARD
This lizard's wide, spiked body makes it harder for predators to swallow. In addition, it frightens predators away by pumping blood into the tissues around its eyes until they burst—spraying blood up to 1.2 m (4 ft).

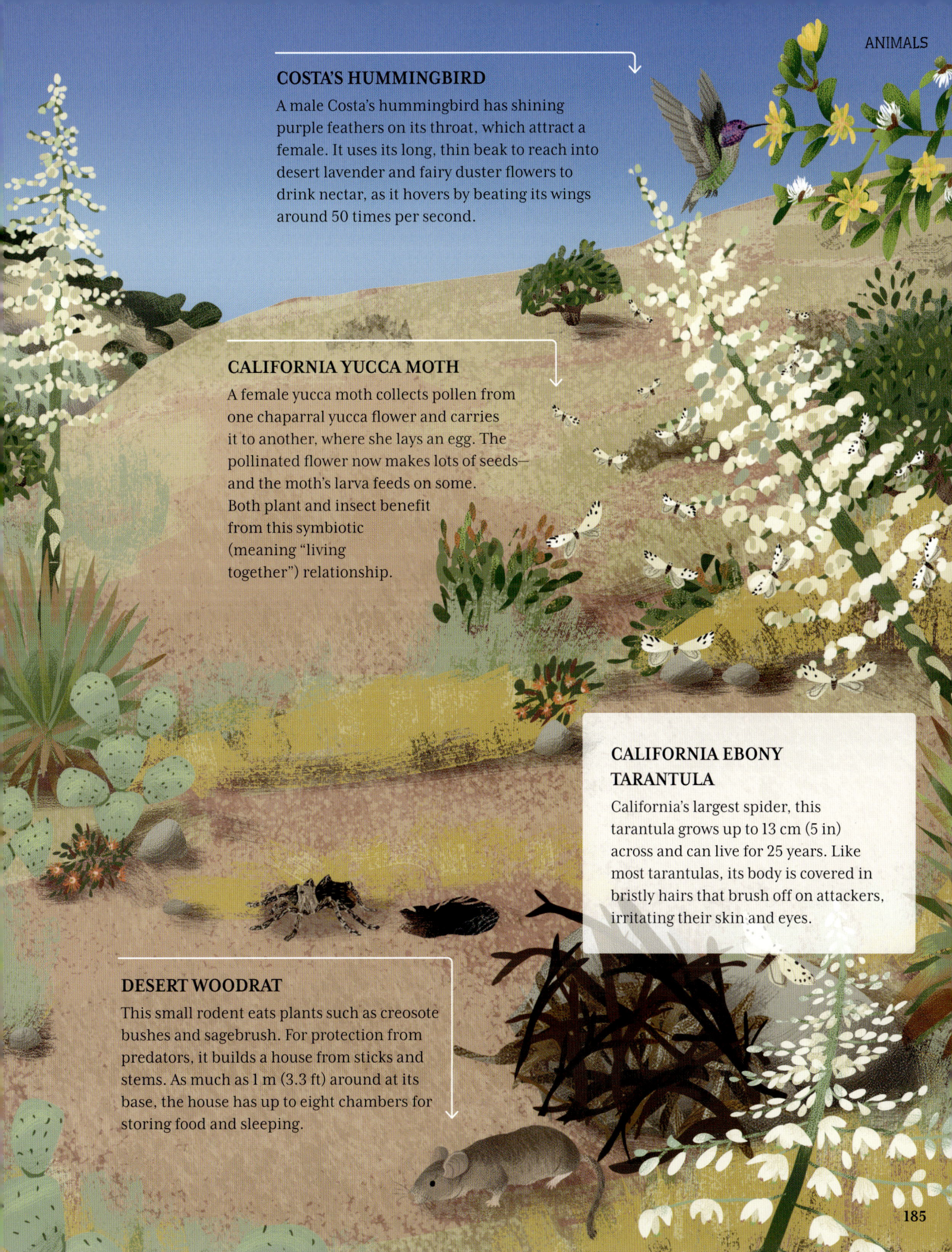

ANIMALS

COSTA'S HUMMINGBIRD
A male Costa's hummingbird has shining purple feathers on its throat, which attract a female. It uses its long, thin beak to reach into desert lavender and fairy duster flowers to drink nectar, as it hovers by beating its wings around 50 times per second.

CALIFORNIA YUCCA MOTH
A female yucca moth collects pollen from one chaparral yucca flower and carries it to another, where she lays an egg. The pollinated flower now makes lots of seeds—and the moth's larva feeds on some. Both plant and insect benefit from this symbiotic (meaning "living together") relationship.

CALIFORNIA EBONY TARANTULA
California's largest spider, this tarantula grows up to 13 cm (5 in) across and can live for 25 years. Like most tarantulas, its body is covered in bristly hairs that brush off on attackers, irritating their skin and eyes.

DESERT WOODRAT
This small rodent eats plants such as creosote bushes and sagebrush. For protection from predators, it builds a house from sticks and stems. As much as 1 m (3.3 ft) around at its base, the house has up to eight chambers for storing food and sleeping.

Jellyfish

These brainless invertebrates have stinging tentacles that inject prey with venom. Adult jellyfish, named medusas, have a soft, umbrella-shaped body known as a bell. In the middle of the bell is the jellyfish's mouth. Adults swim by squeezing their bell, pushing water behind them.

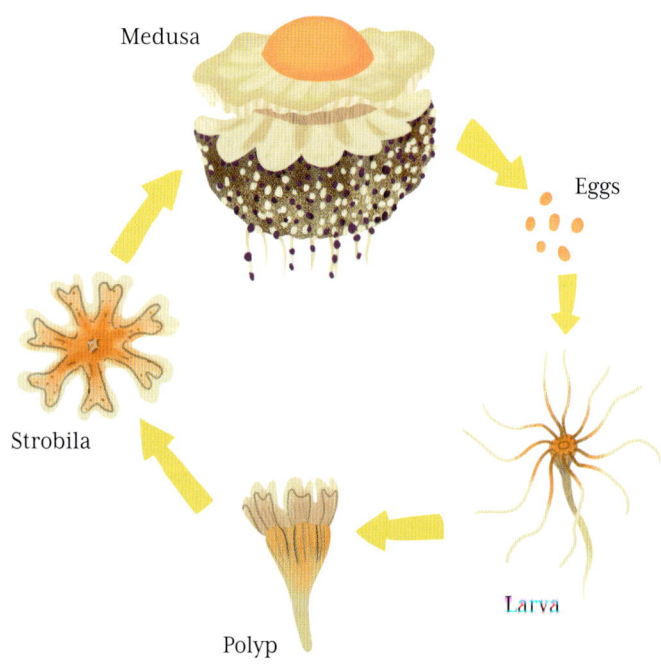

FRIED EGG JELLYFISH

Like other jellyfish, the fried egg has different body forms during its life. After hatching from its egg, it is a bean-shaped, swimming larva. The larva attaches to the seafloor, then turns into a stalk-shaped polyp, with upward-pointing tentacles. Plate-like segments grow then separate from the polyp, each one developing into a medusa.

ATOLLA JELLYFISH

Found in the deep, dark ocean, this jellyfish can make its own light, an ability known as bioluminescence. When the atolla is attacked, it gives a series of blue flashes, which not only startle the attacker but attract the attention of other predators that may attack the attacker.

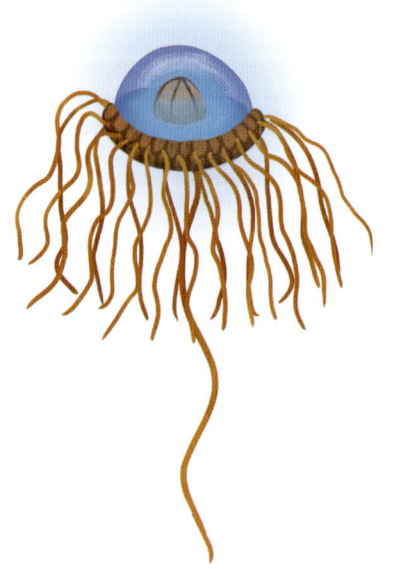

WHITE-SPOTTED JELLYFISH

Unlike most of its relatives, this jellyfish does not have venom strong enough to harm prey. Instead, it has clusters of small mouthlets around the base of its frilly oral ("mouth") arms. As the jellyfish swims, water containing tiny creatures flows into the bell—and the mouthlets swallow the food.

ANIMALS

LION'S MANE JELLYFISH

One of the largest jellyfish, the lion's mane has a bell more than 2 m (6.6 ft) wide. The bell has eight lobes, making it resemble an flower with eight petals. Each lobe has up to 150 tentacles, which trail behind the jellyfish to entangle fish and invertebrates.

CAULIFLOWER JELLYFISH

The cauliflower jellyfish's tentacles have stinging cells that inject some of the most powerful venom of any jellyfish. Each stinging cell houses a tiny needle-like stinger. When touched, the cell opens, letting water rush in. This makes the stinger shoot out, piercing prey and injecting the venom.

PURPLE-STRIPED JELLYFISH

This jellyfish has four frilly oral arms, as well as eight longer tentacles equipped with stinging cells. When the tentacles touch prey, they sting then bend toward the oral arms, passing them the stunned prey. An oral arm grasps the prey and squeezes it toward the mouth.

Jellyfish Facts

CLASS	True jellyfish
PHYLUM	Cnidarians
SIZE	0.05–36.6 m (0.16–120 ft) long
RANGE	All oceans as well as the brackish water of coastal lagoons and estuaries
DIET	Invertebrates, eggs, algae, and fish

ANIMALS

Red Sea Reef

Lying between the continents of Africa and Asia, the Red Sea is an inlet of the Indian Ocean. In the warm, shallow waters along its coasts are around 2,000 km (1,240 miles) of coral reef, which are home to about 200 species of coral and more than 1,200 fish species.

The Red Sea's warm, clear water makes it ideal for reef-building corals. The sea is one of the world's warmest bodies of sea water, with an average summer surface temperature of 28 °C (82 °F) and a winter temperature of 22 °C (72 °F).

However, the reef is at risk from global warming, which is causing a worldwide rise in sea temperatures. When the water gets hotter than 30 °C (86 °F), the coral polyps become stressed and expel the algae from which they get much of their energy. This results in an event known as coral bleaching, when the coral turns white, is weakened, and may fall victim to disease.

SOFTCORAL SEAHORSE

This fish curls its tail around coral while it waits for small prey to pass—then sucks hard through its long snout. A female seahorse lays her eggs in a pouch on the male's belly. When the babies hatch, the male "gives birth" by squeezing them out of his pouch.

FINGER CORAL

This coral and its relatives build much of the stone-like structure of the reef. Living in a colony of many thousands, each polyp builds a hard skeleton around its soft body, one on top of the other, forming a single branching structure. Each polyp, around 2 mm (0.08 in) across, extends tentacles to catch tiny floating animals.

ANIMALS

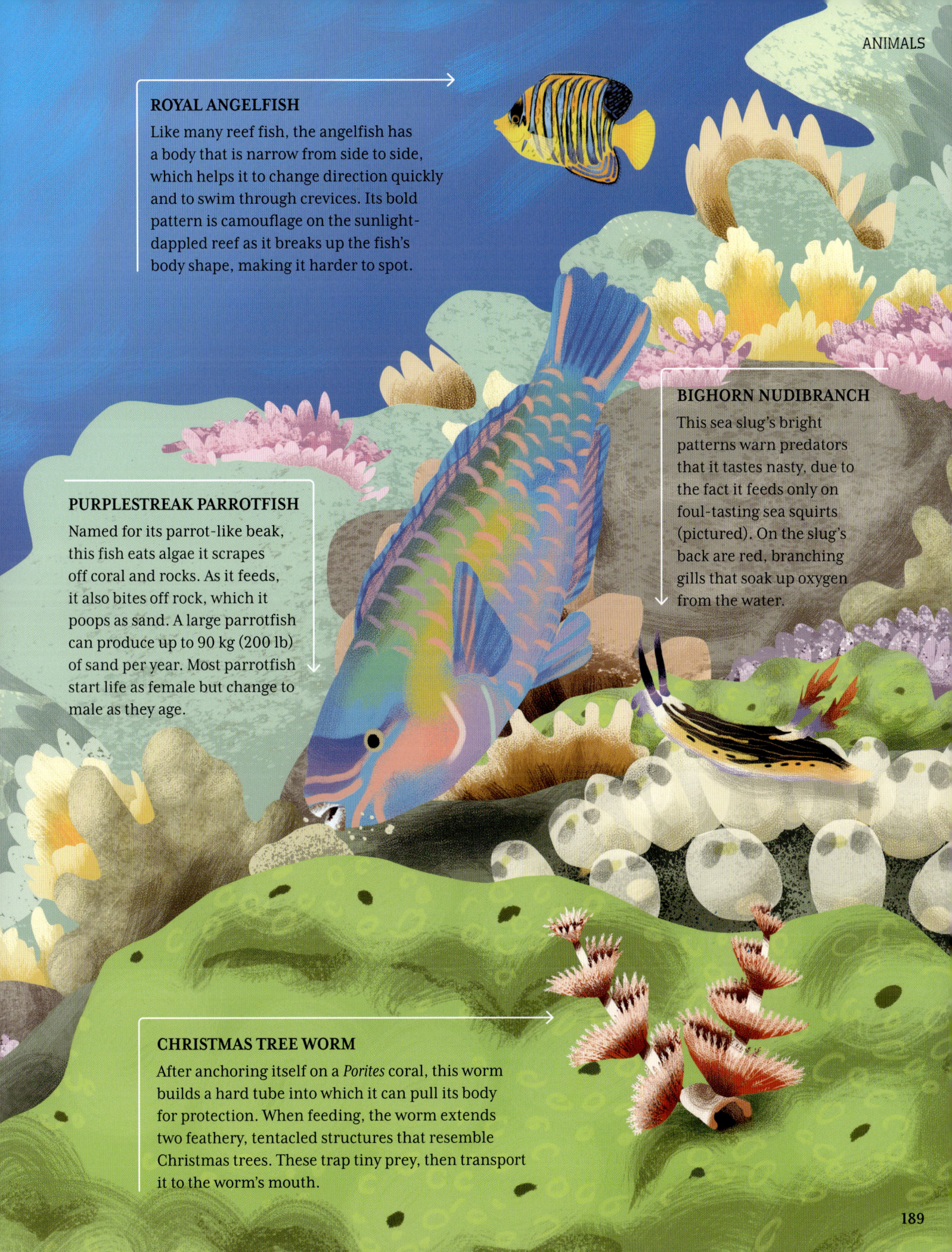

ROYAL ANGELFISH
Like many reef fish, the angelfish has a body that is narrow from side to side, which helps it to change direction quickly and to swim through crevices. Its bold pattern is camouflage on the sunlight-dappled reef as it breaks up the fish's body shape, making it harder to spot.

BIGHORN NUDIBRANCH
This sea slug's bright patterns warn predators that it tastes nasty, due to the fact it feeds only on foul-tasting sea squirts (pictured). On the slug's back are red, branching gills that soak up oxygen from the water.

PURPLESTREAK PARROTFISH
Named for its parrot-like beak, this fish eats algae it scrapes off coral and rocks. As it feeds, it also bites off rock, which it poops as sand. A large parrotfish can produce up to 90 kg (200 lb) of sand per year. Most parrotfish start life as female but change to male as they age.

CHRISTMAS TREE WORM
After anchoring itself on a *Porites* coral, this worm builds a hard tube into which it can pull its body for protection. When feeding, the worm extends two feathery, tentacled structures that resemble Christmas trees. These trap tiny prey, then transport it to the worm's mouth.

Sharks

Sharks are fish that—unlike most fish—have a skeleton made of bendy cartilage rather than bone. Nearly all sharks are hunters that track down prey using their keen senses. Some sharks swim in the open ocean, but others hunt in shallow water where there is plenty of food.

SIXGILL SAWSHARK

Sharks breathe by letting water flow into their mouth and through their gills, which soak up the water's oxygen. Water flows out of sharks' gill slits, on the sides of their body. Unlike most sharks, which have five gill slits, this shark has six. It also has a long, saw-like snout called a rostrum, with which it hits fish and stirs up sand in search of shrimp and crabs.

BLACKTIP REEF SHARK

Named for the black tips to its fins, this shark lives on coral reefs in the Pacific and Indian Oceans. Unlike most fish, which lay eggs, this shark gives birth to live young, called pups. The pups stay in very shallow water close to shore, where large predators cannot swim.

GREAT WHITE SHARK

Up to 6.1 m (20 ft) long, this shark has a sense of smell so powerful that it can smell one drop of blood in 10 billion drops of water. With its strong, flexible jaws, it can seize prey as large as seals and dolphins. It has 300 jagged-edged teeth arranged in rows, so when a front tooth falls out, the tooth behind moves forward to take its place.

GREAT HAMMERHEAD SHARK

The heads of sharks are dotted with tiny organs called ampullae of Lorenzini, which detect the electric charges given off by all animals as they move. Due to this shark's hammer-shaped head, its ampullae cover a wider area, so it can sense the movements even of prey buried in sand.

HORN SHARK

This small shark has a sharp spine at the front of each of its two dorsal (back) fins. If attacked, the horn shark jabs with its spines. The shark spends much of its time on the seafloor, where its big nostrils help it smell prey and its large, high eyes can see over surrounding coral.

BANDED WOBBEGONG

This flat-bodied shark lies motionless among coral, where it is camouflaged by its blotchy skin and fringe of algae-like skin flaps. The flaps also have sensitive cells that help the shark smell prey. When prey comes close, the wobbegong sucks the creature into its large mouth.

Shark Facts

SUPERORDER	Sharks
CLASS	Cartilaginous fish
SIZE	0.2–18.8 m (0.7–61.7 ft) long
RANGE	All oceans plus some rivers in the Americas, Africa, and Asia
DIET	Invertebrates, fish, birds, seals, dolphins, and turtles

ANIMALS

Amazon Rain Forest

The world's largest rain forest, the Amazon covers 5.5 million sq km (2.1 million sq miles) around South America's Amazon River. The forest is home to more than 1 million species of insects, 1,290 birds, 420 mammals, 420 amphibians, and 370 reptiles.

Brazil nut, kapok, and angelim trees are among the tallest emergent trees, growing up to 88.5 m (290 ft) high and living for hundreds of years. Many animals of the emergent layer have wings, including birds, bats, and butterflies.

In the thick canopy below, fruit-eating birds call loudly to communicate with each other through the screen of leaves. Hiding quietly in the dimly lit understory are hungry hunters and their prey, while plant- and insect-eaters snuffle through leaf litter on the forest floor.

WHITE-THROATED TOUCAN
Up to 60 cm (24 in) long, this bird uses its huge beak to reach for fruit as it sits on a tree branch. A toucan communicates with its flock using croaks, barks, and growls, as well as by clattering its beak.

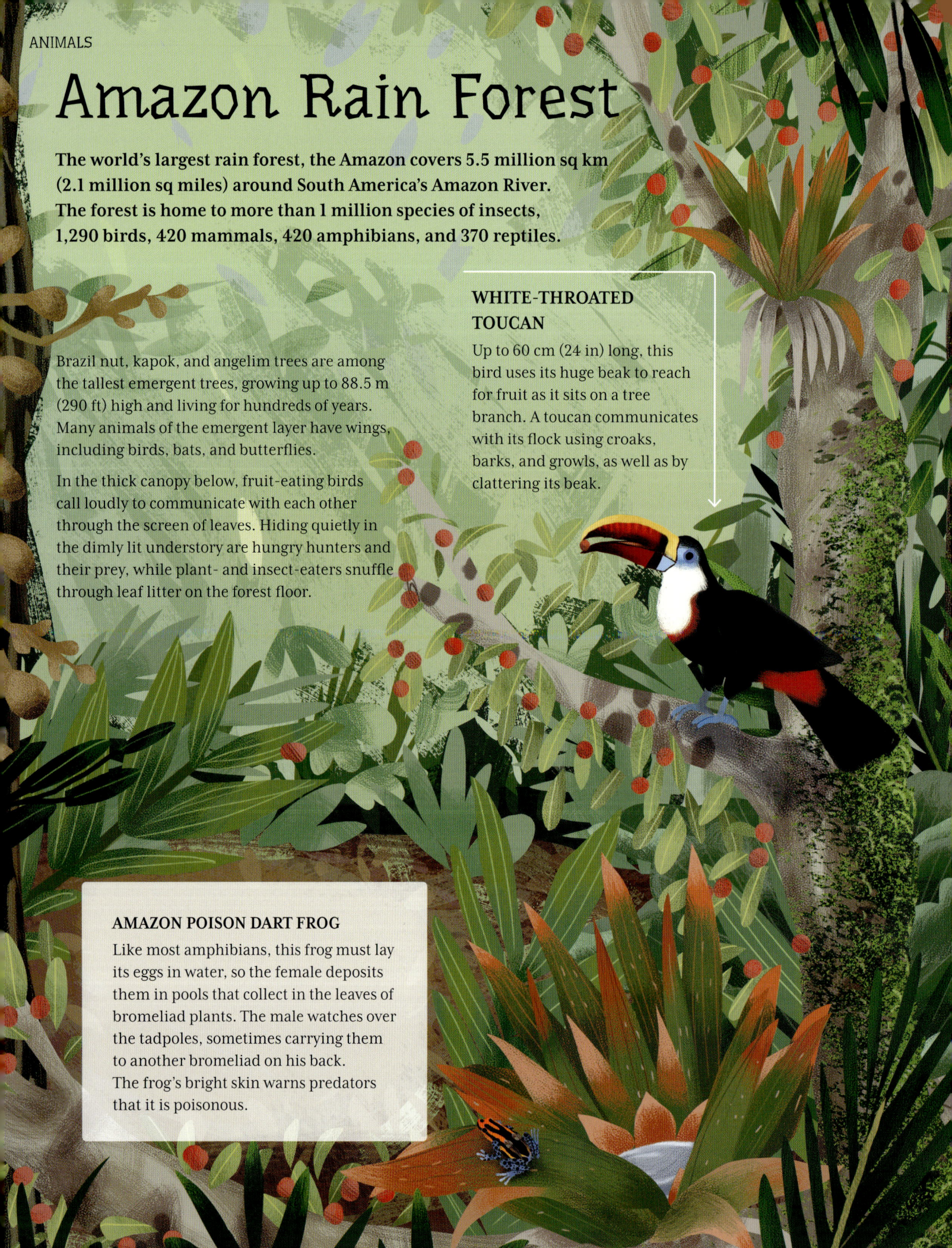

AMAZON POISON DART FROG
Like most amphibians, this frog must lay its eggs in water, so the female deposits them in pools that collect in the leaves of bromeliad plants. The male watches over the tadpoles, sometimes carrying them to another bromeliad on his back. The frog's bright skin warns predators that it is poisonous.

ANIMALS

SCARLET MACAW

This parrot grasps fruits, nuts, and insects with its large, hooked beak. It often flies in a squawking flock, with the bright patches on the birds' plumage making it hard for predators—such as eagles and hawks—to spot the outline of a single bird.

RHETENOR BLUE MORPHO

Measuring 10 cm (4 in) across, this butterfly's wings have bright blue uppersides and brown undersides. As the butterfly flaps, the flickering between blue and brown is hard for a butterfly-eating bird to focus on.

SOUTH AMERICAN TAPIR

This mammal uses it long, bendy, muscular snout to reach for shoots, leaves, fruit, and seeds. It often bathes in water or mud to stay cool and wash insects off its body.

JAGUAR

The jaguar is the Amazon's apex predator ("top hunter"), since it is too fierce to have predators of its own. It hides among the understory vegetation as it waits for an animal such as an anteater or tapir to pass—then it kills with a bite to the skull.

Frogs

These amphibians have large eyes, long back legs suited to jumping, and no tail. They usually lay their eggs in fresh water. Young frogs, known as tadpoles, live in water. Most adult frogs live on land but stay close to fresh water or inhabit damp forests.

Frog

Frog spawn

Tadpole

STRIPED MARSH FROG

Like nearly all frogs, the striped marsh frog goes through changes known as metamorphosis. Eggs, known as frog spawn, are laid in a pond or ditch. After hatching, the tadpoles have a tail and no legs. They swim in the water, feed on algae, and take oxygen from water using body parts called gills. Over several months, the tadpoles grow legs, lose their tail, and develop lungs for taking oxygen from air. Their mouth grows wider for eating insects and slugs.

BRAZILIAN HORNED FROG

Using its strong, sticky tongue, this 30-cm- (12-in-) long frog grabs prey as large as mice. Its wide mouth has sharp teeth in the upper jaw. The frog's leaflike horns and green-yellow pattern help it hide in marshes and wet leaves. Its bulky body and short legs make it a slow crawler rather than a speedy hopper.

MADAGASCAR TOMATO FROG

Named for its red skin, this frog is found in marshes, swamps, and ponds. Its bright shade warns predators that it is poisonous, since venom seeps from its skin. When threatened, this frog also puffs up its body, making itself more frightening and more difficult to swallow.

ANIMALS

INDIAN BULLFROG
Up to 17 cm (6.7 in) long, this frog often lives in holes in flooded rice fields. In the mating season, the skin of male Indian bullfrogs changes from olive green to bright yellow, with blue vocal sacs. The sound of the male's mating calls bounces around inside these elastic throat sacs, making them louder. Brighter, louder males find more mates.

ISHIKAWA'S TORRENT FROG
Most wetland frogs are found around still or slow-moving water, but this Japanese frog lives around swift-flowing mountain streams and waterfalls. It lays its eggs on wet, mossy rocks on the banks. The tadpoles stay in the safety of rock pools, so that they are not washed away.

SOUTHERN LEOPARD FROG
This nocturnal frog lives around ponds, swamps, and flooded caves and mines in North America. Only 9 cm (3.5 in) long, its strong back legs let it jump up to 90 cm (3 ft). Females lay 1,500 eggs on water plants, often in a mass with the eggs of other females to keep them warm.

Frog Facts
ORDER	Frogs
CLASS	Amphibians
SIZE	0.7–32 cm (0.3–12.6 in) long
RANGE	All continents except Antarctica but absent from some isolated islands
DIET	Insects, worms, snails, frogs, mice, and snakes

ANIMALS

Sahara Desert

The world's largest hot desert, the Sahara covers 9.2 million sq km (3.6 million sq miles) of North Africa. Most of the region is rocky, but in sandy areas known as ergs, dunes soar to 180 m (590 ft) high. On summer days, the sand can be heated to 80 °C (176 °F).

In most of the Sahara Desert, the average daily temperature is more than 25 °C (77 °F). However, when the Sun sets, the lack of cloud cover means the air cools swiftly. Nights are always 13 to 20 °C (23 to 36 °F) cooler than days.

Many Saharan animals are nocturnal, staying in the shade or underground during the heat of day, then emerging at night to eat. Most are well camouflaged by dappled or sandy fur, feathers, or scales, which helps them go unnoticed among dunes and rocks.

FENNEC FOX
The smallest member of the dog family, this fox has huge ears. These help it stay cool because their large surface loses lots of body heat to the air. The fox's foot pads have thick fur to protect them from hot sand.

WEST AFRICAN CROCODILE
During dry periods, this crocodile digs a burrow and becomes dormant, sleeping so deeply that its body processes slow. After rain, it gathers with other crocodiles at a guelta, a pocket of water that collects in a valley.

ANICALS

DROMEDARY CAMEL
The dromedary stores fat in its hump, surviving on this energy for up to 2 months if it cannot find plants to eat. Thick eyebrows shade its eyes from sunlight, while long eyelashes protect them from wind-blown sand.

ADDAX
This antelope gets its water from plants and the dew that forms when the temperature drops at night. Cold air can hold less water than hot air, so droplets of dew collect on plants. The addax's pale fur reflects the Sun's heat so it stays cooler.

NORTHWEST AFRICAN CHEETAH
After sunset, this cheetah hunts antelopes, running at 100 km/h (62 miles per hour) as it gives chase. It can survive without drinking as long as it eats, since mammal blood is around 90 percent water.

DEATHSTALKER SCORPION
Up to 7.5 cm (3 in) long, the deathstalker has a curving tail ending in a sharp stinger that injects deadly venom into prey or predators. The scorpion's strong pincers are used for grasping and crushing prey such as insects and other scorpions.

American Alligator

The American alligator is an apex predator in freshwater marshes and swamps in the southeastern United States. It belongs to an order of large, strong reptiles known as crocodilians, which also includes crocodiles, caimans, and gharials.

ALLIGATOR LIFE

Like other crocodilians, the American alligator spends part of its life on land and part in water, where it swims by swinging its muscular tail. It hunts both in water and on land—and will even jump up to 1.5 m (5 ft) into the air to reach birds. The alligator's long snout contains up to 80 sharp, cone-shaped teeth, which give one of the most powerful bites of any animal. Its bite force is more than 13,000 Newtons, with 1 Newton being the force needed to throw a weight of 1 kg (2.2 lb) a distance of 1 m (3.3 ft) in 1 second.

A female American alligator lays 20 to 50 eggs in a nest built from leaves and mud near water. She covers the eggs with leaves, which heat as they rot, keeping the eggs warm. Eggs kept at between 32.5 °C and 33.5 °C (90.5 °F and 92.3 °F) will produce males, while cooler or hotter eggs produce females. The female stays nearby to protect the eggs until they hatch.

A KEY ANIMAL

The American alligator is known as a keystone species, which is an animal that has a great effect on the other animals in its habitat. This is partly because the alligator is the largest predator in its habitat, but also because it makes important changes to the habitat. Using its feet and snout, the alligator digs ponds known as alligator holes. Water remains in these ponds in the dry season, so the alligator can stay cool. Yet the ponds also provide a place for small water-living animals—such as fish, turtles, and frogs—to survive the dry season, although some also become food for the alligator.

American Alligator Facts

- **SPECIES** *Alligator mississippiensis*
- **FAMILY** Alligators and caimans
- **CLASS** Reptiles
- **SIZE** 3.4 to 4.8 m (11.2 to 15.7 ft) long
- **RANGE** Southeastern United States from Texas to North Carolina
- **DIET** Fish, turtles, frogs, birds, snakes, and mammals from raccoons to Florida panthers

A young alligator, called a hatchling, will remain with its mother for up to 2 years.

The American alligator rests on a log or bank to warm itself in the sunshine after swimming. Its tough skin is protected by bony plates covered with horn.

Snakes

Snakes are legless reptiles with wide-opening jaws for swallowing prey. Some snakes make venom, a poison injected into prey with sharp, hollow fangs. Other snakes swallow prey alive or kill prey by coiling tightly around it.

NUBIAN SPITTING COBRA
Like all venomous snakes, the spitting cobra makes venom in glands behind its eyes. As well as injecting venom into prey, this snake defends itself by spraying venom from the front of its fangs, blinding an attacker if the venom enters the eyes. By squeezing muscles around its glands, the snake squirts venom up to 2 m (6.6 ft).

ARIZONA CORAL SNAKE
Unlike most other desert snakes, which are shaded to blend in with desert sand, coral snakes are strikingly patterned. The easy-to-remember pattern warns that the snake is venomous, so predators, such as birds of prey, do not attack. This strategy is known as aposematism (from the ancient Greek for "away sign").

MOJAVE DESERT SIDEWINDER
This rattlesnake has a style of movement suited to slippery, shifting sand: sidewinding. It moves its body in a wave-like pattern, curving both vertically and sideways, which pushes it forward at a diagonal angle. To warn away predators, it shakes horny segments at the tip of its tail, making a rattling noise.

ANIMALS

INLAND TAIPAN

Found in Australia, the inland taipan has the most powerful venom of any snake. The venom it injects with just one bite could kill 100 adult humans. However, this shy snake usually only bites small mammals, such as long-haired rats, which die almost instantly.

SAHARAN HORNED VIPER

This venomous snake lies partly buried in sand until birds or rodents approach—then it bites, holding prey in its mouth until the venom has taken effect. The tall scales above the snake's eyes, known as horns, may protect its eyes from blown sand.

DESERT ROSY BOA

Like many snakes, this species changes its activities depending on the temperature. In the heat of summer, it spends the day beneath rocks. In the cooler night, it hunts for rats and mice, which it circles in its coils until they stop breathing. In winter, when the temperature falls in its North American home, the snake moves into a period of sleep and inactivity known as brumation.

Snake Facts

SUBORDER	Snakes
CLASS	Reptiles
SIZE	0.1–6.95 m (0.3–22.8 ft) long
RANGE	All continents except Antarctica; the Indian and Pacific Oceans
DIET	Lizards, frogs, small mammals, birds, eggs, fish, and invertebrates

Green Sea Turtle

This reptile has paddle-like limbs, a beaklike mouth, and a body covered by a strong shell called a carapace. It can stay underwater for up to 2 hours before swimming to the surface to breathe. It is usually found in warm, shallow coastal waters, where it feeds on seagrasses.

An adult green sea turtle rips seagrasses using the hard, jagged edge of its beak.

ALL IN THE NAME

The green sea turtle gets its name from the green body fat found under an adult's carapace. This fat is tinged green by the turtle's diet of seagrasses. However, young sea turtles live in deeper waters, where they feed on animals such as jellyfish, crabs, and worms. The different diets of young and adult turtles may be helpful in preventing competition for food.

A LONG LIFE

Green sea turtles live for up to 80 years. They are mature enough to mate when they reach around 25 years old. In time for the mating season, adult male and female sea turtles return to the shallow water near the beach

where they were born. This may mean a journey of up to 2,600 km (1,600 miles) between the turtle's feeding and mating sites. Yet this journey is worthwhile because the turtles know they will find a mate and a warm, sandy beach suitable for egg-laying. Scientists think that turtles find their way by sensing Earth's magnetic field, since the planet's iron-rich core makes it a magnet with a north and south pole.

When a female is ready to lay eggs, she uses her back flippers to dig a hole on the beach, in a dry spot above the high tide. After laying up to 200 eggs, she buries them with sand. She may make up to five such nests in each mating season, before swimming back to her feeding site.

After 50 to 70 days, the eggs hatch all at once during the night. The baby turtles, called hatchlings, climb out of the sand and make their way to the water, instinctively knowing which direction to take. Despite the darkness, this is a dangerous journey, since predators such as gulls and crabs may be watching.

A green turtle hatchling is around 5 cm (2 in) long. Only around one in every hundred is likely to live to maturity.

Green Sea Turtle Facts
- **SPECIES** *Chelonia mydas*
- **FAMILY** Sea turtles
- **CLASS** Reptiles
- **SIZE** 0.9 to 1.5 m (3 to 4.9 ft) long
- **RANGE** Warm regions of the Atlantic, Indian, and Pacific Oceans
- **DIET** Seagrasses, algae, small invertebrates, and fish eggs

ANIMALS

Arctic Sea Ice

In winter, when the air temperature can drop to -69 °C (-93 °F), ice covers most of the Arctic Ocean, around 15 million sq km (5.8 million sq miles). Much of the sea ice melts in spring and summer, shrinking to around 4 million sq km (1.5 million sq miles).

Up to 20 m (65.6 ft) thick, sea ice provides resting places for seals and walruses. These ocean-living mammals, which must breathe oxygen from air, also give birth on the ice. Hunting seabirds perch on the sea ice, while even a few land-living mammals venture there in search of food.

Global warming has shrunk the Arctic sea ice: In summer, it is around 13 percent smaller than 10 years ago. This has increased the distance that animals must swim to reach resting, feeding, and birthing spots, as well as cutting off migration routes for land-living mammals.

WALRUS
The walrus has four flippers and a streamlined body suited to swimming. It spends much of its time resting on the ice between dives in search of clams, snails, and worms. The walrus uses its tusks, which are extra-long teeth, for climbing onto the slippery ice and making holes in it.

NARWHAL
The narwhal is a whale, a mammal that spends its entire life in water. In winter, the narwhal dives for fish beneath the ice. Every 25 minutes, it surfaces to breathe at a crack. Male narwhals and a few females have a tusk, up to 3.1 m (10.2 ft) long, which males probably use to attract females.

ANIMALS

PEARY CARIBOU

This deer lives on the islands of the Canadian Arctic. It uses sea ice as a bridge between its winter and summer feeding grounds on different islands. These movements also let caribou from different islands mate with each other, so the population stays large and healthy.

IVORY GULL

During winter, this seabird lives near a polynya, an area of open ocean water surrounded by sea ice. It seizes fish from the water, but also follows polar bears to feed on their leftovers.

ARCTIC FOX

This fox has thick fur, which also covers the pads of its feet. Its body is compact, while its ears and legs are short, so it has less surface from which to lose body heat. In winter, it follows polar bears over the sea ice, so it can eat the remains of their kills.

HARP SEAL

A female harp seal gives birth to one pup each February. An adult has silver and black fur, but a newborn's fur is white for camouflage on the sea ice. A mother feeds her pup on milk for 12 days before returning to the water to hunt. The pup must survive on its stored body fat until it can hunt, at 4 weeks old.

ANIMALS

Polar Bear

The world's largest land-living meat-eater, a polar bear can weigh as much as 700 kg (1,500 lb)—more than eight adult men. Although polar bears are usually born on land, they spend most of their life on the Arctic sea ice, where they hunt for seals.

SEAL HUNTER

The polar bear uses its powerful sense of smell to find the holes in sea ice where seals come up for air or to rest. The bear waits nearby, barely moving for perhaps several hours, as it waits for a seal to appear. Then the bear uses a front paw, which is armed with sharp claws, to drag the seal onto the ice. The bear kills with its strong jaws, which have 42 jagged-edged teeth.

A polar bear is well suited to its life on the sea ice. Its paws are up to 30 cm (12 in) wide, spreading the bear's weight so the ice does not crack as it walks. The paws are also effective paddles when the bear swims between ice floes. The bear is kept warm by a 10-cm- (4-in-) thick layer of body fat, as well as long, pale fur that acts as camouflage.

Polar bears often prey on ringed seals, as well as harp, common, hooded, and bearded seals. After eating, a polar bear washes itself with water or snow.

ANIMALS

Mother polar bears are protective of their cubs, fighting off predators such as male bears. Mothers make a chuffing noise when young cubs wander too far away.

BEAR CUBS

Adult polar bears usually live alone, but males and females meet at seal resting spots during the mating season. After mating, the female eats extra food so that she gains fat. When preparing to give birth, she usually goes ashore, where she digs a den in a snowdrift. A narrow entrance tunnel leads to a chamber where, protected from cold and wind, she normally gives birth to two cubs.

For the first 3 months, mother and cubs stay in their den. Toothless and helpless, the cubs are fed on their mother's milk while she lives off her stored fat. When the pups weigh at least 10 kg (22 lb), their mother leads them to the sea ice, where she hunts for food for them all. The cubs learn to hunt by copying their mother. After around 2.5 years, cubs are left to care for themselves.

Polar Bear Facts

- **SPECIES** *Ursus maritimus*
- **FAMILY** Bears
- **CLASS** Mammals
- **SIZE** 1.8–3 m (5.9–9.8 ft) long
- **RANGE** Arctic Ocean and northern coasts of North America, Europe, and Asia
- **DIET** Seals as well as walruses, musk oxen, fish, birds, eggs, and plants

Rodents

Out of around 4,000 species of mammals, 1,500 are rodents. These mammals have long, sharp front teeth that grow continuously, but are worn down by gnawing food and burrowing. Most rodents are small animals with short limbs and long tails.

NORTHERN FLYING SQUIRREL

This forest-living rodent can glide from higher to lower tree branches due to a thick fold of skin, called a patagium, which runs from each front leg to back leg. When gliding, the flying squirrel spreads its limbs wide, forming a parachute. Its longest glides are more than 45 m (148 ft).

RED SQUIRREL

The red squirrel uses its long tail for balance as it jumps from tree branch to branch. In parts of Great Britain, Ireland, and Italy, this squirrel has been driven out by the eastern gray squirrel, which was brought from North America by humans. Gray squirrels are larger and carry diseases that kill red squirrels but not themselves.

NORTH AMERICAN PORCUPINE

A porcupine has 30,000 quills growing from its skin, apart from on its face, belly, and feet. Quills are thick, hard hairs that are formed into sharp spines. When threatened, a porcupine raises its quills, so that they stick into an attacker's skin—and stay stuck long after detaching from the porcupine.

ANIMALS

NORTHERN RED-BACKED VOLE

Like many other rodents, this vole is camouflaged among trees, rocks, and soil by its dappled brown fur. It nests in a short burrow or beneath a rock. In winter, it stays active by building tunnels beneath the snow that covers its northern forest home, which gives protection from cold and predators such as foxes.

EASTERN DEER MOUSE

This deer mouse makes a nest of grass and moss in tall, hollow trees of North American forests. During the safety of night, it emerges to hunt for seeds, leaves, spiders, and caterpillars. During the winter cold, the deer mouse shares a nest with up to ten others.

SIBERIAN CHIPMUNK

In winter, this chipmunk stays in its underground burrow, where it has stored 3–4 kg (6.6–8.8 lb) of seeds. This food is transported in pouches in the chipmunk's cheeks, which can reach the size of the chipmunk's body when full. The burrow, up to 2.5 m (8.2 ft) long and with separate storage and waste areas, is often shared with another chipmunk.

Rodent Facts

ORDER	Rodents
CLASS	Mammals
SIZE	12–134 cm (5–53 in) long
RANGE	All continents except Antarctica but also absent from some islands
DIET	Seeds, stems, leaves, nuts, insects, worms, and other small animals

Lion

This big cat once roamed across Africa, southern Europe, and southwestern Asia. Today, humans have driven lions from everywhere except savanna and shrubland in Africa and western India. Most lions live in family groups called prides, but young adults may spend years hunting alone before joining a pride.

LIFE IN A PRIDE

Male lions are larger than females, which are called lionesses. When males are around a year old, they start to grow longer hair on their head, shoulders, and chest, called a mane. Healthier, older males have darker and thicker manes. A thick mane may protect the neck from teeth and claws during fights with other males, but it is probably most useful for attracting females. When choosing a mate, lionesses prefer lions with thick manes.

Lions spend around 20 hours a day sleeping or resting, often in the shade of a tree. When the temperature falls at dusk, lions wake and begin to play or groom each other with their tongues.

On the African savanna, lions often hunt blue wildebeest. Lions can open their jaws to up 28 cm (11 in) wide, then stab with sharp canines 7 cm (3 in) long.

SKILLED HUNTERS

Most hunting is done around dusk and dawn, when the temperature is lower than in the heat of day. Lions stalk prey by closing in slowly and silently, relying on their golden fur and the dim light for camouflage among the dry grass.

When lions are close to their prey, they make a sudden rush and leap, killing with a bite to the throat. Male lions hunt alone, but much of a pride's hunting is done by groups of lionesses. Each lioness plays a particular role in hunts, such as stalking prey on the left or right. Usually, food is shared with the rest of the pride.

A lioness gives birth to up to four cubs in a den among rocks or shrubs. For the first six months, she feeds the cubs on her milk.

Lion Facts
- **SPECIES** *Panthera leo*
- **FAMILY** Cats
- **CLASS** Mammals
- **SIZE** 2.3–3 m (7.5–9.8 ft) long
- **RANGE** Africa south of the Sahara Desert, and western India
- **DIET** Mammals including blue wildebeest, plains zebras, giraffes, and deer

ANIMALS

Australian Eucalyptus Forest

Eucalyptus forest covers around 1 million sq km (385,000 sq miles) of Australia. There are over 700 species of eucalyptus trees and shrubs, most of them evergreen, with names such as river red gum, stringybark, and silvertop ash.

Eucalyptus forests are often in areas with long, dry summers where wildfires are common. Yet many eucalyptus trees resprout quickly after a fire. Others have seeds that are cracked open by the heat of fire and start to grow in the sunlit space cleared by the blaze.

Animals of the eucalyptus forests can sense fires before humans do. They flee by flying, hopping, or running to gullies or rivers, climbing higher, or hiding in burrows. However, global warming is resulting in more wildfires, putting these forests and their animals at risk.

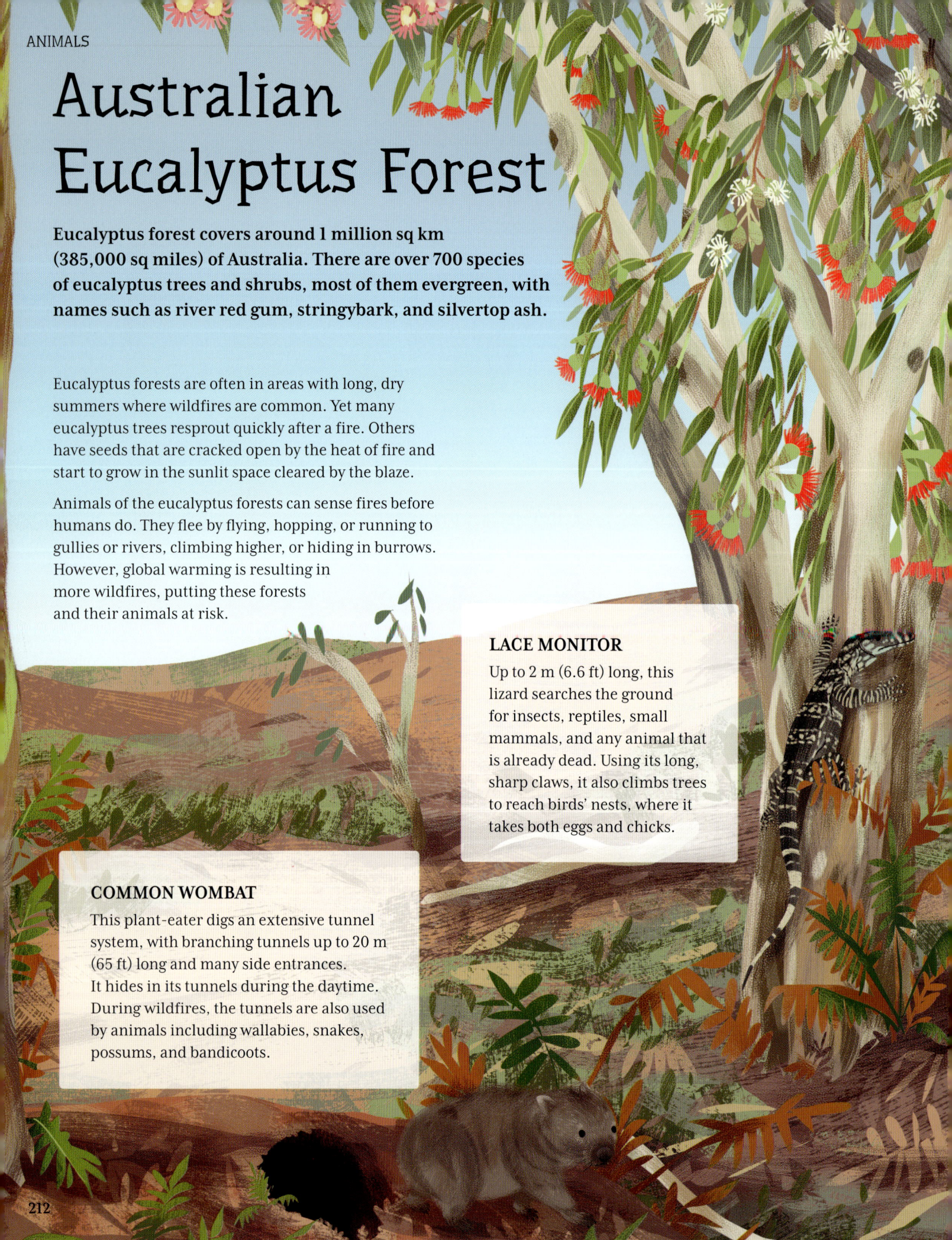

LACE MONITOR
Up to 2 m (6.6 ft) long, this lizard searches the ground for insects, reptiles, small mammals, and any animal that is already dead. Using its long, sharp claws, it also climbs trees to reach birds' nests, where it takes both eggs and chicks.

COMMON WOMBAT
This plant-eater digs an extensive tunnel system, with branching tunnels up to 20 m (65 ft) long and many side entrances. It hides in its tunnels during the daytime. During wildfires, the tunnels are also used by animals including wallabies, snakes, possums, and bandicoots.

ANIMALS

KOALA
The koala has few competitors for food since it eats only eucalyptus leaves, which are poisonous to many animals. These leaves offer little energy, so the koala spends up to 22 hours a day sleeping in the safety of a tree.

RED-TAILED BLACK COCKATOO
This parrot feeds on the seeds of eucalyptus trees such as desert and brown stringybark. It can hold a seed or branch with one clawed foot, usually the left one, while standing on the other foot.

RAINBOW LORIKEET
This bird feeds on nectar and pollen from eucalyptus flowers, using its long, bristle-tipped tongue to reach inside and lap them up. The lorikeet's bright plumage helps it to be recognized by others of its species.

RED-NECKED WALLABY
A wallaby travels by hopping, using its long back legs and strong tail. Like the koala and wombat, it is a marsupial mammal. Found mostly in Australia and South America, marsupials give birth to tiny, undeveloped babies, which they carry in a pouch on their abdomen.

Meerkat

This mammal lives in deserts and dry grasslands in southern Africa, including the Kalahari and Namib Deserts. It lives in a group of up to 40 meerkats, known as a mob or gang. The mob shares a burrow, inside which the temperature remains comfortable throughout the year.

MEERKAT MOB

In each meerkat mob, one pair of adults does the work of mating and giving birth. The other adults help care for the pair's pups. Mob members often groom and play with each other, which helps to maintain their friendships. Closeness between members of the mob is important, because meerkats rely on each other to watch for predators such as jackals, foxes, and eagles.

Meerkat Facts
- **SPECIES** *Suricata suricatta*
- **FAMILY** Mongooses
- **CLASS** Mammals
- **SIZE** 40–60 cm (16–24 in) long
- **RANGE** Southern Africa in dry, treeless regions
- **DIET** Beetles, butterflies, scorpions, small birds, lizards, and plants

In the cool of early morning or late afternoon, a group of adults leaves the burrow to look for food. One of the adults climbs on a rock, stands tall on its back legs, and watches all around. The watching meerkat makes constant "peep" noises to tell the others that all is well. If danger is sighted, the watcher gives a high-pitched bark, and the mob runs into a burrow entrance.

BURROWING AND BATTLING

Each mob has several burrow systems within its territory. The mob moves from one burrow to another if the surrounding food is low. Up to 2 m (6.6 ft) deep, each burrow system has around 15 entrances and exits. When digging a burrow, meerkats scrape with their claws, scoop out the soil with their joined forepaws, then kick it behind with their back legs.

A mob defends its territory by marking the border with a strong-smelling liquid made in a gland beneath their tails. If another mob crosses this border, the mob puts on a threatening display to scare them away: leaping forward while kicking up their legs. If this show of strength fails, the meerkats will fight each other, which can result in injuries.

When a meerkat needs to warm up, it sunbathes on its back. The dark fur and skin of its belly soak up more warmth than its paler back.

A group of adult meerkats searches for insects and plants to eat. A meerkat can survive without drinking water, because it gets the water it needs from eating plant roots and juicy fruits.

Primates

Around 55 million years ago, primates evolved in rain forests, where most still live today. Primates include monkeys, apes, lemurs, and humans. They are large-brained mammals that live in pairs or groups. Many live in trees, which they climb with the help of their strong limbs and grasping fingers and toes.

BORNEAN ORANGUTAN

Orangutans are in the great ape family, along with gorillas, chimpanzees, bonobos, and humans. Like other great apes, orangutans are tailless and clever, often using sticks to open fruit, poke termite nests, or catch fish. The Bornean orangutan is critically endangered due to the cutting down of its rain forest habitat.

LAR GIBBON

Although this gibbon's fur ranges from black to sandy, it always has a black, largely hairless face surrounded by white hair. It swings from branch to branch using its extremely long arms. On the rare times it comes to the ground, it walks on its short back legs while holding its arms over its head for balance.

RED-HANDED HOWLER MONKEY

This tree-dweller has a long tail that can curl around and hold branches, known as a prehensile tail. The howler communicates by making howling calls that can be heard up to 4.8 km (3 miles) away, the volume increased by an extra-large bone in the monkey's throat.

ANIMALS

EMPEROR TAMARIN
The emperor tamarin was named for its white whiskers, which look like the mustache of German emperor Wilhelm II (1859–1941). This monkey eats fruit, flowers, frogs, and insects in the Amazon rain forest canopy. Both males and females help to carry, feed, and wash babies.

BONOBO
Along with the chimpanzee, the bonobo is humans' closest relative. It lives in the Congo rain forest, where it eats fruit, honey, eggs, and small mammals. Although bonobos sometimes fight, they also form lifelong friendships, share food, and hug each other when distressed.

BLACK-AND-WHITE RUFFED LEMUR
Living in the canopy of the Madagascan rain forest, this lemur feeds on fruit. Groups are led by females, which take the first choice of food, ensuring that they have enough energy to raise young. Females build their babies nests of leaves, where they care for them during their first weeks.

Primate Facts
ORDER	Primates
CLASS	Mammals
SIZE	0.2–1.7 m (0.6–5.6 ft) long (excluding humans)
RANGE	Nonhuman primates live in Central and South America, Africa, and southern Asia
DIET	Fruit, leaves, flowers, seeds, insects, and small mammals

Blue Whale

The largest animal ever to exist, the blue whale grows up to 29.9 m (98 ft) long. It weighs as much as 199 tons (219 US tons)—more than 16 African elephants. Like other whales, dolphins, and porpoises, the blue whale belongs to a group of mammals known as cetaceans.

SUITED TO WATER

Cetaceans are water-living mammals with a smoothly shaped body. They swim by swinging their tail up and down, while steering with their paddle-shaped front limbs. Cetaceans that are fast-moving hunters have a tall dorsal (back) fin to help with steering. Yet the blue whale has a very small dorsal fin, around 33 cm (1 ft) high, that has little use. Cetaceans also have a thick layer of fat, known as blubber, which keeps them warm.

Cetaceans are descended from four-legged, land-living mammals, but lost their back legs as they evolved to suit a life spent entirely in water. They give birth in the water to live babies, known as calves, which can swim immediately. Every 2 or 3 years, a female blue whale has a single calf, which is 6 to 7 m (20 to 23 ft) long.

Like all mammals, cetaceans must breathe air into their lungs, so they swim to the water surface regularly. They breathe through holes, known as blowholes, on top of their head. The blue whale has two blowholes, which spurt water and steam more than 12 m (49 ft) into the air when it breathes out. This whale is known to dive as deep as 315 m (1,033 ft) for up to 15 minutes at a time.

A blue whale calf stays with its mother for up for 7 months, drinking as much as 190 l (50 US gallons) of her milk each day. A blue whale may live for 80 to 90 years.

ANIMALS

Bristles of baleen, up to 90 cm (3 ft) long, line the blue whale's upper jaw.

KRILL KILLER

Despite its great size, the blue whale is not a fierce hunter. It feeds almost entirely on tiny invertebrates called krill. When it finds a patch of krill, it swims quickly forward with its mouth open wide. Up to 220,000 l (58,000 US gallons) of water, filled with krill, surges into the whale's mouth. Its mouth has bristly comblike plates made of baleen. Baleen contains keratin, which is also found in human fingernails, bird beaks, and reptile scales. The krill are trapped by these plates, while the whale squeezes the water back out of its mouth.

Blue Whale Facts

SPECIES	*Balaenoptera musculus*
FAMILY	Rorqual whales
CLASS	Mammals
SIZE	21 to 29.9 m (69 to 98 ft) long
RANGE	All oceans, apart from ice-covered portions of the Arctic Ocean
DIET	Mostly krill, plus other small invertebrates and fish

ANIMALS

Andes Mountains

The Andes Mountains stretch for 7,000 km (4,350 miles) through western South America. In the central Andes is the Altiplano (meaning "high plain"), a vast region of flat, mostly treeless land with an average height of 3,750 m (12,300 ft).

Most plants on the Altiplano are grasses and low shrubs, so animals find little shelter from heat or cold. They face extremes of temperature: Summer days reach 24 °C (75 °F), but winter nights fall to -20 °C (-4 °F). Many animals stay comfortable by swapping between basking in the sunshine and sheltering in a burrow or beneath rocks.

Altiplano mammals have evolved to survive the thin air, often by having very efficient hearts and extra blood cells for carrying oxygen around their body. Birds are among the most common animals here, because their lungs can extract more oxygen from air than those of mammals.

DARWIN'S RHEA
A relative of ostriches and emus, the rhea is a flightless bird with weak wings. Up to 1 m (3.3 ft) tall, it uses its long legs to run from predators, such as Andean mountain cats, at 60 km/h (37 miles per hour).

MONTANE GUINEA PIG
This wild guinea pig is an ancestor of pet guinea pigs. It shelters from the weather and predators by trampling runways through grasses, so it stays hidden as it searches for leaves and fruit to eat.

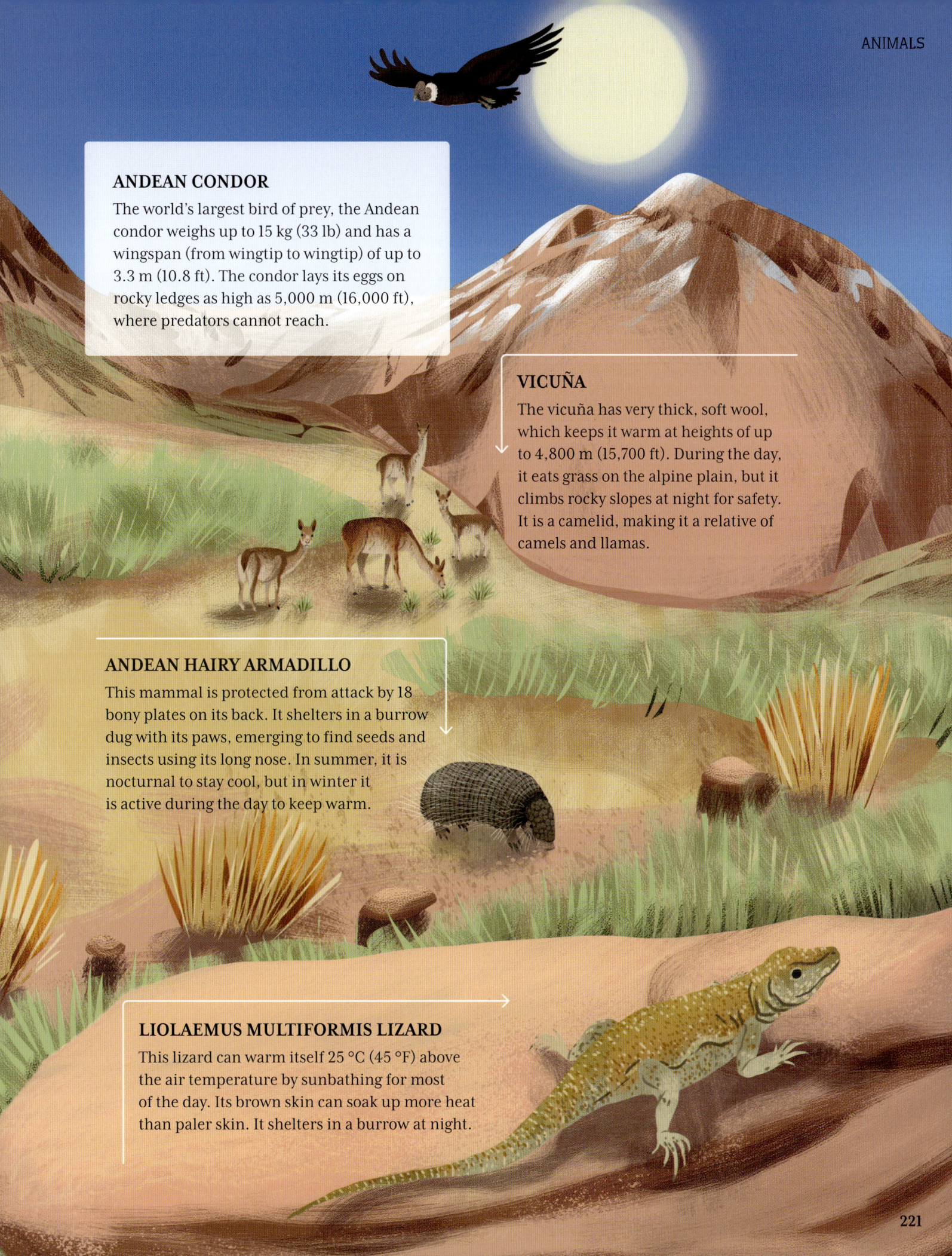

ANDEAN CONDOR

The world's largest bird of prey, the Andean condor weighs up to 15 kg (33 lb) and has a wingspan (from wingtip to wingtip) of up to 3.3 m (10.8 ft). The condor lays its eggs on rocky ledges as high as 5,000 m (16,000 ft), where predators cannot reach.

VICUÑA

The vicuña has very thick, soft wool, which keeps it warm at heights of up to 4,800 m (15,700 ft). During the day, it eats grass on the alpine plain, but it climbs rocky slopes at night for safety. It is a camelid, making it a relative of camels and llamas.

ANDEAN HAIRY ARMADILLO

This mammal is protected from attack by 18 bony plates on its back. It shelters in a burrow dug with its paws, emerging to find seeds and insects using its long nose. In summer, it is nocturnal to stay cool, but in winter it is active during the day to keep warm.

LIOLAEMUS MULTIFORMIS LIZARD

This lizard can warm itself 25 °C (45 °F) above the air temperature by sunbathing for most of the day. Its brown skin can soak up more heat than paler skin. It shelters in a burrow at night.

Penguins

Penguins have flipper-shaped wings that are suited to swimming but useless for flight. There are 18 penguin species, all found in the southern hemisphere apart from the Galápagos penguin, which lives on the equator. These six species spend part of their life on Antarctica or nearby islands.

GENTOO PENGUIN

The gentoo is the fastest-swimming penguin, reaching 36 km/h (22 miles per hour) as it dives for small invertebrates called krill. Like all penguins, the gentoo spends three-quarters of its life at sea, but returns to land to nest. Females lay two eggs among grass on the northernmost portion of Antarctica, known as the Antarctic Peninsula, or on islands around Antarctica.

ADÉLIE PENGUIN

During the long Antarctic winter, Adélies stay at sea, where temperatures are a little warmer. At the start of summer, in late October, they return to the Antarctic coast to build nests from stones. Females lay two eggs, which both parents take turns sitting on to keep them warm.

CHINSTRAP PENGUIN

The chinstrap is named for the black line in the feathers across its throat. Like other penguins, the chinstrap has an upright stance on land, waddling slowly on its short legs and webbed feet. To move faster across snow, chinstraps slide on their belly while pushing with their feet.

ANIMALS

MACARONI PENGUIN

Like all penguins, the macaroni has a form of camouflage known as countershading: Its belly is white, while its back and flippers are black. When swimming, the penguin's pale belly is difficult to spot against the sunlit water by a predator or prey swimming below. Viewed from above, the penguin's black back blends into the dark depths.

Penguin Facts
FAMILY	Penguins
CLASS	Birds
SIZE	0.3–1.1 m (1–3.6 ft) tall
RANGE	Coastal oceans and coasts of the southern hemisphere
DIET	Fish, krill, and squid

EMPEROR PENGUIN

The only penguin that lays eggs during the Antarctic winter, when temperatures fall to -40 °C (-40 °F), the emperor has thick layers of fat and feathers to keep warm. After a female lays her single egg, her mate balances it on his feet, warming it under skin and feathers.

KING PENGUIN

The second largest penguin after the emperor, the king is up to 1 m (3.3 ft) tall. King penguin chicks move into groups called crèches when they are a few weeks old. In a crèche, chicks huddle together for warmth, watched over by a few adults. Their parents hunt at sea, returning regularly with food.

Snowy Owl

The snowy owl is the largest bird of prey in the northernmost tundra. It has mostly white plumage, which keeps it camouflaged against snow. Like other birds of prey, it eats animals that are large compared with its own size, helped by a sharp, hooked beak and claws.

SKILLED HUNTER

The snowy owl watches for prey from a rock or mound. Like other owls, it can turn its head by 270 degrees, so it can see nearly all around and can pinpoint the direction of sounds by sensing when they are loudest in each ear. When the owl detects small animals—particularly rodents such as lemmings, mice, and voles— it swoops, thumping down hard on the animal with its strong claws, which are known as talons.

Small prey is often swallowed whole. Powerful stomach juices break down the flesh, while the indigestible bones, teeth, fur, and feathers are pressed into pellets that are brought back up 18 to 24 hours later.

TUNDRA TRAITS

A snowy owl can withstand temperatures as low as -62 °C (-80 °F) without appearing distressed. It has very dense feathers, with a thick layer of fluffy "down" feathers underneath its longer, stronger "flight" feathers. The feathers on its feet are longer than those of any other owl. During storms, the snowy owl is often seen sheltering behind rocks. Most owls hunt at night, but this owl must endure both the long winter night and the endless summer day, so it hunts for short periods during both night and day.

In the milder weather of May or early June, a female snowy owl lays around seven to nine eggs on higher ground on the tundra. For around a month, she sits on her eggs to warm them, while her male partner brings food. Newly hatched chicks are blind and rely on their parents for food. By late September, when the tundra is growing icier, the chicks can hunt on their own, just in time to fly southward to escape the winter. However, many adults, particularly older and larger birds, stay in the far north all year.

The fringed edges of the snowy owl's flight feathers help to dampen the sound of air passing over its wings as they beat, so the owl can hunt noiselessly.

Snowy Owl Facts

- **SPECIES** *Bubo scandiacus*
- **FAMILY** True owls
- **CLASS** Birds
- **SIZE** 52–71 cm (20–28 in) long
- **RANGE** Far northern North America, Europe, and Asia
- **DIET** Small mammals and birds

Unlike its parents, a snowy owl chick has brown feathers, which keep it hidden among lichen and rocks.

Songbirds

There are around 4,000 species of songbirds, also called oscines, a group of birds with a great variety of songs and calls. These small birds have anisodactyl feet—with three toes pointing forward and one backward—which are ideal for perching on the branches of trees and shrubs.

GREATER DOUBLE-COLLARED SUNBIRD

This South African bird drinks nectar by reaching into flowers with its long, curving beak. It also eats insects and spiders, which are plucked from their web. The male has iridescent (shining in a rainbow of shades) feathers, which he shows off to attract a female by bobbing on a high branch.

RED-CAPPED ROBIN

Found in Australian shrubland, this species is named for its "cap" of red feathers. The male has a larger and brighter cap than the female, as well as a red belly. This bird perches on a low branch to watch for crawling beetles and ants—then pounces to seize them in its beak.

CHINESE WHITE-BROWED ROSEFINCH

This rosefinch's strong, cone-shaped beak is suited to grasping and cracking seeds. A male has a pink face and belly, while a female is brown, which helps her stay unnoticed while she sits on her nest. This is cup-shaped, hidden in a bush, and made of grass, twigs, and moss.

ANIMALS

CYPRUS WARBLER

The Cyprus warbler is known for its fast, loud song, which it uses to communicate with its mate, to keep other warblers out of its territory, and perhaps just for pleasure. Females lay three to five eggs in a nest hidden in a bush or gorse thicket.

HOODED YELLOWTHROAT

The hooded yellowthroat lives on hillsides in Mexico. It usually hides quietly in a thicket, but flutters to a high branch to sing when it wants to attract a mate. A female lays only two eggs, fewer than songbirds that must migrate to warmer regions in winter, since she is more likely to survive to lay eggs for several years.

WHITE-WINGED FAIRYWREN

Outside the mating season, all white-winged fairywrens have brown plumage that camouflages them among the saltbushes of Australian shrubland. In spring and summer, one male in each flock grows bright blue plumage and mates with several females, while the brown-feathered males help care for the chicks.

Songbird Facts

ORDER	Songbirds
CLASS	Birds
SIZE	6.5–70 cm (2.6–28 in) long
RANGE	All continents except Antarctica in all regions except polar ice
DIET	Seeds, fruits, nectar, insects, and other small animals

Dinosaurs

Dinosaurs were an amazing group of reptiles, both fierce and peaceful, huge and tiny, speedy and lumbering. They walked the Earth from around 233 million years ago until 66 million years ago. Today's reptiles include crocodiles, lizards, and snakes. Most modern reptiles have skin covered by scales, breathe air using their lungs, and lay tough-shelled eggs on land. Dinosaurs shared these characteristics, although a few had feathers as well as scales. The first reptiles lived around 312 million years ago. Over time, reptiles changed—or evolved—into many different groups, including flying reptiles, known as pterosaurs, and the dinosaurs, which usually lived on land.

Over the 167 million years that dinosaurs hatched, ate, drank, slept, and fought, more than 1,000 dinosaur species evolved. A species is a group of animals that look similar and can make babies together. Evolution takes place because parents pass on their characteristics—such as a long neck—to their babies. A useful characteristic such as a longer neck, which allows a plant-eating dinosaur to reach higher branches than its rivals, gives that dinosaur a better chance of surviving until it is mature enough to have its own, longer-necked babies. These babies pass on their longer necks to their babies ... and over time, the useful characteristic becomes more and more common. When a species has changed so much that it looks distinctly different, scientists call it a new species. In this way, a new species of extremely long-necked dinosaurs evolves.

As new species of dinosaurs evolved, others became extinct. Some species became extinct because larger, sharper-toothed dinosaurs evolved to kill them. Others became extinct because faster or taller dinosaurs evolved to steal their prey or eat their conifer trees. In the end, all the dinosaurs became extinct when a space rock, known as an asteroid, hit Earth. Yet we could say that some dinosaurs are alive and well today! Before the asteroid struck, some dinosaurs had evolved beaks, feathers, and wings—and flown into the sky as birds.

Opisthocoelicaudia was a plant-eating dinosaur that lived around 70 million years ago. In addition to its usefully long neck, it had a long, flexible tail that helped it balance as it fed on high branches.

Around 130 million years ago, two dinosaurs splash through a wetland in what is today central Spain. Hump-backed *Concavenator* tries to seize a frightened *Pelecanimimus* in its sharp-toothed jaws.

Dinosaur Life

Paleontologists are scientists who study the fossils of dinosaurs and other extinct living things. They have pieced together a picture of how dinosaurs looked and how they may have behaved. There are still many mysteries that may never be solved, including what kinds of noises dinosaurs made to show friendliness or fear.

DIFFERENT FROM THE REST

Dinosaurs had an advantage over other reptiles. Other reptiles have legs that sprawl to the sides, so they must wriggle their body from side to side when they run, making them both breathless and slower. Dinosaurs walked with their back legs directly beneath their body, so the legs could take longer strides and carry more weight. This allowed dinosaurs to be faster and grow bigger.

The dinosaur *Dubreuillosaurus*

The early reptile *Nanoparia*

MEAT AND PLANTS

The earliest dinosaurs were meat-eaters, also known as carnivores. Meat-eating dinosaurs preyed on many different animals, including insects, fish, amphibians, mammals, and reptiles, including dinosaurs. Over time, around two-thirds of dinosaurs evolved to be plant-eaters, also known as herbivores. They ate plant parts such as leaves, fruit, twigs, and bark.

Lucianovenator

DINOSAURS

LAYING EGGS

Like most reptiles and all birds, dinosaurs laid eggs. Female dinosaurs laid up to 30 eggs in a nest, which they scraped in the ground or built from piled-up mud and leaves. Some dinosaurs sat gently on their eggs to keep them warm, then watched over their young dinosaurs after they hatched. Yet some meat-eating dinosaurs buried their eggs safely, then walked away, leaving their sharp-clawed babies to care for themselves after hatching.

Oviraptor

Omeisaurus herd

LIVING TOGETHER

Although large meat-eaters probably hunted alone, many plant-eaters moved in a herd. Living in a group was safer, since all the dinosaurs could bite, claw, and kick a predator—or all run in different directions, leaving the predator unsure which to chase. Dinosaurs probably made calls to communicate with their herd. Some paleontologists think these calls included rumbles and booms.

SCALES AND FEATHERS

Most dinosaurs had skin covered by scales, which are small plates made of keratin. This tough material is also found in hair, horns, and hooves. Scales protected dinosaur skin from being damaged. A few dinosaurs had bigger, bonier plates known as scutes, which offered even better protection. Some meat-eating dinosaurs had feathers, which are also made of keratin. While early feathered dinosaurs had short, soft feathers for warmth, some later dinosaurs grew longer, stiffer feathers—and evolved into birds.

Oksoko

Panoplosaurus

Dinosaur Groups

Dinosaurs can be divided into groups based on their similarities. Dinosaurs that looked very similar are placed in the same species. Similar species are placed in larger groups such as families, which are placed in even larger groups, such as suborders. Many paleontologists group dinosaurs into four suborders: theropods, sauropodomorphs, cerapods, and thyreophorans.

THEROPODS

Most theropods were meat-eaters—and nearly all meat-eating dinosaurs were theropods. These dinosaurs usually walked on their back legs, freeing their shorter front limbs for grasping prey. Theropods had hollow bones, making them more lightweight. They usually had three main toes and three main fingers. Most feathered dinosaurs were in the theropod suborder, but some groups of theropods had scales. Theropods ranged from around 34 cm (13 in) to 14.3 m (47 ft) long. It was a group of small theropods that evolved into birds.

Megalosaurus

SAUROPODOMORPHS

These dinosaurs were plant-eaters. They had long necks for reaching high or distant food, and long tails to balance the weight of their necks. Early sauropodomorphs walked on their back legs, but later sauropodomorphs were so big and heavy that they walked on all fours. The largest sauropodomorphs were the largest dinosaurs of all, reaching 35 m (114.8 ft) long.

Diplodocus

Triceratops

CERAPODS

The cerapods were plant-eaters, with hard, keratin-covered beaks for cutting twigs and stems. Their teeth had sharp ridges, which helped to mush plants. Some cerapods walked on two legs, and others walked on four. Cerapods included ceratopsians, which often had horns and neck frills; and pachycephalosaurs, which had domed skulls.

THYREOPHORANS

These plant-eaters had thick bony plates known as scutes, which protected them from attack. Due to the weight of their scutes, most thyreophorans walked on four, sturdy legs, with their front legs usually shorter than their back legs. Thyreophorans included stegosaurs, which had rows of tall scutes down their back; and ankylosaurs, which sometimes had a bony tail club.

Stegosaurus

Ankylosaurus

Pterodactylus

Gryposuchus

DINOSAUR RELATIVES

The dinosaurs were in the archosaur superorder of reptiles. These reptiles had the advantages of teeth set deep into sockets, so they did not fall out easily; and extra openings in their skulls, making them more lightweight. Other archosaurs included pterosaurs, which were flying reptiles; and pseudosuchians, which were crocodile-like reptiles. Today, the only surviving archosaurs are birds and crocodiles and their relatives.

Fossils

Fossils have taught us everything we know about dinosaurs and other extinct living things. Fossils are the preserved remains of animals and plants. Some, known as body fossils, preserve an animal's body—or parts of it. Others, known as trace fossils, preserve traces of the animal, such as its footprints or poop.

BODY FOSSILS

Most body fossils form when a dead animal is quickly covered with mud or sand, which can happen in water or in deserts. Usually, the animal's soft body parts, such as skin, fat, and muscle, rot away. It is the hard body parts—such as bones, teeth, and horns—that have the best chance of being preserved. More mud or sand pile on top of the body and, over thousands of years, harden into rocks such as mudstone and sandstone. Water seeps into the bones and teeth, turning them to rock as it deposits tough materials known as minerals.

Sometimes, an animal's body is preserved by a different method. Animals that lived in an icy climate, such as woolly mammoths, can be frozen. Many insects were fossilized by being covered in sticky tree resin that hardened into amber. Some animals were even preserved by falling into tar.

TRACE FOSSILS

Fossils of footprints, burrows, and nests can form when they are baked by the sun, then covered by sand or mud. Footprints are particularly useful trace fossils because they tell us how an animal walked or ran.

Paleontologists make guesses about which dinosaur made which footprints by comparing the number and sizes of toes with the fossils of feet found nearby. To make estimates of walking or running speed, paleontologists measure the distance between footprints as well as their depth. When several tracks are found together, paleontologists can figure out if the dinosaurs lived in a herd.

Fossilized poops, known as coprolites, preserve the remains of bones, shells, or leaves, telling paleontologists about an animal's diet and chewing habits. Paleontologists cannot always know which dinosaur made which coprolite, but there are clues in a coprolite's size, shape, and location.

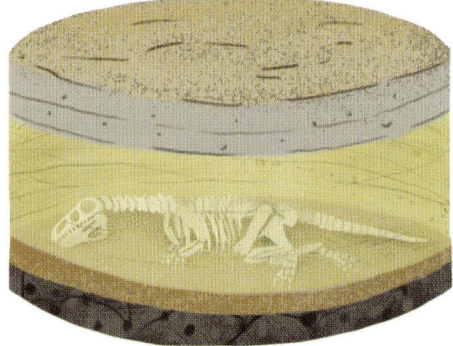

A dinosaur dies on the seashore, sinks to the water bottom, then is quickly buried by sand and mud.

Beneath layers of rock, the dinosaur's bones and teeth are replaced by minerals.

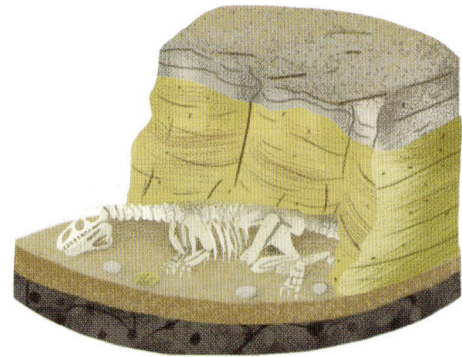

The fossil is lifted by movements of the great plates of rock that form Earth's surface. The surrounding rock is worn away, revealing the fossil.

Paleontologists uncover fossils very carefully, documenting each bone and its position. By examining the shapes of a dinosaur's bones and teeth, paleontologists find out how the animal looked and how it might have behaved. They also examine the layers of rock around a fossil to discover its age.

DINOSAURS

Djadokhta

In Mongolia's Gobi Desert is the Djadokhta Formation of 75-million-year-old sandstone rocks. The formation is rich with fossils of dinosaurs and their eggs. When the rocks formed, this area was dry, sandy, and windblown, just as it is today.

Many of the dinosaurs fossilized at Djadokhta were killed when they were buried in sand by sandstorms or collapsing dunes. The dunes may have collapsed after they became unsteady during sudden heavy rain. Some dinosaurs were trapped while sitting on their nest.

The sand prevented the bodies from being eaten by hungry dinosaurs or birds, although some were nibbled by burrowing invertebrates. The water-soaked sand—and the buried dinosaurs—slowly turned to rock and fossil.

ALMAS
Named after a part-man, part-monster creature in Mongolian stories, this small, birdlike theropod dinosaur preyed on lizards and insects. Females laid their eggs in hollows scraped in the ground, then sat on the eggs to keep them warm. Like *Saurornithoides*, *Almas* was a member of the troodontid group.

HALSZKARAPTOR
Just 60 cm (24 in) long, this dinosaur was a close relative of the small predators *Velociraptor* and *Tsaagan*. While some paleontologists think that *Halszkaraptor* lived only on land, others think it spent time in water, using its jagged-edged beak for catching fish.

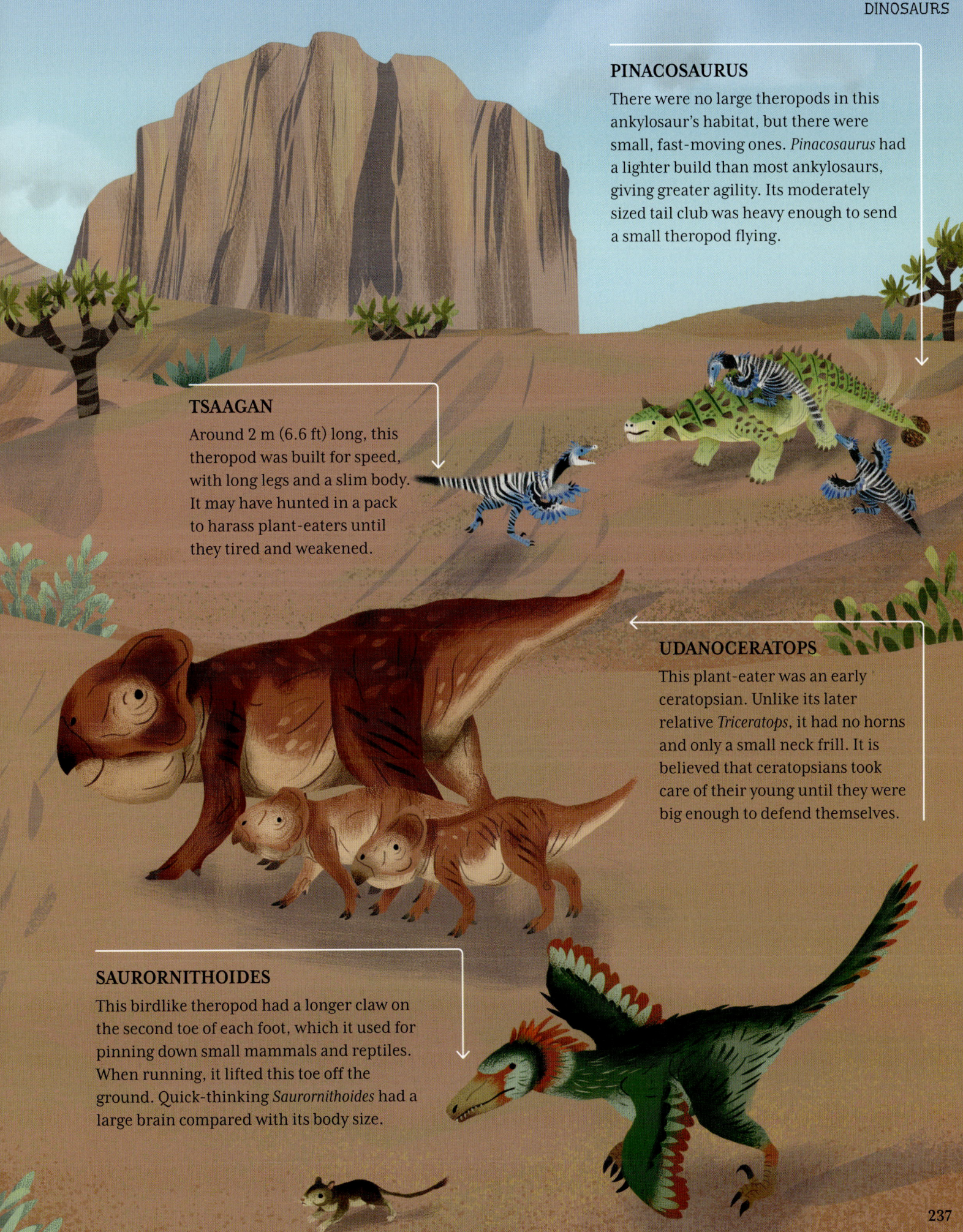

DINOSAURS

PINACOSAURUS
There were no large theropods in this ankylosaur's habitat, but there were small, fast-moving ones. *Pinacosaurus* had a lighter build than most ankylosaurs, giving greater agility. Its moderately sized tail club was heavy enough to send a small theropod flying.

TSAAGAN
Around 2 m (6.6 ft) long, this theropod was built for speed, with long legs and a slim body. It may have hunted in a pack to harass plant-eaters until they tired and weakened.

UDANOCERATOPS
This plant-eater was an early ceratopsian. Unlike its later relative *Triceratops*, it had no horns and only a small neck frill. It is believed that ceratopsians took care of their young until they were big enough to defend themselves.

SAURORNITHOIDES
This birdlike theropod had a longer claw on the second toe of each foot, which it used for pinning down small mammals and reptiles. When running, it lifted this toe off the ground. Quick-thinking *Saurornithoides* had a large brain compared with its body size.

Parasaurolophus

Parasaurolophus (meaning "near crested lizard" in ancient Greek) was named for its tall head crest. Paleontologists have suggested many different purposes for this crest, from attracting a mate to making loud calls. The crest may have been bigger in adult males than in young males and females.

PERFECT PLANT-EATER

Parasaurolophus belonged to the cerapod suborder of dinosaurs. These dinosaurs were plant-eaters with horny, sharp-edged, beaklike jaws for snipping off twigs. *Parasaurolophus* was in the hadrosaur family of cerapods, which are often called duckbilled dinosaurs due to their flattened snout that resembled a duck's beak.

A hadrosaur's beak was toothless, but at the back of its jaws were several rows of grinding teeth that easily chewed tough plant material. A hadrosaur also had muscly cheeks that helped it hold lots of food in its mouth. These advantages allowed hadrosaurs to eat and digest large amounts of leaves, twigs, and pine needles—and also helped them become the most common plant-eating dinosaurs of the Late Cretaceous Period. One member of the family, *Edmontosaurus*, was one of the last surviving dinosaurs.

Parasaurolophus could walk on either two or four legs. When wandering slowly from plant to plant, it probably balanced its great weight—of up to 5,000 kg (11,000 lb)—on all four legs. Yet when it was threatened by a theropod dinosaur, *Parasaurolophus* could run fast on its long back legs.

CURIOUS CREST

Many paleontologists think that *Parasaurolophus*'s head crest helped it communicate. The long, curving crest was hollow. When *Parasaurolophus* called to its herd, the sounds bounced around inside the crest, which made them louder. In the same way, the hollow body of a guitar makes the sound of a plucked string louder.

Another possible use for the crest was to cool *Parasaurolophus* down when it got hot. The crest had a large surface area, which allowed lots of body heat to escape. An adult male *Parasaurolophus* may also have shown off his large crest at mating time, with larger-crested males having more success with females.

Parasaurolophus's hollow crest was formed by extended premaxilla and nasal bones. In other dinosaurs, the premaxilla bones are small bones at the tip of the upper jaw. The nasal bones usually form the top of the snout.

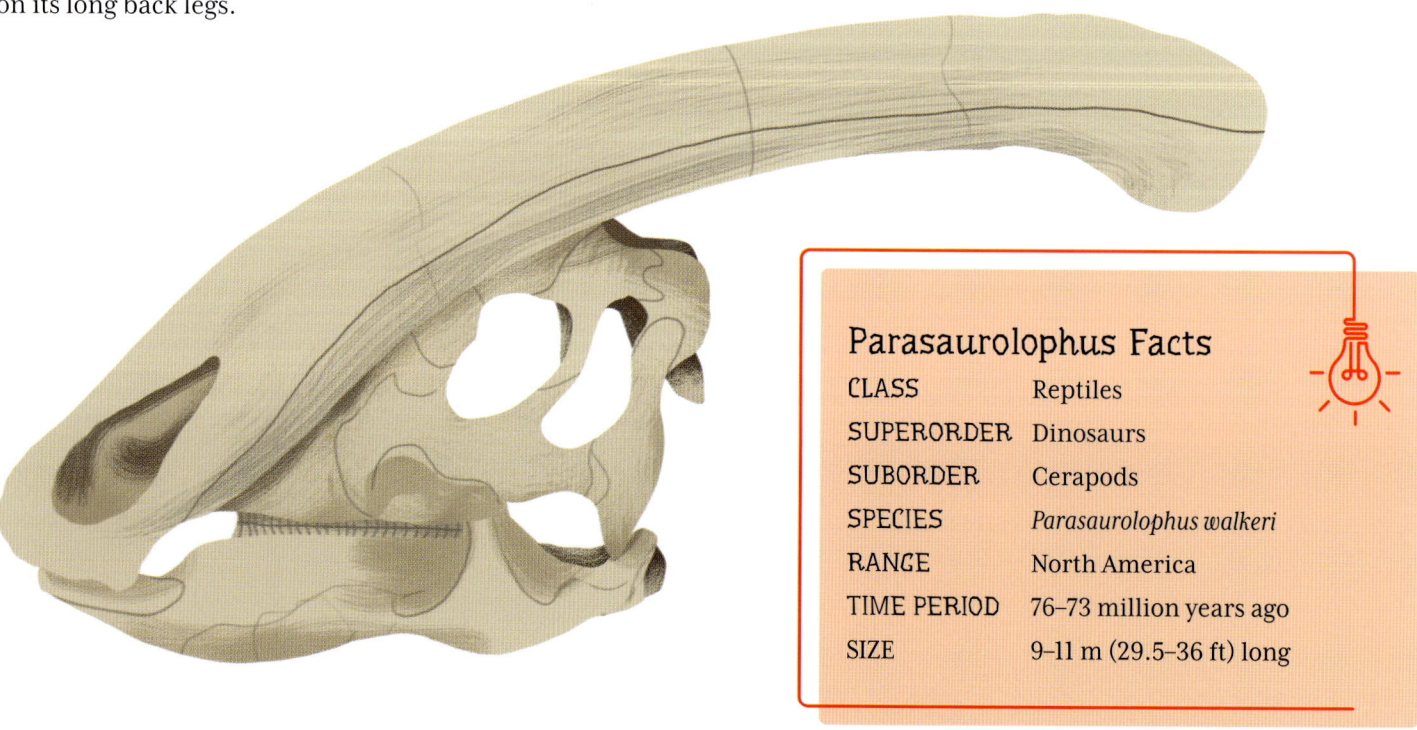

Parasaurolophus Facts
CLASS	Reptiles
SUPERORDER	Dinosaurs
SUBORDER	Cerapods
SPECIES	*Parasaurolophus walkeri*
RANGE	North America
TIME PERIOD	76–73 million years ago
SIZE	9–11 m (29.5–36 ft) long

Like a modern deer, *Parasaurolophus* may have lived in a large herd, ranging from several hundred during the mating season to a dozen or less at other times. A range of calls helped the herd stay together and keep safe from predators.

Solnhofen

The limestone of Germany's Solnhofen region preserved fossils of insects, pterosaurs, and dinosaurs. The most extraordinary find was *Archaeopteryx*, a birdlike dinosaur that gives clues about how dinosaurs evolved into birds.

Around 150 million years ago, Solnhofen lay at the edge of a shallow ocean that was dotted with many small islands. Dead animals that fell or were washed into the water were gently covered by fine-grained mud, in which even their feathers and wings were preserved.

The islands were home to more than 20 species of flying reptiles known as pterosaurs, which plucked fish from the sea and nested on rocks and cliffs. Among the largest pterosaurs here was *Rhamphorhynchus*, with a wingspan of 1.8 m (5.9 ft). *Ctenochasma* was one of the smallest, just 25 cm (10 in) from wingtip to wingtip.

RHAMPHORHYNCHUS

This pterosaur had forward-pointing, needle-like teeth suited to trapping wriggling fish and squid. Its long tail, ending in a vane of tissue and skin, helped steady its flight. *Rhamphorhynchus* snatched prey from the water surface or dived right in, powering through the waves with its broad, flat feet.

ARCHAEOPTERYX

Up to 50 cm (20 in) long, *Archaeopteryx* (meaning "old wing" in ancient Greek) was a theropod dinosaur with features of both dinosaurs and their descendants—birds. Its arms had developed into wings, which were covered in long, strong feathers. It could make short, flapping flights. However, like a dinosaur, it still had teeth in its beak, clawed fingers, and a long bony tail.

PTERODACTYLUS

Like all pterosaurs, *Pterodactylus* (meaning "winged finger") had wings made from skin stretched between its long fourth finger and its legs. It probably showed off its head crest when trying to attract a mate.

CTENOCHASMA

Ctenochasma (meaning "wide comb") was a pterosaur. It had over 400 bristle-like teeth that formed a comb, sticking outward to create a basket-like structure. This was probably used for sieving small fish out of the water using a scooping action.

MESUROPETALA

Mesuropetala was a dragonfly, one of a group of winged insects that is largely unchanged today. Insects were the first animals in the air, around 325 million years ago. Pterosaurs followed 230 million years ago, around 80 million years before birdlike dinosaurs made it off the ground.

COMPSOGNATHUS

Around 1 m (3.3 ft) long, *Compsognathus* was a theropod dinosaur. It may have had short feathers on its body and scales on its back legs and tail. It chased insects and lizards, running fast on its back legs.

Velociraptor

Velociraptor was a small, fast-moving meat-eater. It was a member of the dromaeosaurid group of feathered theropod dinosaurs. *Velociraptor* chased small prey such as lizards and mammals, but was also quick-thinking enough to attack a weakened dinosaur when it saw one.

CATCH AND CLAW

Velociraptor means "swift snatcher" in Latin. With its lightweight build, this dinosaur could run fast on its long back legs, reaching 40 km/h (28 miles per hour) for short bursts. It had an extra-long, curved claw on the second toe of each foot, which it held off the ground as it ran. This claw measured 6.5 cm (2.6 in) around its outer edge.

When it caught up with prey, *Velociraptor* leaped on top, pinning down the animal with its claws. This method is used by modern birds of prey such as eagles. Then *Velociraptor* may have torn flesh from its living victim until the unlucky animal died from blood loss or shock. *Velociraptor* had around 30 teeth, which were small and curved with jagged edges that helped it slice flesh. It had a long, narrow snout that was suited to feeding on small animals—or ripping at larger ones.

FIGHTING DINOSAURS

In 1971, a fossil was discovered of a fighting *Velociraptor* and *Protoceratops*, which grew to around 2.5 m (8.2 ft) long. Since *Protoceratops* was much more sturdily built than *Velociraptor*, this fossil tells us this *Velociraptor* might have been extremely fearless, perhaps because it was desperately hungry or because it was young and inexperienced. Alternatively, this *Velociraptor* may have noticed that the *Protoceratops* was old, sick, or injured.

The two animals were locked in combat when they were buried by a sandstorm or sand dune collapse in the desert where they lived. The *Velociraptor* was underneath its prey, with one of its extra-long claws stuck in the *Protoceratops*'s throat. The *Protoceratops* was biting the right arm of its attacker with its hard beak. If the *Velociraptor* had managed to pierce its victim's windpipe, or one of the major blood vessels in its throat, it would have won this battle.

Velociraptor Facts

CLASS	Reptiles
SUPERORDER	Dinosaurs
SUBORDER	Theropods
SPECIES	*Velociraptor mongoliensis*
RANGE	Asia
TIME PERIOD	75–71 million years ago
SIZE	1.5–2 m (4.9–6.6 ft) long

Velociraptor (right) and *Protoceratops* lived in Asia in a dry, sandy habitat. Hardy, low-growing shrubs provided food for plant-eaters.

Pachycephalosaurs

Pachycephalosaurs (meaning "thick-headed lizards" in ancient Greek) had very thick, dome-shaped skulls. These dinosaurs may have used their heads to butt each other, like male mountain goats do today. These dinosaurs were plant-eaters or possibly omnivores.

PACHYCEPHALOSAURUS

The dome of *Pachycephalosaurus's* skull was made of bone up to 25 cm (10 in) thick, which would have cushioned the dinosaur's small brain when headbutting. The dinosaur had a beak for snipping stems, while the sides of the jaw had tiny, leaf-shaped teeth suited to grinding leaves. Yet the beak also bore sharp teeth that could have caught insects.

PRENOCEPHALE

Like their relatives, male *Prenocephales* (meaning "sloping heads") may have had headbutting competitions with rivals, over access to females or the best feeding spots. The winners of these competitions may have become leaders of the herd.

ALASKACEPHALE

This dinosaur was named after the US state of Alaska, where its fossils were first discovered, in an area that was a muddy coastal plain during the Late Cretaceous Period. *Alaskacephale* found plentiful food here, including the leaves of flowering trees, shrubs, herbs, and ferns.

STEGOCERAS

When young, *Stegoceras* may have had a flat skull, which grew into a dome with age. The dome was edged by a shelf ornamented with knobs. An adult *Stegoceras* may have showed off its head to attract a mate, with the largest and most ornamented skulls having most success.

COLEPIOCEPHALE

Like its relatives, *Colepiocephale* (meaning "knuckle head") had large eyes. The region of its brain used for processing smells was unusually big for a dinosaur. Both these features helped *Colepiocephale* sense approaching predators and find food.

Pachycephalosaur Facts

CLASS	Reptiles
SUPERORDER	Dinosaurs
SUBORDER	Cerapods
RANGE	North America and Asia
TIME PERIOD	92–66 million years ago
SIZE	2–4.5 m (6.6–15 ft) long

GOYOCEPHALE

Goyocephale (meaning "decorated head") may have had a flatter skull than most pachycephalosaurs. However, only one skull has yet been found, in the Gobi Desert of Central Asia. It may have belonged to a young *Goyocephale* whose skull was still growing.

Tyrannosaurus

Tyrannosaurus (meaning "tyrant lizard") was one of the largest meat-eaters that ever walked the Earth. Although theropods such as *Spinosaurus* were slightly longer, *Tyrannosaurus* had a stronger bite than any other dinosaur—more than 100 times more powerful than a human's jaws.

BUILT FOR KILLING

Tyrannosaurus had 60 curving teeth up to 30.5 cm (12 in) long. Each sharp tooth had jagged edges that helped *Tyrannosaurus* carve through scales, skin, muscles, and bones. The dinosaur's skull was up to 1.5 m (5 ft) long, with exceptionally thick, strong jaw bones that were snapped closed by powerful muscles.

Although *Tyrannosaurus* had short arms, they were muscled enough to hold on to struggling prey while the dinosaur inflicted a deep and deadly wound with its jaws. *Tyrannosaurus* had only two fingers, but each was armed with a long, sharp claw.

This dinosaur's eyes were forward-facing, which helped the two eyes work together to judge the distance and speed of fast-fleeing prey. In contrast, many plant-eating dinosaurs had eyes on the sides of their head to watch all around for predators. The shape of *Tyrannosaurus*'s skull suggests that a large portion of its brain was dedicated to analyzing smells, which helped it detect prey more than 1,000 m (3,280 ft) away.

Overall, *Tyrannosaurus* had a relatively large brain compared with its body size, giving it around the same intelligence level as a modern bird. This meant that *Tyrannosaurus* could think quickly, respond fast to changing situations, and even plan ahead the best way to corner its unlucky prey.

TOP HUNTER

Like today's large meat-eaters, such as lions and wolves, *Tyrannosaurus* probably hunted live prey as well as feeding on dead animals it found, which is known as scavenging. At 4 m (13.1 ft) tall, this dinosaur's size and strength made it an apex predator, with no predators of its own unless it was young or sick. *Tyrannosaurus* could take its pick of plant-eating dinosaurs as big as 9-m- (29.5-ft-) long *Triceratops* and 8-m- (26.2-ft-) long *Ankylosaurus*. Like lions and wolves, *Tyrannosaurus* may have hunted in a pack to bring down the largest prey of all: sauropodomorphs such as *Alamosaurus*.

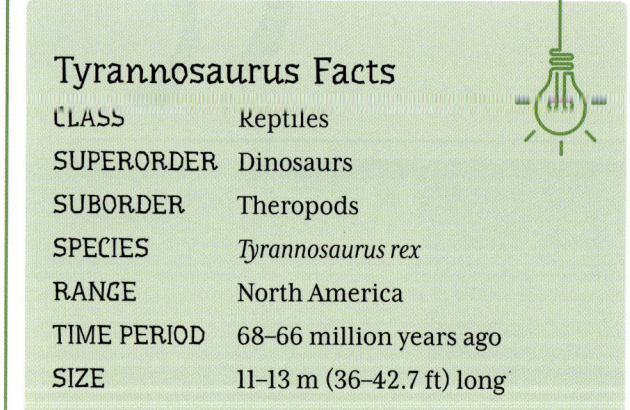

Tyrannosaurus Facts

CLASS	Reptiles
SUPERORDER	Dinosaurs
SUBORDER	Theropods
SPECIES	*Tyrannosaurus rex*
RANGE	North America
TIME PERIOD	68–66 million years ago
SIZE	11–13 m (36–42.7 ft) long

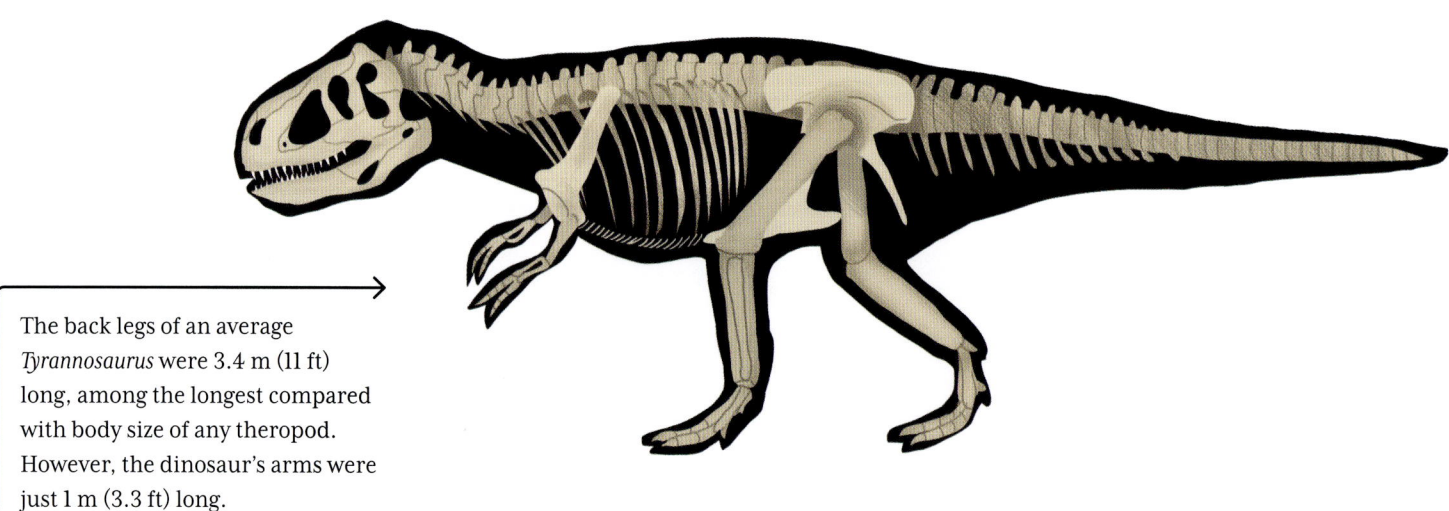

The back legs of an average *Tyrannosaurus* were 3.4 m (11 ft) long, among the longest compared with body size of any theropod. However, the dinosaur's arms were just 1 m (3.3 ft) long.

Tyrannosaurus bite marks have been found on *Triceratops* fossils. The marks suggest that *Tyrannosaurus* often tried to rip off the plant-eater's neck frill to reach its soft neck.

Glossary

absorb
To take in or soak up.

alga (plural: algae)
A plantlike protist that usually lives in and around water, such as a seaweed.

amphibian
An animal that usually spends part of its life on land and part in water, such as a frog.

animal
A living thing that has many cells, feeds on other living things, and breathes oxygen.

antenna
A slender feeler found on the head of some invertebrates.

antibiotic
A medication that is used to kill or damage bacteria.

archaeon (plural: archaea)
A tiny, simple living thing with one cell.

artery
A tube through which blood travels from the heart to the rest of the body.

asexual reproduction
A type of reproduction in which offspring are made by one parent.

asteroid
A small rocky or metal object that orbits the Sun in space.

astronomer
A scientist who studies planets, stars, and space itself.

atmosphere
The gases surrounding a planet, moon, or other space object, held by its gravity.

atom
The smallest building block of matter. An atom has a central nucleus, containing particles called protons and neutrons, usually surrounded by one or more electrons.

aurora
Lights in the sky made by particles from the Sun exciting gases in the atmosphere.

axis
An imaginary line through the middle of a planet or other space object, around which the object rotates.

bacterium (plural: bacteria)
A tiny living thing with one cell. Some bacteria can cause disease.

biome
A widespread community of plants and animals that are suited to their region's climate.

bird
An animal that lays tough-shelled eggs and has a beak, wings, and feathers.

bird of prey
A bird that hunts animals that are large compared with its own size.

black hole
An area of space with such strong gravity that not even light can escape from it.

blood vessel
A tube that carries blood around the body.

brittle
Hard, but easy to break or snap.

camouflage
The way the pattern and shape of an animal make it less visible.

carbon dioxide
A substance made of carbon and oxygen atoms. Carbon dioxide is a gas at room temperature.

carnivore
An animal that eats other animals.

cartilage
A strong, bendy material found in the body.

cell
The smallest working part of a living thing's body.

cerapod
A plant-eating dinosaur with a beak and ridged teeth.

chemical bond
A strong attraction between atoms that enables them to join together as molecules. The bond often results from the sharing of electrons.

chemical reaction
A change that takes place when two or more substances combine to form a new substance or substances.

chromosome
A long, coiled molecule of deoxyribonucleic acid (DNA).

class
A scientific group that includes animals with the same body plan, such as birds or mammals.

climate
The usual weather in a region over many years.

climate change
Long-term changes in Earth's temperature and weather. Since the 19th century, human activities have been the main cause of climate change, largely due to the burning of fossil fuels, which releases heat-trapping gases.

comet
A small icy object with an elliptical (like a stretched circle) orbit that takes it close to and far from the Sun.

command module
The section of a space capsule, such as the Apollo capsule, that holds the crew.

compound
A substance made of many identical molecules, each containing atoms of more than one element.

condensation
When a gas changes state into a liquid.

conduction
A process by which heat or electricity travels through a material. Heat energy travels through the vibrations and collisions between molecules or atoms. Electrical energy travels by the movement of electrons between atoms.

conifer
A tree that produces seeds inside cones and has needle-like or scale-like leaves that usually remain on the tree year-round.

constellation
A group of stars that seem to make a shape in the night sky.

continent
A large area of land, usually separated from other continents by ocean. Today, there are seven continents: Africa, Antarctica, Asia, Australia, Europe, North America, and South America.

convection
A process by which heat travels through a flowing liquid or gas. Convection happens when there is a difference in temperature: The hot part of the liquid or gas rises, while the cooler part sinks.

coral reef
An underwater structure made of the skeletons of millions of tiny coral animals.

core
The inner region of a planet, star, or other space object.

crest
A growth of bone, scales, feathers, skin, or hair on the head or back of an animal.

Cretaceous Period
A period of Earth's history lasting from 145 to 66 million years ago.

crust
The outer layer of a planet or moon.

dense
Tightly packed with molecules.

deoxyribonucleic acid (DNA)
A molecule found in cells that carries instructions for the growth and function of the body.

digest
To break down food into smaller, simpler parts.

dinosaur
An extinct, land-living reptile that walked with its back legs held directly beneath its body.

dwarf planet
An object orbiting a star that is massive enough for its gravity to pull it into a ball-like shape, but is not massive enough to clear other objects out of its path.

dwarf star
A star of average or low brightness and size.

eclipse
When an object such as a star, planet, or moon passes into the shadow of—or passes behind—another body.

electric charge
A property of electrons and protons, which are particles found in atoms.

electric current
A flow of electrically charged particles, usually electrons.

electromagnetic radiation
A type of energy that travels through space at the speed of light. This energy travels in packets called photons, which also—confusingly—behave like a wave of electric and magnetic force. Radiations are given different names depending on the amount of energy their photons carry, from low-energy radio waves, through microwaves, infrared, visible light, ultraviolet, and X-rays, to the highest-energy gamma rays.

electron
A particle found in atoms, outside the nucleus. An electron has a negative electric charge.

electron shell
An orbit that electrons follow around an atom's nucleus. An atom can have several shells, each at a different distance from the nucleus and each holding up to a certain number of electrons.

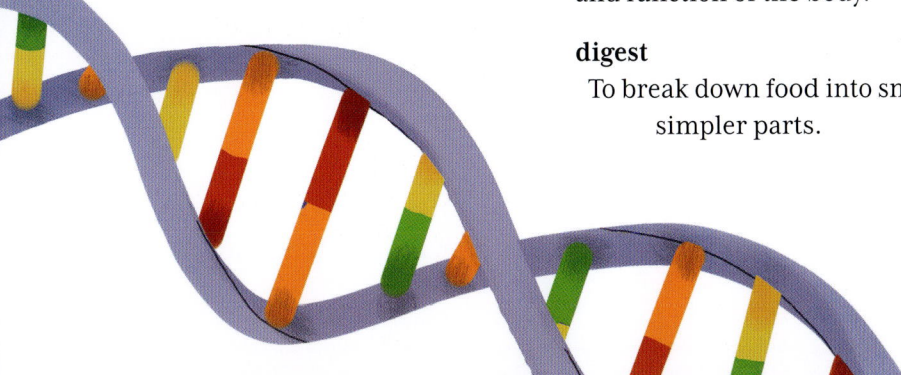

element
A material that cannot be broken down into simpler substances. An element is made up of identical atoms, each with the same number of protons in its nucleus. There are 118 known elements.

ellipse
An oval shape, like a stretched circle.

energy
The ability to exert a force or cause change.

enzyme
A substance that brings about change, such as breaking up food into simpler materials.

equator
An imaginary line drawn around a planet or star, halfway between its poles.

eukaryote
A living thing made of a cell or many cells that have a central part called a nucleus. Animals, plants, fungi, and protists are eukaryotes.

evaporation
When a liquid changes state into a gas.

evolve
To change gradually over time.

exoplanet
A planet outside our Solar System.

extinction
When a species dies out.

family
A group of species that are closely related, so that they look and behave much alike. For example, lions and tigers are in the cat family.

feather
A light, fringed growth from the skin of birds and some dinosaurs. A feather has a tough central stem, with softer threads growing from either side. Feathers are made from keratin, which is also found in scales and hair.

fern
A flowerless plant that has feathery or leafy fronds and makes new plants by releasing tiny spores.

fin
A body part that juts from the body of fish and some other water-living animals, helping them swim.

fish
A water-living animal, usually with fins and scales, that takes oxygen from the water using gills.

flowering plant
A plant that bears flowers and makes new plants by producing seeds contained within fruit.

force
A push or pull that can make an object speed up, slow down, or change shape.

fossil
The remains of an animal or plant that died long ago, preserved in rock.

fossil fuel
Coal, oil, and natural gas are fossil fuels, which formed underground from the remains of dead plants and animals. Like all fuels, a fossil fuel can be burned to release energy in the form of light and heat.

fresh water
Unsalted water, such as in rivers, lakes, and ponds.

fungus (plural: fungi)
A living thing that usually feeds on decaying material.

galaxy
Thousands, millions, or trillions of stars, as well as planets, gas, and dust, all held together by gravity.

gas
A substance, such as air, that can move freely and has no fixed shape.

gene
A section of deoxyribonucleic acid (DNA) that contains a particular instruction.

generation
A group of people—or other living things—who are born at around the same time.

gill
An organ that takes oxygen from water.

gland
A body part that makes a substance for use in the body or for release.

glucose
A sugar that is used by animal and plant cells to make energy.

gravity
A force that pulls all objects toward each other. The greater an object's mass, the greater the pull of its gravity.

habitat
The natural home of an animal, plant, or other living thing.

helium
The second most common and second lightest atom in the Universe. Helium is a gas at room temperature.

hemisphere
Half of a sphere, such as a planet.

herbivore
An animal that eats plants.

hibernate
To spend the winter in a dormant, or resting, state.

horn
A hard material, also called keratin, that is found in scales, feathers, beaks, claws, nails, and hair. Another meaning of "horn" is a pointed, bony growth on the head.

hydrogen
The most common and lightest atom in the Universe. Hydrogen is a gas at room temperature.

impact crater
A bowl-shaped dip on a planet or moon caused by a collision with an asteroid or other object.

infinite
Endless in size or number.

inheritance
The passing on of characteristics from parents to their offspring, through asexual or sexual reproduction.

insect
An invertebrate with six legs and a three-part body.

invertebrate
An animal without a backbone, such as a squid, spider, or insect.

isotope
One of two or more forms of the same element, with atoms that have the same number of protons in their nuclei but different numbers of neutrons.

keratin
A hard material that is found in scales, feathers, beaks, claws, nails, and hair.

kinetic energy
The energy of an object or particle that is moving.

larva (plural: larvae)
A young stage in the life cycle of some invertebrates, fish, and amphibians, during which the animal looks different from its adult form.

lava
Melted rock that has spilled from a volcano.

light-year
The distance light travels in 1 year: 9.46 trillion km (5.88 trillion miles).

liquid
A substance, such as water, that can flow to fit the shape of any container but takes up a particular amount of space.

lung
An organ that takes oxygen from air.

magma
Melted rock beneath the surface of a planet or moon.

magnetism
A force caused by the movement of electric charges, which results in pulling and pushing forces between objects.

mammal
An animal that grows hair at some point in its life and feeds its young on milk, such as a cat or human.

mantle
A layer inside a planet or moon that lies between the core and crust.

marine
Found in saltwater, in the ocean.

mass
A measure of the amount of matter in an object; often called "weight."

mate
A partner for making babies.

matter
Anything that takes up space and has mass ("weight"). All ordinary matter is made of atoms. Matter has four forms: solid, liquid, gas, or plasma.

metal
A material that, at room temperature, is usually solid, hard, shiny, and bendy. Metals include iron, nickel, and gold.

metamorphosis
The change in body shape that most amphibians and some invertebrates and fish go through as they grow into adults.

microorganism
A living thing too tiny to be seen without a microscope.

migrate
To move from one region to another at particular times of year.

Milky Way
Our home galaxy.

mineral
A solid, natural substance that forms in the ground or in water.

molecule
A group of atoms that are chemically bonded to each other.

moon
A rounded object orbiting a planet.

multicellular
Made of many cells.

mycelium (plural: mycelia)
The rootlike body of a fungus, made of many branching threads.

nectar
A sugary liquid made by flowers.

neutron
A particle found in atoms, located inside the nucleus. A neutron has no electric charge.

nocturnal
Active at night.

nucleus
The central part of an atom; the part of a eukaryotic cell that contains deoxyribonucleic acid (DNA).

nutrient
A substance needed by a living thing's body for growth and health.

offspring
The young (or "babies") of an animal, plant, or other living thing.

omnivore
An animal that eats both plants and animals.

orbit
The curved path of an object around a star or planet.

order
A group of families that are closely related. For example, the cat and dog families are in the meat-eating Carnivora order.

organ
A body part that does a particular job, such as the heart or brain.

organelle
A structure, found in cells, that has one or more jobs to do.

oxygen
The third most common atom in the Universe. Oxygen is a gas at room temperature. Found in air and water, it is needed by the cells of most living things so they can make energy.

paleontologist
A scientist who studies fossils.

particle
A tiny portion of matter.

photon
A particle that carries electromagnetic energy.

planet
An object orbiting a star that is massive enough for its gravity to pull it into a ball-like shape and to remove other large objects from its path.

plant
A living thing that makes its own food from sunlight.

plasma
A gas in which the atoms have ripped apart, losing electrons.

pole
The far north or far south point where a planet's axis meets its surface.

pollen
A powder made by flowers. It can fertilize other flowers of the same species, so they make seeds.

potential energy
Energy that is stored in an object, due to its materials, position, size, or shape.

predator
An animal that hunts other animals.

prey
An animal that is killed by another animal for food.

prokaryote
A simple living thing made of a single cell that does not have a nucleus. Bacteria and archaea are prokaryotes.

protist
A eukaryote that may be either multicellular or unicellular and is not an animal, plant, or fungus.

proton
A particle found in atoms, located inside the nucleus. A proton carries a positive electric charge.

pterosaur
A flying reptile with wings made from skin stretched over a long fourth finger.

radiation
Energy that travels through space at the speed of light.

radioactivity
A release of energy from the decay of the unstable nucleus of an atom.

radio wave
A form of electromagnetic radiation that can be used to carry information between communication devices such as phones and computers.

rain forest
A thick forest found in areas that are rainy throughout the year.

range
The area where an animal is found.

reproduction
The process by which living things

make new living things, known as offspring.

reptile
An animal with a dry skin, covered in scales or larger plates called scutes, that usually lays eggs on land.

rigid
Unable to bend or change shape.

rock
A solid material made of a mixture of minerals, which are themselves made of elements such as oxygen and silicon.

room temperature
A comfortable indoor temperature.

rotation
Turning around an axis.

scale
A small, hard plate that grows from the skin of most fish and reptiles.

scute
A bony plate with a horny covering.

sea ice
Ice that forms on the surface of the cold ocean.

sensor
A device that detects changes in its surroundings, such as light, heat, or sound.

service module
The portion of a space capsule that holds machines and fuel tanks. It does not return to Earth.

sexual reproduction
A type of reproduction in which offspring are made by two parents.

snout
The nose and mouth of an animal.

solar panel
A device that turns sunlight into electricity.

Solar System
The Sun and all the objects, from planets to asteroids, that are orbiting it.

solid
A substance that takes up a particular amount of space and, usually, has a definite shape.

space capsule
A wingless spacecraft.

species
A group of living things that look similar and can reproduce together.

sphere
A ball-shaped object.

spore
A tiny, single-celled package—released by fungi, simple plants, and some protists—that can grow into a new fungus, plant, or protist.

star
A glowing ball of plasma, held together by its own gravity.

Sun
The star at the middle of our Solar System, around which Earth and the other planets orbit.

telescope
A device used to observe distant objects by detecting the light or other energy they give off or reflect.

temperate
In the area between the tropics and polar regions, where it is neither very hot nor very cold.

theropod
A usually meat-eating dinosaur with hollow bones and, in many cases, three main toes.

tide
The rising and falling of the ocean at the shore, caused by the pull of the Moon's gravity on the water.

tissue
A group of similar cells that work together.

tree
A plant with a thick, woody stem.

tropical
In the area around the equator, where it is hot year-round.

tundra
A cold, treeless region.

unicellular
Made of one cell.

vein
A tube through which blood travels from the body to the heart.

venom
A poison made by an animal.

vertebrate
An animal with a backbone: a fish, amphibian, reptile, bird, or mammal.

virus
A tiny package of material, which some scientists call living and others call non-living. It can reproduce only inside a living thing and can cause disease.

visible light
The portion of electromagnetic radiation that human eyes can see.

volcano
A hole in a planet or moon's surface through which lava can spill out.

water
A substance made of oxygen and hydrogen atoms. Water is essential for life as we know it.

wavelength
The distance between the peaks of waves of energy.

work
The use of force to move an object.

X-ray
A high-energy form of electromagnetic radiation that can travel through many materials.

Index

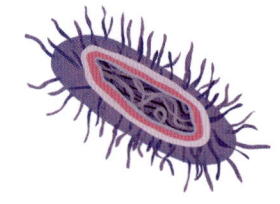

acceleration 34
acids 26–7
active galactic nuclei 133
addax 197
air 25, 50, 102–3
air resistance 32
Alaskacephale 244
alligators, American 198–9
alloys 25
Almas 236
Alpha Centauri system 120–1
Amazon rainforest 192–3
amphibians 146, 172, 174, 192, 194–5
Andes Mountains 220–1
Andromeda galaxy 137
animals 145, 146, 172–227
apex predators 193, 198, 246
archaea 142, 143, 149
Archaeopteryx 240
archosaurs 233
Arctic sea ice 204–7
armadillo 221
artificial intelligence (AI) 59
Asteroid Belt 78–9
astronauts 118–19
atmospheres 70, 76–7, 84, 102–3, 106, 115
atomic nucleus 8, 28–9, 38
atomic number 10
atoms 4, 6, 8–9, 14–16, 18, 20, 24–6, 28, 30, 41, 50, 54, 62, 80, 120, 127, 138–9
auroras 18, 106–7
Australia 212–13
axolotl 172

bacteria 142, 143, 148
bases 26–7
bears, polar 206–7
bees, Cape honeybee 180–1
beetles 178–9
Big Bang 136, 138–9
bioluminescence 22
biomass 61
biomes 112–13
birds 147, 174, 176–7, 184–5, 192–3, 205, 213, 220–1, 224–7, 233, 240
black holes 127–9, 133, 135
blood 158–60, 167, 220

boiling point 21
bones 159, 160–1
bonobos 217
brain 156, 162–3
breathing 158, 166
butterflies 4, 175, 192–3

calendars 104, 105
camels 197
Cannon, Annie Jump 124–5
carbohydrates 169
carbon dioxide 22, 56, 60, 110, 151, 154, 166–7
caribou, Peary 205
cars 56–7
cats 193, 197, 210–11
cells 140, 142–4, 147, 156
division 144
cerapods 232, 238–9
Ceres 78
cetaceans 218
changes of state 20–1
chaparral, Californian 184–5
chemical bonding 9, 15
chemical energy 38, 56
chemical reactions 22–3
chipmunks, Siberian 209
chromosomes 145
circuits 52
climate 112
climate change 56, 60, 110–11
clouds 109
Colepiocephale 245
combustion (burning) 22
comets 94–5, 114
compounds 6, 9, 21, 24
Compsognathus 241
computers 58–9
condensation 20, 21
conduction 50, 51
conductors 50, 52
constellations 120, 122–3
convection 51
coral reefs, Red Sea 188–9
coronal loops 69
crabs 182–3
crocodiles 196, 198, 228, 233
Ctenochasma 241
Curie, Marie 7

dark matter 133
deforestation 110
deoxyribonucleic acid (DNA) 142–6, 149, 171
deserts 196–7, 214
diamonds 14, 84
digestive system 158, 168–9
digital devices 58
dinosaurs 147, 228–47
Djadokhta Formation 236–7
dwarf planets 62, 78, 90, 92–3, 97

ears 165
Earth 55, 64, 84, 95, 98–113
atmosphere 102–3
axis 105
crust 98, 100–1
mantle 98, 100
orbit 104–5
Earth-like planets 130, 131
earthquakes 100
eclipses 116–17
eggs 169, 170–2, 174–6, 178–83, 185, 188, 190, 192, 194–5, 198, 203, 221–4, 227, 228, 231, 236
electric charge 8, 18, 26, 41, 52, 66, 68, 106, 120
electrical energy 29–30, 39, 52–3, 56, 58, 80
electromagnetic radiation 31–2, 39, 40–3, 51, 66
electromotive force 52
electrons 8–9, 18, 28, 30, 41, 52–5, 66, 80, 106, 138
elements 6–13, 17–18, 20–1, 24, 28
energy 30–61, 66, 127
Eris 97
Eucalyptus forest 212–13
eukaryotes 142, 143, 147
evaporation 20, 21, 108–9
event horizon 128
evolution 140–1, 142, 146–7, 228
exoplanets 130–1
extinction 146, 172, 228
eyes 164

farming 110
fats 169

254

feathers 174, 231
fields 53, 54, 68–9, 76–7, 106, 203
fingerprinting 23
fish 146, 174, 188–9, 190–1
Fleming, Alexander 155
flowers 152–3
food 140, 158, 169
forces 30–61
fossil fuels 60–1, 110
fossils 230, 234–6, 240, 243–4, 247
foxes 196, 205
freezing 20
friction 32
frogs 192, 194–5
fruit 153
fuel 56, 60–1, 110, 127
fungi 145, 147, 154–5

galaxies 120–39
Galileo Galilei 82, 83, 86
gamma rays 41
Ganymede 62, 82–3
gas giants 80, 84, 130
gases 9, 18–21, 50–1
genes 144
genomes 144
geothermal heat 61
germination 153
gibbons 216
glass 15
global warming 110, 184, 188
Goyocephale 245
gravity 30, 32–3, 35, 38, 62, 70, 74–5, 78, 90, 94, 96, 102, 114, 119, 120, 127–9, 133, 139
greenhouse gases 110
see also carbon dioxide
guinea pigs 220

habitats 112–13, 118–19, 146, 176–7, 184–5, 192–3, 196–7, 204–5, 212–13, 220–1
Halszkaraptor 236
Haumea 93
hearing 165
heart 158, 159, 166–7
heat (thermal) energy 29, 39, 50–1, 61, 66
helium 19–21, 25, 62, 80, 127, 138–9
human body 156–71
hydrogen 6, 8–10, 25–8, 62, 64, 66, 80, 106, 127, 138–9
hydroxide 26–7

ice 111, 112, 204–7
ice giants 88, 130
in vitro fertilization (IVF) 171
infrared 40, 51
inheritance 145, 146, 228
insulators 50
internet 59
intestines 168–9
invertebrates 146–7, 174–83, 185–9, 193, 197
ions 26, 27
iron 22, 25, 54, 74, 76, 80, 106, 139
isotopes 28–9

jellyfish 172, 186–7
joints 160
Jupiter 62, 64–5, 78, 80–3, 95, 106

keystone species 198
kinetic energy 39
koala 213
krill 172, 219, 222
Kuiper Belt 90, 92–3, 94, 96–7

lemurs 217
life 66, 77–8, 82, 98, 130, 140–55
characteristics of 140
life sciences 4
light 30–1, 40–5, 66, 102, 120
light-years 120
lions 210–11
liquids 9, 16–17, 20–1, 50–1
lizards 184, 212, 221
Local Group 136–7
lungs 158, 166–7

machines, simple 36–7
magma 100–1
magnetism 30, 53–5, 68–9, 76–7, 106, 203
Makemake 93
mammals 147, 172, 174–7, 185, 193, 196–7, 204–11, 214–21
Mars 64, 74–7
marsupials 213
mass 33, 34, 126–8
matter 6–29, 30, 138
meat-eaters (carnivores) 172, 206, 210–11, 230–2, 236–7, 240–3, 246–7
mechanical energy 39, 56
medicine 157
meerkats 214–15
melting 20
Mercury 62, 64, 70–1, 106
Mesuropetala 241

metals 11, 12–13, 25, 50, 52, 54–5, 64, 98
mice 209
microorganisms 143, 145, 148–9
microwaves 40
Milky Way 120, 129, 134–6, 139
mitochondria 143, 156
mixtures 21, 24–5
molecules 6, 9, 14–16, 18, 20–1, 23, 26, 50
monkeys 216
Moon 98–9, 114–19
moons 62, 74–5, 78, 82–3, 86–93, 106
motion, laws of 34–5
mouth 168
muscles 159, 160–1
mycelium 154–5

narwhal 204
natural sciences 4
natural selection 146
Neptune 64–5, 90–1, 96
nerves 159, 164
neutrons 8, 28–9, 138
Newton, Sir Isaac 32, 34–5
nuclear energy 38, 60
nuclear fission 29
nuclear fusion 66

observable Universe 136–7
oceans 111, 114, 140, 147, 188–9
oil 56, 60, 61
Oort Cloud 94, 96–7
orangutans, Bornean 216
Orcus 93
organ systems 158–69
organs 156, 158–9, 162–3, 166–7
owls, snowy 224–5
oxygen 6, 8–9, 22, 24–6, 74, 102, 106, 139, 151, 156, 166–7, 220

pachycephalosaurs 232, 244–5
paleontologists 230–2, 234, 236, 238
Parasaurolophus 238–9
penguins 176, 177, 222–3
penicillin 155
periodic table 10–11
pH scale 26–7
photons 40–1, 66
photosynthesis 151
physical sciences 4
Pinacosaurus 237
Pisces–Cetus Complex 137